Alternative Dispute Resolution in Business

Lucille M. Ponte | Thomas D. Cavenagh

Australia • Brazil • Japan • Korea • Mexico • Singapore • Spain • United Kingdom • United States

**Alternative Dispute
Resolution in Business**

Lucille M. Ponte
Thomas D. Cavenagh

Executive Editors:
 Michele Baird

 Maureen Staudt

 Michael Stranz

Project Development Manager:
 Linda deStefano

Senior Marketing Coordinators:
 Sara Mercurio

 Lindsay Shapiro

Senior Production /
Manufacturing Manager:
 Donna M. Brown

PreMedia Services Supervisor:
 Rebecca A. Walker

Rights & Permissions Specialist:
 Kalina Hintz

Cover Image:
 Getty Images*

For product information and
technology assistance, contact us at **Cengage Learning
Customer & Sales Support, 1-800-354-9706**

For permission to use material from this text or product,
submit all requests online at **cengage.com/permissions**
Further permissions questions can be emailed to
permissionrequest@cengage.com

ISBN-13: 978-0-324-03125-6

ISBN-10: 0-324-03125-4

Cengage Learning
5191 Natorp Boulevard
Mason, Ohio 45040
USA

Cengage Learning is a leading provider of customized learning
solutions with office locations around the globe, including
Singapore, the United Kingdom, Australia, Mexico, Brazil, and Japan.
Locate your local office at: **international.cengage.com/region**

Cengage Learning products are represented in Canada by
Nelson Education, Ltd.

For your lifelong learning solutions, visit **custom.cengage.com**

Visit our corporate website at **cengage.com**

Cengage Learning purchased South-Western from
Thomson on July 5, 2007

Printed in the United States of America

CONTENTS

Contents

Contents

Part I

INTRODUCTION

Chapter 1: Litigation and Dispute Resolution

Chapter 2: The ADR Response to Resolving Business Disputes

Chapters 1 and 2 begin our discussion of the relationship between business and alternative dispute resolution. Chapter 1 describes and assesses the civil litigation system, the principle method of formally resolving business disputes, both in this country and abroad. Chapter 1 addresses the impact of the litigation system on business as well as several judicial and legislative options for mitigating some of the negative consequences of litigation for business. Chapter 2 describes the nature and sources of business disputes and summarizes some alternative dispute resolution mechanisms that may be used to resolve those disputes. This chapter also lays out the advantages and disadvantages of ADR for business dispute resolution purposes.

1

LITIGATION AND DISPUTE RESOLUTION

CHAPTER HIGHLIGHTS
In this chapter, you will read and learn about the following:

1. The major civil litigation systems of the world.
2. The stages of the lawsuit in the United States and the ꜀   ꜀pro-
   priate to consider using ADR to resolve a dispute.
3. The ways in which civil litigation affects business.
4. Several judicial and legislative suggestions for re
   its adverse impact.

A variety of processes exist to resolve disputes a
Some of these processes, such as litigation, are
Others, like the minitrial or mediation, may b
lays the groundwork for our comprehensive
lution (ADR) by describing the impact on b
ers are an alternative—the civil lawsuit. W}
process, by default he or she is, in most c;
be aware of the costs of litigation and t
the systems used around the world bef/
ADR.

   ADR is any formal or semiformal
a business dispute. The premise of *
because litigation does not work w

does not, however, suggest that the trial process is inferior in any general sense to alternative dispute resolution. This chapter presents an overview of major civil litigation systems and their impact on American business, and addresses judicial and legislative legal reforms intended to reduce that impact.

AN OVERVIEW OF MAJOR CIVIL LITIGATION SYSTEMS

Essentially two models of civil litigation are used throughout the world: the **adversarial, common law model** and the **inquisitorial, civil law model.** The adversarial system is used most prominently in the United States. It involves the introduction of evidence in a process governed by extensive procedural rules following which a jury renders a judgment on the basis of legal instructions given by a judge. The inquisitorial system is used in civil law nations, including Japan and the European Union (excluding England). It too considers evidence, but in different ways and to different ends.

One can draw distinctions between the adversarial and inquisitorial systems on any one of three bases. The first is the sources of law from which the systems draw their direction. The adversarial approach is normally encompassed within a common law system as it is in the United States. As such, it draws from many sources of legal regulation, including: constitutional law, treaties, state and federal statutes, municipal ordinances, administrative regulations, and precedential case law. These various sources of legal authority are interpreted and applied by judges at both the trial and appellate levels.

In inquisitorial jurisdictions such as Japan, which normally use civil law systems, all of the applicable law is drawn from statutes. These statutes attempt to distill all legal authority into an orderly and comprehensive code of law. As a result, while adversarial common law systems develop over time as judges interpret and apply the various authorities to which they are subject, inquisitorial civil law is contemporaneous, with statutes developed on an "as needed" basis. In addition, while judges in common law countries have considerable power, inasmuch as they not only apply the law but develop it by interpreting it, civil law countries relegate virtually all legal authority to the legislative branch. Judges in civil law countries simply apply the law as laid down in the code.

The second basis for distinction is the processes used to resolve conflict. Adversarial law countries rely heavily on the trial because the various sources of law have a common nexus in the judge, who applies the laws to individual litigants. Conversely, civil law countries use a wide variety of processes including many of the negotiated processes described later in this text. Because the law is clear, the ___ concentrate less effort on applying the law than on resolving the diffi___ the parties. Civil law countries have other procedural differences as ___, while the adversarial system, particularly in the United States,

http://

For a comparison of the inquisitorial and adversarial systems see: http://www. ozemail.com.au/ ~dtebbutt/oj/ ojeurope3.html makes extensive use of pretrial discovery (the exchange of information related to the case), civil law systems permit little, if any, discovery. Curtailing discovery reduces the time and expense of the trial, but it may also diminish the accuracy of the result.

The third basis for distinction is the outcomes available under each system. Common law countries normally use juries to resolve legal disputes; some, like the United States, make access to a jury an almost absolute right. However, civil law countries normally do not provide a jury trial, preferring instead to allow a judge to act within the code to solve a dispute. In common law countries, juries may award punitive damages and a fairly wide range of compensatory damages such as for pain and suffering. In civil law systems damages are much more limited, normally excluding punitive damages and very significantly restricting noneconomic compensatory damages.

Each system has its strengths and weaknesses. The common law system tends to be less consistent, more costly, and more acrimonious than the civil law system because of the multiple sources of legal authority at both the state and federal levels and the difficulty of interpreting and applying them. It does, however, provide

FIGURE 1.1   Summary Comparisons of Major Civil Litigation Systems

Category	United States	European Union	Japan
Nature of system	Win-lose; adversarial	Win-win; primarily inquisitorial	Win-win; primarily inquisitorial
Types of actions	Individual plaintiffs; class actions	Individual plaintiffs; no class actions	Individual plaintiffs; no class actions
Discovery process	Highly detailed process; 80% of legal fees	Civil law—not allowed; common law— very limited	Not allowed
Legal fee arrangements	Hourly rates; contingency fees— % of money recovered	Hourly rates; no contingency fees— loser pays other's legal fees	Commencing fees—up to 8% of attorney fees, court costs and damages, no contingency fees
Right to jury trial	Guaranteed in most civil cases	No guarantee	No guarantee
Damage awards	Usually determined by juries	Determined by judges	Determined by judges
Types of damages	Compensatory, including pain and suffering; punitive	Compensatory, with very limited pain and suffering; no punitive	Compensatory, with very limited pain and suffering; no punitive
Costs of tort system	Totals @ 2.5% of U.S. GNP; about 1.5 million per case	Totals @ 0.5% of EU GNP	Most costs confidential, yet damages seldom exceed 150,000 per case

a wider and therefore more complete range of remedies, a greater degree of flexibility to address the exigencies of a particular case, and the opportunity for plaintiffs to create new causes of action by successfully relying on the novel application of precedent and the broad legal dictates of the common law. The civil law system is relatively consistent, easily accessible, and comparatively expeditious and inexpensive. It does not, however, allow for meaningful variances between cases and parties, and it limits damages in ways that may leave significant gaps between harm done and recompense paid. Furthermore, some case types are simply excluded from consideration altogether. Both systems are costly and time-consuming. Although the American civil law system can be quite expensive, the civil law systems of Europe and Asia, though less costly, are not without many of the same shortcomings.

ADR IN ACTION

Religious Law Systems

Some countries rely on neither the common law system nor the civil law system. These countries exercise a third option, resembling the civil system of law but based on religious doctrine and practice. These **religious law systems** tend to be more monolithic and insular than standard civil law systems. Consider, for example, India. Its system of law is considered a nominally civil law system. Yet the country's law, particularly in the area of family law, is based significantly on Hindu teach-ing as codified in books of Hindu law called *Smitris*. This law is highly personal and is based on religious faith rather than on public consensus or judicial decision. Similarly, Muslim countries like Saudi Arabia apply Islamic law, called *Sharia,* which is drawn from the *Koran* and related sacred writings. Even some Western European countries weave religion into their law; consider, for example the ban on abortion present in Irish law, which is steeped in Catholic religious belief.

THE STAGES OF THE LAWSUIT AND THE USE OF ADR

The civil justice system in the United States is an adversarial, common law system in which a neutral party, normally a jury, decides both questions of law and fact to reach a conclusion regarding the claims made by the parties. Civil cases, those in which ADR is normally used, are very different from criminal cases. While a criminal trial requires a jury to determine guilt "beyond a reasonable doubt," the jury in a civil trial must determine liability based on a "preponderance of evidence." This means that the claims made by the plaintiff simply must be more likely true than not. It is, consequently, easier to prevail in a civil trial than in a criminal trial. Also, while the criminal case seeks to establish guilt, the civil case seeks to establish liability. Liability means finding that an error was made; guilt entails a finding of intentional culpability. While criminal cases typically end with the imposition of punishment, civil cases are generally resolved through the payment of damages. Jail is not an option for the civil judge or jury. Indeed, money is likely all that a civil tribunal can award. Those money damages may simply compensate a plaintiff or go beyond compensation to deter future conduct in the form of punitive damages. Finally, while the criminal trial is a public matter between the state, the "victim" of a crime, and a defendant, the civil trial is a private matter between two parties.

The American civil lawsuit consists of three stages: pretrial, trial, and appeal. Each of these three stages can entail considerable time and expense. The **pretrial stage** of the lawsuit begins with the preparation of formal documents commencing the lawsuit. After the parties have exchanged these documents and filed them with a court, **discovery** takes place. This is the point at which parties provide extensive information to each other in the form of witness statements and documents; this process can be quite lengthy. Indeed, discovery may account for the bulk of the time spent in litigation and as much as 80 percent of the cost. Finally, during the pretrial stage, additional documents (called motions) prepared as a result of the information gleaned from discovery might be filed by one party or the other seeking a final judgment prior to trial or a ruling on some aspect of the forthcoming trial.

The **trial** consists of the orderly presentation of evidence to a judge or jury with arguments on the meaning and importance of the evidence made by the attorneys trying the case. The presentation of evidence is highly structured and governed by formal rules of procedure. Following the presentation of evidence and the arguments on the meaning of the evidence, the judge will render a decision or prepare the jury with instructions to deliberate and render a decision.

Finally, parties dissatisfied with the ruling at trial usually have the right to **appeal** to a higher court, and many do so. Indeed, litigants who lose at trial may appeal through several levels of state and federal courts seeking a new trial or a reversal of the trial court's ruling. When a party wins an appeal, it may begin the entire trial and appeal process again.

The movement of civil litigation through these three stages can be very costly and time-consuming. Remember, though, that there is no legal obligation to file suit to resolve a dispute—it can be resolved informally. It is also possible to settle a case at any stage of litigation, including during appeal, because there is no obligation to complete the process of litigation once commenced. Indeed, as many as 90 percent of all civil cases filed are settled prior to trial. As a result, disputing parties may initiate ADR at many points during litigation or instead of litigation altogether.

Parties may, for example, try to directly negotiate a resolution to the dispute before filing suit. If they cannot reach a negotiated agreement, they may use mediation to more formally attempt to settle. This may take place prior to filing suit, or after filing suit and on the basis of some discovery. A minitrial or summary jury trial may also be used after filing suit and taking discovery, but in an attempt to settle the matter without an actual trial. Parties may even substitute arbitration for a jury trial or try to negotiate *following* a trial if a lengthy and costly appeal is likely. In short, ADR is possible throughout the life of the dispute and at any stage of formal litigation.

Parties who use ADR prior to, or at some point during, litigation do so for a variety of reasons. Although we cover many of these reasons later in the text, four warrant attention here. First, the cost of litigation, in legal fees and trial expenses, can be prohibitively high. (Later in this chapter we address the formidable economic impact of litigation on business.) In addition, the length of time to reach a judgment through litigation may compel parties to seek resolution outside of the courthouse. The pretrial stage itself is known to take months, even years. The appeals process may be just as lengthy and could start the entire time-consuming process over. Moreover, the longer the process takes, the more expensive it becomes. This is true partly because legal fees accrue throughout the process and partly because the process distracts key people from important business pursuits. For example, instead of devoting undivided attention to managing the business, a CEO may be obligated to give deposition testimony. Or, rather than working on new product development, an engineer may be forced to spend time preparing extensive answers to interrogatories or preparing documents for the opposing party. At every stage of the process is the risk of an adverse ruling that will end the case unfavorably. Litigation is a winner-take-all event. Even when the evidence would seemingly ensure a favorable outcome, a judge or jury may perceive it differently. The result may be an adverse verdict with significant costs incurred. Finally, important business *relationships* may be lost in the acrimony of a trial.

THE IMPACT OF LITIGATION ON BUSINESS

http://

A Study of the U.S. and Illinois tort systems can be found at: http://www.icjl. org/data2/ niu2.htm

The American legal system bears the brunt of blame for the high cost of doing business. Indeed, some people, claim that a **liability crisis** exists. Clearly, the effects of the American legal system on business can be significant, and occasionally businesses find themselves defending against cases that lack merit. However, whether the system is to blame for all the negatives ascribed to it is another question altogether.

Fair-minded people can and do disagree on how extensively the litigation system affects business, on whether its impact is uniformly negative, and on whether there is a need to change the system. There is even debate about whether a lawsuit or liability crisis exists at all. In the case that follows, considering whether a plaintiff has a right to question a jury on its predispositions toward the liability crisis, it becomes clear that very different perspectives on the liability crisis or lack thereof abound. It is also evident that the belief or lack of belief in the liability crisis is perceived to affect jury decision making.

BABCOCK V. NORTHWEST MEMORIAL HOSPITAL
767 S.W.2d 705 (1989)

FACT SUMMARY

Artaruth Babcock broke her pelvis and was hospitalized. During her hospitalization, Mrs. Babcock developed blisters on her heels, which allegedly ultimately resulted in the amputation of both her legs. Mrs. Babcock and her husband sued the hospital and her doctors, alleging negligence in their care of Mrs. Babcock. During voir dire, the trial judge refused to allow the Babcocks' attorney to question the jury panel about the alleged lawsuit crisis, which he believed would bias the jury against the claim.

The trial court granted two pretrial motions. The first motion prohibited "[a]ny mention of the alleged 'liability insurance crisis,' 'medical malpractice crisis,' or any similar mention of or questions to potential jurors regarding the current state of affairs in the liability insurance industry." The second motion prohibited "calling the jury's attention to any advertisements either on radio, television, in newspapers or magazines which speak of malpractice crisis and are paid for by and credited to insurance companies." During voir dire, a member of the jury panel stated that he had read articles and advertisements discussing the alleged liability crisis, and his concern for the effect of jury awards on insurance premiums might impede his ability to be impartial. After that juror was struck for cause, the Babcocks renewed their request for permission to question the entire jury panel about the alleged "lawsuit crisis." The trial court again denied the request. The following exchange took place

before the bench:

Counsel for Babcocks: Your Honor, while everybody is still up here and on the record, I would like to bring—bring out the Court's ruling on my motion—on their Motion in Limine. It's my understanding that the Court has precluded me from asking questions as to whether the jury has heard or read about, not necessarily the insurance crisis, but the liability crisis and the lawsuit crisis. This man obviously is very influenced by it and I think his answer that he was concerned about malpractice, the insurance premiums specifically, I think that that brings forth the need and the necessity for a fair trial that the Plaintiff be allowed to go into this in a little more depth with all the rest of the jurors.

The Court: All right. Let the record show that was made, carefully considered, and the same ruling is in effect. Otherwise, it would open the door completely to both sides to go into that, which would completely prejudice the jury. We couldn't get a fair trial.

After the jury was selected, the Babcocks for the third time objected to the trial court's refusal to allow questions concerning the alleged "lawsuit crisis" and asked for an opportunity later in the day to include the questions they would have asked the jurors on the record. The objection was overruled and the request denied. The Babcocks' motion for a new trial included an affidavit that delineated the questions they would have asked during voir dire about the "lawsuit crisis."

OPINION: *MAUZY, Justice*

At issue in this case is whether the trial court abused its discretion by prohibiting voir dire examination inquiring about the "lawsuit crisis" or "liability insurance crisis."

In Texas, the right to a fair and impartial trial is guaranteed by the Constitution and by statute. It is widely recognized that Texas courts permit a broad range of inquiries on voir dire. At the time of trial, tort reform and the debate concerning the alleged "liability insurance crisis" and "lawsuit crisis" were the subject of much media attention. No one can deny the media blitz spurred by the controversy over tort reform during the 1987 legislative session. Advertisements proclaiming a "lawsuit crisis" asserted that personal injury lawsuits had created an economic crisis and that excessive jury awards resulted in higher premiums. Media coverage of the alleged "lawsuit crisis" has unquestionably created the potential for bias and prejudice on both sides of the personal injury docket.

In a recent opinion, the Second Court of Appeals, when confronted with the same issue, held that the plaintiffs had a right to question the jury to determine if anyone was prejudiced against plaintiffs' rights by such advertising. The defendants [in that case] alleged error by the trial court because the plaintiffs were allowed to question prospective jurors about certain advertisements on tort reform. They contended that such questioning interjected liability insurance into the case. The court of appeals held that such questions were necessary to ask and that the questions in no way indicated the defendants were insured.

Similarly, the respondents in this case contend that allowing such questions would interject insurance into the case.

We are unpersuaded by this argument. The mere mention of insurance is not necessarily grounds for reversal. When the Babcocks requested to ask the prospective jurors questions about the "liability crisis" and the "lawsuit crisis," they specifically stated they did not want to question the jury about insurance. The proposed voir dire questions that were subsequently filed with the trial court avoid any mention of insurance.

Both the Fourteenth Court of Appeals and the Second Court of Appeals have concluded that litigants have a right to question prospective jurors about their exposure to media coverage of the "lawsuit crisis." This right is based on the fundamental right to trial by a fair and impartial jury. We hold that the trial court abused its discretion by refusing to allow the Babcocks to question the jurors about the alleged "lawsuit crisis."

A broad latitude should be allowed to a litigant during voir dire examination. This will enable the litigant to discover any bias or prejudice by the potential jurors so that peremptory challenges may be intelligently exercised. Although we recognize that voir dire examination is largely within the sound discretion of the trial judge, a court abuses its discretion when its denial of the right to ask a proper question prevents determination of whether grounds exist to challenge for cause or denies intelligent use of peremptory challenges.

In the instant case, the Babcocks were denied the opportunity to intelligently exercise challenges. The trial court's refusal to allow questions directed at exposing bias or prejudice resulting from the controversy over tort reform denied the Babcocks the right to trial by a fair and impartial jury.

Respondents contend that the trial court's refusal to allow the questions was harmless error. We disagree. The trial court's action, which resulted in the denial of the Babcocks' constitutional right to trial by a fair and impartial jury, was harmful. Therefore, we hold that the trial court's refusal to allow questions during voir dire addressing the alleged "liability insurance crisis" and "lawsuit crisis" was an abuse of discretion and was reasonably calculated to cause and probably did cause the rendition of an improper judgment.

The judgment of the court of appeals is reversed and the cause is remanded to the trial court.

Discussion Questions

1. Do you believe there is a genuine litigation crisis? Why or why not? Do you believe you possess sufficient information to reach a conclusion?
2. Should jurors be permitted to consider cases based on their personal feelings about the litigation system if doing so would prejudice their decision?
3. Assuming a liability crisis exists, would greater use of ADR alleviate it? How?

One impact of litigation on business is that on world competitiveness. U.S. businesses must operate within a common law system that allows for larger, more frequent, and more easily obtained judgments. Thus, it may be somewhat more difficult for business to be profitable here versus abroad, in systems implementing civil law. Another significant impact of the U.S. legal system is cultural. Harvard law scholar Mary Ann Glendon argues in her book *Rights Talk: The Impoverishment of Political Discourse* that the pervasive use of litigation to resolve claims, particularly those involving questions of individual rights, has decreased our sense of community and increased our feelings of cynicism and indifference. Others besides Glendon think we are a more acrimonious and adversarial society as a result of the ready access to our system of civil justice. UCLA Law Professor Carrie Menkel-Meadow argues, for example, that the adversarial system makes justice less likely in a modern, multicultural society. She criticizes the adversarial system in four ways. First, she asserts that the adversarial system relies on "oppositional thinking" that may leave important information undisclosed and undiscussed. In addition, she asserts that the structure of the adversarial system limits cases unreasonably to two sides, despite the possibility that many sets of interests may be at stake in a case. Third, she contends that the adversarial system is unnecessarily and deleteriously limited in the economic remedies it permits, remedies she describes as "binary" or win-lose. Finally, she, like Glendon, believes that adversarial processes create adversarial cultures.[1]

In all likelihood, however, economic costs top the list of impacts of the civil litigation system on the business world. Proponents of legal reform estimate that the

---

1. Carrie Menkel-Meadow, "The Trouble with the Adversary System in a Post-Modern, Multicultural World," *The Institute for Study of Legal Ethics*, 49, 1996.

annual cost to the American economy of the civil justice system may reach as high as $130 billion. The cost can be measured both in terms of the expenses associated with the process of law and the cost of the outcomes permitted by the law. Because of the tremendously disparate nature of the cases brought, it is difficult to calculate accurately the average cost of trying a civil suit in the United States. It is equally difficult to calculate the average length of time it takes to pursue a case to its legal conclusion, particularly because different jurisdictions at both the state and federal levels have very different docket sizes and waiting times. What can be said is that legal fees are high—reaching as high as $500 an hour for litigation in some cities—and that the litigation process takes years to complete, up to ten years in some jurisdictions.

Another contributor to high economic costs associated with litigation is the **frivolous lawsuit.** Defining a frivolous suit is difficult. The following case considers the question of whether the judgment in a particular lawsuit should be set aside. Consider the analysis of that question in terms of what has been said here regarding the American common law system, because such a suit would likely never be filed or considered in a civil law system.

FERLITO V. JOHNSON & JOHNSON PRODUCTS, INC.
771 F. Supp. 196 (E.D. Michigan 1991)

FACT SUMMARY

Plaintiffs Susan and Frank Ferlito, husband and wife, attended a Halloween party in 1984 dressed as Mary and her little lamb. Mrs. Ferlito had constructed a lamb costume for her husband by gluing cotton batting manufactured by defendant Johnson & Johnson Products (JJP) to a suit of long underwear. She had also used defendant's product to fashion a headpiece, complete with ears. The costume covered Mr. Ferlito from his head to his ankles, except for his face and hands, which were blackened with Halloween paint. At the party Mr. Ferlito attempted to light his cigarette by using a butane lighter. The flame passed close to his left arm, and the cotton batting on his left sleeve ignited. Plaintiffs sued defendant for injuries they suffered from burns which covered approximately one third of Mr. Ferlito's body. Following a jury verdict entered for plaintiffs, the Honorable Ralph M. Freeman entered a judgment for plaintiff Frank Ferlito in the amount of $555,000 and for plaintiff Susan Ferlito in the amount of $70,000.

OPINION: *GADOLA, District Judge*

To recover in a "failure to warn" product liability action, a plaintiff must prove each of the following four elements of negligence: (1) that the defendant owed a duty to the plaintiff, (2) that the defendant violated that duty, (3) that the defendant's breach of that duty was a proximate cause of the damages suffered by the plaintiff, and (4) that the plaintiff suffered damages. To establish a prima facie case that a manufacturer's breach of its duty to warn was a proximate cause of an injury sustained, a plaintiff must present evidence that the product would have been used differently had the proffered warnings been given. In the absence of evidence that a warning would have prevented the harm complained of by altering the plaintiff's conduct, the failure to warn cannot be deemed a proximate cause of the plaintiff's injury as a matter of law. Similarly, a failure to warn cannot be deemed a proximate cause of injury if the plaintiff knew of the danger about which he claims the defendant failed to warn. A manufacturer has a duty "to warn the purchasers or users of its product about dangers associated with intended use." Conversely, a manufacturer has no duty to warn of a danger arising from an unforeseeable misuse of its product. Thus, whether a manufacturer has a duty to warn depends on whether the use of the product and the injury sustained by it are foreseeable. Whether a plaintiff's use of a product is foreseeable is a legal question to be resolved by the court. Whether the resulting injury is foreseeable is a question of fact for the jury.

In the instant action no reasonable jury could find that JJP's failure to warn of the flammability of cotton batting was a proximate cause of plaintiffs' injuries because plaintiffs failed to offer any evidence to establish that a flammability warning on JJP's cotton batting would have dissuaded them from using the product in the manner that they did.

Plaintiffs repeatedly stated in their response brief that plaintiff Susan Ferlito testified that "she would never again use cotton batting to make a costume." However, a review of the trial transcript reveals that plaintiff Susan Ferlito never testified that she would never again use

cotton batting to make a costume. More importantly, the transcript contains no statement by plaintiff Susan Ferlito that a flammability warning on defendant JJP's product would have dissuaded her from using the cotton batting to construct the costume in the first place. At oral argument counsel for plaintiffs conceded that there was no testimony during the trial that either plaintiff Susan Ferlito or her husband, plaintiff Frank J. Ferlito, would have acted any differently if there had been a flammability warning on the product's package. The absence of such testimony is fatal to plaintiffs' case; for without it, plaintiffs have failed to prove proximate cause, one of the essential elements of their negligence claim.

In addition, both plaintiffs testified that they knew that cotton batting burns when it is exposed to flame. Susan Ferlito testified that she knew at the time she purchased the cotton batting that it would burn if exposed to an open flame. Frank Ferlito testified that he knew at the time he appeared at the Halloween party that cotton batting would burn if exposed to an open flame. His additional testimony that he would not have intentionally put a flame to the cotton batting shows that he recognized the risk of injury of which he claims JJP should have warned. Because both plaintiffs were already aware of the danger, a warning by JJP would have been superfluous. Therefore, a reasonable jury could not have found that JJP's failure to provide a warning was a proximate cause of plaintiffs' injuries.

The evidence in this case clearly demonstrated that neither the use to which plaintiffs put JJP's product nor the injuries arising from that use were foreseeable. Susan Ferlito testified that the idea for the costume was hers alone. As described on the product's package, its intended uses are for cleansing, applying medications, and infant care. Plaintiffs' showing that the product may be used on occasion in classrooms for decorative purposes failed to demonstrate the foreseeability of an adult male encapsulating himself from head to toe in cotton batting and then lighting up a cigarette.

ORDER

Defendant's motion for judgment notwithstanding the verdict is GRANTED.

Discussion Questions

1. How, exactly, should a frivolous suit be defined? Under what circumstances should a person be permitted to try to prove a loss? Should the basis for judicial consideration of a suit be whether or not its cost to the system outweighs the benefits of a decision to the litigants?

2. In the present case, can it not be said that the system worked well? In other words, did the court not prevent an unjust judgment?

3. If so, can business bear the expense of defending such suits all the way through to a judgment notwithstanding the verdict or appeal? Is this cost of justice too high?

4. Would more extensive use of ADR lead to an *increase* in frivolous claims by encouraging parties to sue, secure in the knowledge that they could negotiate a settlement without judicial interference?

ADR IN ACTION

The Case of the Scalding Coffee

Perhaps no case has so inflamed the American people against the civil legal system in recent years as the case of *Liebeck v. McDonald's*. The case prompted House and Senate floor debates in Washington and was cited regularly as representative of every excess in the legal system that could be cured with meaningful legal reforms. One congressional representative, Christopher Cox of California, described the tort reform movement this way: "If there is a Robin Hood aspect, it is to take from the lawyers and give to the average working American." The *Liebeck* case presents some interesting facts, very few of which were widely publicized, and all of which present a simple question: Was it really a frivolous suit?

Stella Liebeck spent one full week in the hospital and three weeks recuperating at home after suffering third-degree burns on her thighs, genitalia, and buttocks following a spill of a cup of McDonald's coffee purchased at a drive-through window. She was eighty-one years old at the time of the accident. She spilled the coffee while her car was parked and as she endeavored to remove the cap to add cream and sugar to the coffee. During her recovery, she lost more than 20 pounds and underwent a series of very painful skin grafts. She incurred just over $2,000 in out-of-pocket medical expenses plus the lost wages of her daughter, who stayed home to care for her. The case was litigated to a jury, members of which said later that they began the case insulted to have to hear it at all; they believed, in short, before the testimony even began that this was a truly frivolous case. They later awarded Ms. Liebeck $2.9 million; $200,000 in compensatory damages including pain and suffering, but reduced by 20% for her negligence; and $2.7 million in punitive damages. The damages were later reduced to about $650,000 and reportedly privately settled for still less. Here are some of the facts the jurors heard that may have changed their initial opinions of the suit:

- McDonald's had received more than 700 complaints of burns from coffee spills in the ten years preceding the Liebeck burn but did not lower the temperature of the coffee because, in the words of one of their safety consultants, 700 complaints was "basically trivially different than zero."

- McDonald's coffee in the city in which the burn occurred was served at about 190 degrees—at least 20 degrees hotter than any other venue tested. This is a temperature that causes a third-degree, full-thickness burn to skin, muscle, and fatty tissue in 3.5 seconds. (Following the case, the temperature was reduced to 158 degrees, which causes a similar burn—after 60 seconds.)

- McDonald's own witnesses testified that they believed that consumers were unaware of the risk posed by a liquid of this temperature but that McDonald's was and had been aware of the danger for years.

- McDonald's own witnesses also admitted that McDonald's coffee is "not fit for consumption" as and when sold because it will cause severe burns if spilled *or* ingested.

- Ms. Liebeck offered to settle the case before the trial for her out-of-pocket expenses and a promise to turn down the temperature of the coffee; McDonald's countered with an $800 offer, less than one third of Ms. Liebeck's actual losses.

- McDonald's sells more than one billion cups of coffee each year, with daily coffee profit exceeding $1.3 million; Ms. Liebeck's awarded damages, therefore, equaled roughly two days' coffee profits; after the reduction, she recovered less than one day's profits.

It is not just the public that perceives a problem in the justice system. Courts have become concerned about and responsive to the economic impact of litigation on the participants. The following case illustrates this point. The opinion addresses the right of a third party to intervene in a suit that is subject to an agreement to use private ADR to settle a matter that has been in litigation for several years. The court balances the rights of the proposed intervenor against those of the parties already involved in the suit and engaged in settlement negotiation. In doing so, the court provides some astonishing facts and figures related to the impact of litigation—on both the parties and the judicial system.

HAWORTH, INC. V. STEELCASE, INC.
1992 WL 457284 (1992)

FACT SUMMARY

This matter comes before the Court pursuant to Herman Miller's *Motion to Intervene for the Purpose of Discovery.* Haworth filed suit in this Court, charging Steelcase with infringement of two Haworth Patents. Steelcase's answer denied the validity, infringement, and enforceability of the two patents in suit. In addition, Steelcase counterclaimed for judgment holding the patents invalid, not infringed, and unenforceable. Judge Enslen conducted a bench trial, the parties submitted post-trial briefs to the Court, and Judge Enslen entered judgments in favor of Steelcase on Haworth's infringement claim, in favor of Haworth on its validity claim, and in favor of Haworth on its unenforceability claim. Both parties appealed the judgment. The Federal Circuit reversed the findings of non-infringement but affirmed that the defendant had not proven inequitable conduct on the part of the plaintiff. The case was remanded to this Court for further proceedings. On remand, Judge Enslen scheduled a settlement conference to attempt settlement of this case.

James F. Davis, a former judge in the United States Court of Claims, was appointed to serve as a neutral advisor in the settlement negotiations between the plaintiff and defendant. Thereafter, by consent of the parties and pursuant to the inherent power of this Court, the parties entered into a special ADR agreement to settle the issues presented in the civil actions. Judge Enslen also appointed James F. Davis as a special master "for the purposes of encouraging and facilitating settlement, supervising the orderly progress of discovery, and conducting a trial of and deciding the issues between the parties if trial should become necessary." The ADR agreement allowed the parties to include for resolution all claims of which they were aware.

Subsequent to the creation of the ADR agreement, the plaintiff filed suit against Herman Miller, Inc. In its complaint, the plaintiff alleged Herman Miller had been willfully and deliberately infringing, contributorily infringing, and/or actively inducing infringement of the plaintiff's patents. Herman Miller filed its *Motion to*

Intervene in the instant case. Herman Miller alleges it needs discovery of documents connected with the proceedings before the special master, including documents produced in discovery by Haworth and others, for these reasons: (1) to prevent the plaintiff from taking inconsistent positions before the special master and in the lawsuit against Herman Miller, thereby avoiding collateral estoppel on adverse rulings and (2) to prevent the plaintiff from having witnesses change their testimony depending on the proceeding.

The plaintiff vigorously opposes Herman Miller's *Motion to Intervene*. It argues intervention by Herman Miller is not appropriate in this case, given the private nature of the ADR proceedings it has entered into for the purpose of settling its complaints. Furthermore, the plaintiff asserts that allowing Herman Miller's intervention in this case would have a chilling effect on the usefulness of the ADR proceedings and could jeopardize the existence of the ADR procedure, thereby causing the cases to revert back to the federal court for resolution.

OPINION: *DENSLEN, District Judge*

Central to my decision is the importance of alternative dispute resolution methodologies this Court utilizes to manage its case docket, in particular the alternative dispute resolution methodology set up by both parties in this case.

Following a lengthy trial and appellate process, on July 26, 1989, plaintiff and defendant commenced negotiations for settlement purposes. The two lawsuits pending between these litigants were consolidated for this purpose. On December 13, 1989, their settlement negotiations culminated in the order of reference of the disputes to James F. Davis, as Special Master, for resolution. James F. Davis was

invested with the power to encourage and facilitate settlements, to supervise the orderly progress of discovery, to conduct the trial and decide all issues between the parties, if necessary. The alternative dispute resolution procedure covered all patent-based claims between plaintiff and defendant; as well as any other patent related issues arising after December 15, 1989, included by mutual agreement between both parties and the Special Master. Thus, both civil actions pending in the Western District of Michigan were stayed pending the conclusion of the alternative dispute resolution proceedings. Both parties agreed to relinquish any right to appeal to any court any decision by the Special Master, either of discovery or procedural matters or the relief granted in final disposition of the civil actions. All transcripts, documents, and other information produced and testimony given during the alternative dispute resolution proceeding would be kept confidential, and neither party to the agreement could disclose any information concerning the conduct of the proceedings without the express written permission of the other. Both plaintiff and defendant specifically agreed in Paragraph 21 that the purpose of the proceedings was for settling the existing litigation between them.

The explosion of litigation in the federal courts, and the resulting burdens placed on the courts as well as all litigants, is well documented. In 1975, it was estimated that assuming the then present growth of litigation, by the year 2010 the federal court system would experience well over 1,000,000 appellate cases, requiring 5,000 appellate judges to decide them, and 10,000,000 cases initiated each year. Among the reasons noted for the expansion of litigation in the federal court system was the decline of church and family as traditional dispute resolution mechanisms, as well as the increasing complexity of modern society. Typically, it takes from two to six years to get a case to trial. However, business litigation, such as in this case, takes longer. The amount of discovery necessary in business litigation is both extensive and expensive. It is fair to say that most business litigation cases take at least two weeks and not uncommonly months to try. The personnel commitment which is essential for that kind of a trial, and especially the breadth and the depth of the preparation, represents a huge demand and an enormous drain on all the staff and officers of a corporation involved in the trial. But for the litigation they would be using their ingenuity and their capability for business purposes of the corporation and for the benefit of the shareholders. Furthermore, in a case such as this one involving patent disputes, time is of the essence. High technology moves quickly. By the time a complex trial has been completed, the issue may no longer be an issue.

Although approximately 96 percent of all cases are settled prior to judgment, many are settled too late, often after the expenditure of too much effort and money. Accordingly, the exigencies of modern dockets demand the adoption of novel and imaginative means lest the courts, inundated by a tidal wave of cases, fail in their duty to provide a just and speedy disposition of every case. Experimentation with new methods in the judicial system is imperative given growing caseloads, delays, and increasing costs. Federal and state judges throughout the country are trying new approaches to discovery, settlement negotiations, trial and alternatives to trial that deserve commendation and support. The bar should work with judges who are attempting to make practical improvements in the judicial system. Greater efficiency and cost-effectiveness serve both clients and the public.

In order to reduce their caseloads, many federal judges have been utilizing alternative dispute resolution methods. Such methods have served to reduce the time and cost to the litigants. One judge empirically estimated that by utilizing a summary jury trial five times, he had netted a savings in time of about 60 days. Furthermore, use of alternative dispute resolution techniques preserves the trial process for those cases which can be resolved only by trial. In particular, the use of special masters has been endorsed for the facilitation of just, speedy, and inexpensive resolution of complex cases. As the Sixth Circuit has recognized, pursuant to Fed.R.Civ.P. 83, district courts have the authority to enact rules to regulate their practice in matters not inconsistent with the federal rules, including rules requiring the litigants to submit to some variety of alternative dispute resolution. Former Chief Justice Burger referred to those judges who make efforts to formulate alternative dispute resolution mechanisms as "judicial pioneers [who] should be commended for their innovative programs. We need more of them in the future." W. Burger, 1984 Year End Report on the Judiciary.

Aside from relieving the burdens on federal courts' dockets, and saving the litigants time and money, alternative dispute resolution methods produce other favorable results. Summary jury trials allow the litigants to vent their grievances in a forum which does not entail the time and costs of a full-blown trial, and accordingly, they can walk away having had their day in court. Furthermore, the proceeding allows each litigant the opportunity to reassess the strengths and weaknesses of their and their opponent's cases, so that a fresh assessment can be made of the costs and benefits of fully litigating the case. In mediation, the parties can reorient themselves by helping them achieve a new and shared perception of their relationships. Mediation helps the parties to avoid or at least minimize conflicts in the future, and so helps to preserve and enhance relationships between parties which need to be maintained. In virtually all cases, the solution that two parties can work out themselves, voluntarily, will be better than the solution that the most Solomonic court could come up with, as the court is limited in the remedies that it can prescribe.

Reacting to these needs, the Western District of Michigan has promulgated the Local Rules of Practice and Procedure, which includes provisions for various forms of alternative dispute resolution. The judges of this District favor initiation of alternative formulas for resolving disputes, saving costs and time, and permitting the parties to utilize creativity in fashioning non-coercive settlements.

Herman Miller argues it wants to intervene in this case only to conduct discovery. It argues this would expedite the process of discovery in its lawsuit with plaintiff in the pending case in the Northern District of Georgia, thereby producing judicial economy because many of the issues presented to the Special Master may be similar or the same as issues presented to the Court in Georgia. Accordingly, the decisions made by James F. Davis could be asserted as having a collateral estoppel effect on the same issues presented in the Northern District of Georgia. Herman Miller further argues it wants to intervene in order to ascertain

what positions plaintiff has taken on issues in the alternative dispute resolution proceedings before the Special Master, because these positions may be inconsistent with the positions plaintiff is taking before the Court in the Northern District of Georgia. Finally, Herman Miller expresses its need to openly discuss its litigation with the attorneys representing Steelcase, and plaintiff is taking its position with respect to intervention to create a "steel curtain" between the attorneys. Herman Miller asserts plaintiff's characterization of the Special Master proceeding as a settlement agreement is wrong, because the Order of Reference incorporates provisions for discovery and trial in addition to settlement conferences. In conclusion, Herman Miller argues it has demonstrated a clear need to intervene to have access to the materials and documents generated in the course of the proceedings before the Special Master. Herman Miller argues plaintiff can show no harm if intervention is allowed, because intervention would not have a chilling effect on plaintiff's and defendant's proceedings before the Special Master. Herman Miller argues that allowing intervention would not constitute a breach of the Order of Reference, because plaintiff must have known it would at a later date sue other parties on the patents in dispute, and therefore the possibility of intervention was something plaintiff could have and should have contemplated.

In response, plaintiff argues its proceedings before the Special Master are part and parcel of its agreement to settle the case with defendant. The preparation of the Order of Reference was the culmination of lengthy negotiations between the parties, and confidentiality was a very important ingredient to the ultimate

package. Plaintiff further asserts Herman
Miller's argument it needs to ascertain
whether plaintiff is taking inconsistent
positions in the two proceedings is wrong.
Plaintiff asserts its positions regarding
both patents involved in the disputes with
Herman Miller have been made abun-
dantly clear in the proceedings before
Judge Enslen as well as in the appeal to
the Federal Circuit. The alternative dispute resolution methodology was carefully constructed in order to resolve all the
disputes in litigation as well as additional
patent disputes between plaintiff and
defendant should they mutually agree to
include the disputes in the ADR proceeding. Plaintiff argues the methodology was
set up in order to give both parties the
unfettered right to compromise with the
other in order to resolve their disputes,
and such a proceeding is not regular in the
course of litigation. Allowing Herman
Miller to intervene would place plaintiff
in a position to look over its shoulder during the course of negotiations, and if
plaintiff did take a position which could
be construed to be inconsistent, Herman
Miller would then race to the federal court
in the Northern District of Georgia with
this argument. Plaintiff argues this
prospect would have a chilling effect on
the possibility of its engaging in the give
and take essential to compromising which
is necessary to resolve issues, as well as
bringing a close to the patent disputes
between it and defendant. Plaintiff argues
Herman Miller has failed to show the special need to discover inconsistent positions, especially in light of Herman
Miller's representation to the Court it has
no evidence plaintiff is taking inconsistent
positions in the different court proceedings. In fact, Herman Miller presumes that
plaintiff's attorneys, as officers of the
court, are not being deceitful. Plaintiff

argues that should Herman Miller be able
to demonstrate a special need for the
material it seeks to obtain through intervention, it can file a second motion.
However, in this instance, Herman Miller
is only engaging in a giant fishing expedition, based on mere suspicion. Allowing
intervention would undermine the confidentiality contemplated by both plaintiff
and defendant, essential for facilitating
the open exchange of information in order
to resolve their disputes, and to be cre-
ative in resolving their disputes, without a
showing of substantial need on the part of
Herman Miller.

Plaintiff further argues that allowing
Herman Miller to intervene would potentially destroy the alternative dispute resolution procedure because of Herman
Miller's desire to argue the collateral
estoppel effects of the Special Master's
decision to the Northern District of
Georgia. Essential to the alternative dispute resolution proceeding was the provision whereby each party would forego its
right to appeal any decision made by the
Special Master. If the decisions by the
Special Master thus could be given binding effect in other proceedings, neither
party would want to continue with having
waived its right to appeal because of the
prospect of irreparable damage.

Steelcase has informed the Court it
opposes Herman Miller's *Motion to
Intervene*. Allowing intervention into this
proceeding most certainly would result in
plaintiff attempting to either undo or significantly alter the ADR methodology.
Steelcase represents this would be vigorously opposed. Therefore, allowing intervention would at a minimum produce a
dispute between plaintiff and defendant,
wholly collateral to their ADR proceeding, and indeed, potentially destructive of
all the progress they have made in resolv-

ing their many disputes. In either case, the progress which has been made in these cases would be seriously jeopardized, if not delayed for an undetermined length of time for no substantial purpose.

I conclude Herman Miller's *Motion to Intervene* should be denied. Plaintiff has demonstrated a legitimate need to maintain the confidentiality of the documents and materials generated in its alternative dispute resolution proceeding before the Special Master. Allowing Herman Miller to intervene in order to discover these materials cannot be accomplished without harming plaintiff's and defendant's legitimate secrecy interest. Plaintiff would be inhibited from engaging in the give and take essential for compromising disputes if presented with the possibility Herman Miller, Inc., would race to the Northern District of Georgia with the argument plaintiff was taking inconsistent positions in the two proceedings. A scenario such as this cannot reasonably be construed as enhancing judicial economy. Furthermore, the possible use of the Special Master's decisions for collateral estoppel purposes very well may lead to the destruction of the alternative dispute resolution procedure both parties painstakingly constructed, or at a minimum could produce a modification in the Order of Reference, inevitably causing delay in the ultimate resolution of these cases.

Weighed against Herman Miller's need for the information is plaintiff's need to maintain the confidentiality of its proceedings in the alternative dispute resolution methodology. Plaintiff needs the confidentiality to engage in the give and take essential to resolve disputes. Furthermore, the specter of the collateral estoppel effect of the Special Master's decisions in other court proceedings, without the full panoply of appeals from

those decisions, may jeopardize the existence of the entire alternative dispute resolution method designed by the litigants and approved by the Court in this case. This alternative dispute resolution method was painstakingly hammered out over the course of settlement discussions which lasted about six months. Plaintiff and defendant entered into these settlement discussions only after a 23-day bench trial, the following appeal to the federal Circuit, and the denial of a writ of certiorari by the United States Supreme Court. Allowing intervention would jeopardize the settlement of not one but two lawsuits which were filed in the Western District of Michigan and later consolidated, as well as the resolution of other disputes between these parties. Furthermore, it is unlikely future elaborate alternative dispute resolution methods, such as the one fashioned in this case, would be utilized if confidentiality could not be maintained.

My conclusion should not be read to indicate intervention will not be allowed any time two litigants are engaged in alternative dispute resolution. However, in light of the facts of this case, with its extensive procedural history, the importance of encouraging and utilizing alternative dispute resolution methods, the uniqueness and comprehensive nature of the alternative dispute resolution methodology agreed to by plaintiff and defendant, the danger to the viability of the alternative dispute resolution method should intervention be allowed, and the consolidation of the lawsuits in the alternative dispute resolution proceeding before the Special Master, I conclude plaintiff's privacy interests clearly outweigh Herman Miller's needs for the documents and materials generated during the proceedings before the Special Master.

Discussion Questions

1. Do you agree that the circumstances in this case dictate supporting the ADR agreement even if it works to the disadvantage of Herman Miller, Inc.?

2. Should a litigant ever receive different treatment in a case because the overall expenses in the judicial system are so high? Under what circumstances, if any, should a judge decide that "judicial economy" dictates dismissing a claim?

3. Does the use of ADR as a way to reduce judicial dockets mean some litigants receive second-class treatment?

LEGAL REFORMS

The American Tort Reform Association can be found at: http://www.aaabiz.com/ATRA/Default.html

Visit the Association for California Tort Reform at: http://www.sna.com/actr/

Because of concerns raised by both litigants and courts, legislatures at both the state and the federal levels have begun to consider reforms calculated to reduce the economic impact of litigation. It is difficult to decide whether the impact of law on business is extensive enough to warrant legislative intervention. Nevertheless, legislatures have begun to consider and pass legislation to reform the civil justice system. Some reforms are explicitly designed to increase the use of ADR, perhaps by mandating it in some cases. Others, such as the ones that follow, attempt to reduce the costs and complexities associated with litigation. Some of these reforms have passed judicial scrutiny and stand, while others have been voided by state and federal appellate courts. The Illinois Supreme Court recently voided the complete set of tort reform measures enacted by the Illinois Legislature.[2] Descriptions of a few of the most popular approaches to reforming the civil justice system beyond the increased use of ADR follow.

Legal **reforms addressing the awarding of damages** are popular means of reducing the cost of litigation. One approach is to eliminate punitive damages or cap them to a percentage of the actual loss or the net worth of the defendant. Doing so serves the important public policy of punishing and deterring intentional or reckless legal wrongdoing without forcing a company into bankruptcy. Dow-Corning, rather than face, among other things, the possibility of punitive damages in its breast implant litigation, simply declared bankruptcy. A second approach involves eliminating or capping noneconomic losses like pain and suffering damages by providing compensation for actual, physical harm only. Although capping any sort of damages may mean plaintiffs are not fully compensated for real losses, and defendants are not truly deterred from similar conflict. Statutes of repose, those placing absolute time limits on the bringing of a suit may also help. A final, relatively novel approach to reducing the cost of damages in lawsuits is to make punitive damages payable in some percentage to the government, to reduce the incentive to lawyers and plaintiffs to file suit in the hope of turning small actual losses into large

---

2. *Best v. Taylor Machine Works,* 1997 NL 777822 (Ill. Sup. Ct., 1997).

punitive losses. Alaska is one state using this approach; it hopes to receive some of the five billion dollars in punitive damages assessed against Exxon as a result of the *Valdez* oil spill.

In addition to reforms addressing damages, **reforms addressing attorneys** have been offered. Some suggest limiting attorneys' fees. One way to do this is to eliminate contingency fees, which allow the lawyer to obtain a percentage of any recovery. Some argue that doing so would discourage the filing of frivolous suits. Others suggest reducing the number of attorneys by raising the standards to obtain a law degree and license to practice law. Still others advocate the elimination of the attorney right to share in a punitive damages award.

However, reforms that make it more difficult to obtain legal counsel have significant downsides. It is unlikely, some argue, that eliminating contingency fees would have any measurable curtailing effect on frivolous suits. Indeed, some counter that it would have precisely the opposite effect—compelling lawyers to file suit more often to make up income lost to tort reform. Similarly, reforms reducing the number of attorneys likely run afoul of the law as an impermissible restraint on free trade at the same time they fail to address the real problem—it is not necessarily true that fewer lawyers results in fewer or more meritorious suits.

Reforms addressing party rights have also been proposed. One option is a "loser pays" system that allows the prevailing party to collect from the opposing party costs and fees associated with the case. Requiring a preliminary case evaluation prior to suit, perhaps by a board empowered to certify cases as either meritorious or meritless, also has support in some quarters. The practice of certifying cases for merit has been adopted, though largely ruled unconstitutional, in several states, when the process interferes with a litigant's right to justice. The elimination of joint and several liability, the legal concept that holds the defendant responsible for the entire verdict regardless of the percentages of negligence, has also been attempted, though courts generally have ruled this reform unconstitutional.

The U.S. system of civil law has traditionally been an open one, allowing virtually free access to litigants. Reforms that represent barriers to potential litigants are viewed with suspicion both judicially and legislatively. Those who oppose such reforms note that motions to dispose of cases prior to trial can be made and that such motions suffice to assure parties of the dismissal of a frivolous suit while leaving the doors to the courthouse largely open to all.

Procedural reforms such as more narrowly defined "causation" and "duty" in tort cases would make it more difficult to prevail in civil suits. In addition, raising the civil burden of proof beyond a mere preponderance of evidence has also been suggested. Some have even argued that elimination of comparative negligence in favor of contributory negligence, so that a plaintiff who contributes to an injury receives nothing or vastly reduced compensation, is an appropriate response to the effects of litigation. Establishment of a system of independent, judicially appointed and paid expert witnesses, which would eliminate the need for paid partisan experts, may provide juries with clearer and more easily understood direction. Finally, some have suggested elimination of civil juries in all technical areas, as

http://

An Illinois plaintiff attorney has written articles opposing tort reform that can be found at: http://www. cliffordlaw.com/

http://

The Ohio Tort Reform Act can be found at: http://www. alliancecourtwat ch.com/ppts/ ktunn997/index. htm

http://

An audio file of a speech on tort reform is at the Illinois Institute of Continuing Legal Education site: http://www.icle. org/products/ audio/dcooper. htm they have been in part in the patent area, to ensure competent deliberation in all cases.

Legal reform is a difficult endeavor. The rights and protections offered by the civil justice system are justifiably cherished by most people and guarded carefully by the courts. In addition, the U.S. Constitution, as well as those of most states, provide relatively easy access to the courts and strong presumptions in favor of permitting a jury to decide a case on the merits as presented at trial. The result is that courts have, in many instances, ruled that tort reform measures are unconstitutional. ADR provides a remedy to those parties for whom and in those cases where the system, because of cost, time, risk, or business relationship factors, is not appropriate. Although some of the reforms described above may at some point be adopted and affirmed by courts, for now, ADR stands as the best alternative to civil litigation.

http://

Comments of Senator Tom Harkin on federal tort reform can be read at: http://www.policy.com/vcongress/tort/tort-harkin.html

CHAPTER CONCLUSION

Litigation in either an adversarial or inquisitorial system is expensive, time-consuming, risky, and sometimes counterproductive. We have reviewed in this chapter the prevailing public, adjudicative systems used to resolve civil disputes involving businesses. We are now ready to examine the range of processes that stand as alternatives to the public courts, representing perhaps the most significant legal reform of all: far wider use, both voluntary and compelled, of alternatives to trial that reduce the risks, expenses, and time lost on judicial proceedings.

BEST BUSINESS PRACTICES

Here are some practical tips for managers on the use of ADR for the resolution of business disputes.

- Perhaps no other matter affects business as completely as law and the legal process. It is virtually impossible to avoid business disputes and almost as difficult to avoid litigation. As a result, a thorough understanding of the avenues available for the resolution of civil disputes is essential to the businessperson.

- A careful pre-suit analysis of the costs, duration, and likely outcomes of litigation is very useful. Although attorneys cannot predict the outcome of a trial with absolute certainty, they can assess the likely costs and disposition of the case before it is litigated.

- The data are mixed on the question of whether a liability crisis exists, and the ways of resolving it, if it does exist, are far from clear. How one responds to the crisis should be dictated by independent research and analysis.

KEY TERMS

Adversarial, common law model, p. 4
Appeal, p. 7
Discovery, p. 7
Frivolous lawsuit, p. 12
Inquisitorial, civil law model, p. 4
Legal reforms: attorneys, p. 23
Legal reforms: damages, p. 22

Legal reforms: party rights, p. 23
Legal reforms: procedure, p. 23
Liability crisis, p. 8
Pretrial stage, p. 7
Religious law systems, p. 6
Trial, p. 7

ETHICAL AND LEGAL REVIEW

1. Unser purchases a new automobile from BMW, Inc. The car, unbeknownst to plaintiff, was damaged in transit to the seller and has been partially repainted. Instead, Unser is told the car is new and perfect. Following the purchase, the defect is uncovered, and the damage is estimated at $4,000. Unser asks for the amount from BMW and is rebuffed. He sues and receives four million dollars, virtually all of which is in punitive damages. Assuming that the conduct of the defendant is willful and that punitive damages in some amount are appropriate, how much is Unser entitled to? On what do you base your amount? [*BMW v. Gore,* 517 U.S. 559, 116 S. Ct. 1589 (1996)]

2. Acme Corporation produces devices known as breast implants. These devices are used in both elective and nonelective reconstructive cosmetic surgery on women. They are filled with a substance known as silicon. Acme is sued by a class of women who allege that ruptured silicon breast implants cause a range of maladies that are permanent and very serious. They offer as proof a study they commissioned and for which they paid. They have no additional evidence beyond the anecdotal stories told by the plaintiffs themselves. Moreover, your medical experts say that no such harm occurs following rupture of the device. Should a judge dismiss the suit for lack of evidence in response to the defendant's motion for summary judgment? When should cases involving conflicting theories be tried? [*In re Dow Corning,* 86 F. 3d 482 (6th Circ. 1996)]

3. You are retained to draft a state tort reform statute. Which elements of tort reform would you include? Which elements of tort reform would you ignore and why? What constitutional hurdles would you expect to face as you drafted your statute? See for assistance, *Best v. Taylor Machine Works,* 1997 WL 777822 (Supreme Court of Illinois, 1997).

SUGGESTED ADDITIONAL READINGS

Abramson, J. *We, the Jury: The Jury System and the Ideal of Democracy.* Basic Books/Harper Collins Publishers, 1994.

Adler, S. *The Jury: Disorder in the Court.* Doubleday/Main Street Books, 1994.

Glendon, M. A. *A Nation under Lawyers: How the Crisis in the Legal Profession Is Transforming American Society.* Harvard Press, 1994.

Glendon, M. A. *Rights Talk: The Impoverishment of Political Discourse.* Free Press, 1991.

Harr, J. *A Civil Action.* Random House, 1995.

Howard, P. *The Death of Common Sense: How Law Is Suffocating America.* Random House, 1994.

Kritzer, H. *Let's Make a Deal: Understanding the Negotiation Process in Ordinary Litigation.* University of Wisconsin Press, 1991.

Lebedoff, D. *Cleaning Up: The Story Behind the Biggest Legal Bonanza of Our Time.* Free Press, 1997.

Nader, R., and W. Smith. *No Contest: Corporate Lawyers and the Perversion of Justice in America.* Random House, 1996.

2

THE ADR RESPONSE TO RESOLVING BUSINESS DISPUTES

CHAPTER HIGHLIGHTS

In this chapter, you will read and learn about the following:

1. The general characteristics of alternative dispute resolution.
2. The unique features of business conflict.
3. The major alternative dispute resolution processes.
4. The advantages and disadvantages of alternative dispute resolution for business.

In the preceding chapter, we considered adversarial litigation systems and how they impact business. This chapter provides a general overview of alternative dispute resolution (ADR) while examining the nature of conflict in business. It also briefly describes the various alternative dispute resolution processes covered at length in later chapters. Moreover, it considers the advantages and disadvantages of alternative dispute resolution for resolving business disputes, presenting several cases and scenarios designed to develop an ability to evaluate and choose among the various nonlitigation processes for resolving business disputes.

INTRODUCTION TO ADR

The phrase **alternative dispute resolution** describes a series of processes available to resolve disputes without formal, public litigation. All alternative dispute resolution processes share several features.

- They are typically less formal than litigation.
- They provide a rapid, relatively inexpensive alternative to litigation.
- They usually encourage negotiated settlement rather than adjudicated decisions.
- They are often highly confidential in relation to litigation.
- They are flexible enough to be adapted on a case-by-case basis, because they are not governed by legal rules.
- They are typically provided by private practitioners for a fee, rather than by judges and lawyers.

ADR processes are well suited to the resolving of business disputes because they recognize the unique features of business conflict. First, unlike disputes involving private individuals, business conflicts may involve many constituencies. Even when one business disputes another, these constituencies can range from shareholders to employees to customers and vendors. Many business disputes involve multiple companies, which vastly increases the number of affected constituencies. One type of dispute resolution mechanism is unlikely to address the disparate needs of all constituencies involved. ADR processes can be tailored to satisfy the interests of all parties.

Second, businesses encounter internal and external disputes, while individuals generally do not. **Internal disputes** involve members of the business, such as managers or employees. **External disputes** apply to business members and some outside party, such as customers or vendors. In both instances, businesses desire resolutions that are prompt, amicable, and foster valuable future relationships. ADR achieves this by focusing on party negotiated outcomes, a result of nonadversarial processes.

Third, businesses, unlike individuals, face economic competition. As a result, businesses must recognize the potential competitive disadvantages associated with litigation, which is often a costly, protracted, public affair. Clearly, maximizing profit while solving corporate disputes is the principal competitive business consideration. However, businesses also want to maintain a favorable corporate image by privately resolving matters. Protecting trade secrets and proprietary information is another matter of importance. Alternative dispute resolution processes are generally less expensive, less time consuming, and more private than litigation.

Fourth, businesses are regulated in ways and to an extent that individuals are not and therefore must resolve disputes more frequently. Businesses value processes that amicably resolve claims brought under, for example, the Americans with Disabilities Act, the Age Discrimination in Employment Act, or Title VII.

THE MAJOR ALTERNATIVE DISPUTE RESOLUTION PROCESSES

Though many ways to address conflict in the business world exist, the major dispute resolution processes consist of two main classes: (1) those that reserve authority for resolution to the parties themselves and (2) those in which a third party decides the matter. By **authority** we mean the power to reach and enforce a resolution to a dispute. The first class includes negotiation, mediation, the summary jury trial, and the minitrial. The second applies to arbitration, private judging, and a hybrid mediation process called mediation-arbitration. Often, parties will attempt to resolve a matter through a process that they control before turning over the case to a third party.

Party-Driven Processes

The first four processes we will briefly define are the party-driven processes. We will begin with the least formal process and arrange the others according to their increasing formality.

Negotiation. **Negotiation** (Chapter 3), the most widely used, is simply the process of refining and agreeing to the issues and establishing a range of compromise options. Negotiation is often done directly, without legal representation. Introducing legal agents entails a much more formal and often acrimonious negotiation process. Negotiation normally does not bring third parties to the case and is therefore the most private of all dispute resolution processes. Since there are no external rules or protection for the parties, it can also be risky.

Mediation. **Mediation** (Chapter 4) uses a specially trained, neutral third party to help the disputants present their positions and generate and evaluate options to resolve the dispute. Mediation is more formal than negotiation, since it involves a third party and is often conducted pursuant to rules agreed to by the parties. Like negotiation, it may be done either through legal representatives or directly. Mediation is virtually always voluntary and private.

Minitrials. **Minitrials** (Chapter 5) allow parties to carefully structure a process blending negotiation, mediation, and litigation. "Minitrial" is a somewhat deceptive term to describe a novel approach to structured negotiations first used to resolve a dispute between TRW, Inc., and Telecredit, Inc., in the late 1970s. In the process, attorneys each semiformally present the case to senior management representatives of each party. The parties structure in advance the length, content, and nature of the presentation so what the executives will hear is balanced and useful. Parties are normally permitted to engage in limited discovery prior to the presentation. Following the presentation, the executives may negotiate directly or with the assistance of a mediator, who often will have presided over the presentation. The minitrial process is voluntary and generally private.

Summary Jury Trial.   The **summary jury trial** (Chapter 5) enables parties to litigate in an abbreviated and mock courtroom proceeding designed to demonstrate the strengths and weaknesses of each side's case. Typically, a six-member jury is impaneled to hear the case *without* being advised that it will render a nonbinding and advisory verdict. Prior to the "trial," parties can engage in discovery, often including depositions and document requests. The parties then present an abbreviated version of their respective cases, including witnesses and evidence. Following this, the jury deliberates and presents its verdict from which the parties then endeavor to negotiate an outcome to the dispute. Like the minitrial, the summary jury trial is designed to preface negotiations with an objective review of the evidence.

Adjudicative Processes

Three adjudicative processes that are used widely by parties for resolution of disputes are arbitration, mediation-arbitration, and private judging. All three entail a decision, generally binding, made by an impartial third party.

Arbitration.   **Arbitration** (Chapters 6–8) is a private version of the public courtroom trial and is based on the presentation of evidence, rather than a negotiated understanding of the facts. It results in a third-party judgment by an arbitrator normally experienced in the subject matter of the case.

Because arbitration involves both evidence presentation, sometimes through witnesses and on the record, and third-party decision making, it is less private than other ADR processes. Arbitration is usually governed by either statutory or private rules. In either event, the parties will have agreed on the exact regulations for the procedure prior to the hearing. Due to these preexisting agreements, arbitration is largely a mandatory process. However, parties may, and often do, submit cases for arbitration without any obligation to do so.

Mediation-Arbitration.   **Mediation-arbitration** (Chapter 4), a blend of mediation and arbitration, initially calls upon a mediator to assist parties in reaching an agreement. If unsuccessful, the case is immediately transferred to arbitration for a binding judgment by a neutral party. Normally, the same neutral party works as both mediator and subsequently as arbitrator. Mediation-arbitration offers parties the advantages of a party-driven, informal process, while at the same time assuring them a specific timeframe within which their dispute will be resolved. In addition, this process, developed primarily in the labor context, motivates parties to settle through mediation so that they can avoid bringing in a neutral to render a judgment.

Private Judging.   Numerous states provide litigants with the opportunity to present their case before a privately hired judge, called **private judging.**[1] This retired state or federal court judge will hear testimony, review evidence, and render a decision in a dis-

---

1.   California (Cal. Civ. Proc. Code sec. 638–645), New Hampshire (N.H. Rev. Stat. Ann. sec. 519:9), and New York (N.Y. Civ. Proc. L. & R. 4301–21) are some examples.

pute. The private judging statutes in several states allow for juries to be impaneled and decisions to be appealed, though few parties actually appeal. States that specifically allow private judging hope to benefit from reduced demands on public court dockets. Litigants should also benefit from much quicker resolution of cases, though once commenced there is likely to be little economic savings as the process is essentially identical to public litigation. Litigants also have the advantage of the procedural experience and talents of one who has actually tried cases. Disputants are generally free to "rent a judge" in states that do not have authorizing statutes. However, they do not have the right to appeal the decision to a state court, nor are they assured of the enforceability of the decision reached in the process, as they would be in a conventional legal judgment.

THE ADVANTAGES OF ALTERNATIVE DISPUTE RESOLUTION

While all nonlitigation dispute resolution processes have unique advantages and disadvantages, some general observations can be made about those of alternative dispute resolution. We will discuss the advantages first.

Timeliness

Any alternative dispute resolution process will likely provide closure more rapidly than litigation. Less time is spent between occurrence and resolution due to the avoidance of vastly overcrowded court dockets. ADR processes can begin as soon as parties have prepared their cases, whereas it may take months to go to trial in federal courts and even years for state courts. Timeliness is also achieved because significantly less time is invested throughout the resolution process where such things as motions, witness preparation, and appeal are unnecessary.

Cost

Many alternative dispute resolution processes can be substantially less expensive than litigation. While a complete arbitration proceeding is unlikely to save much, mediation, for example, can significantly reduce the cost of resolving a dispute. ADR reduces expenses in several ways. First, attorney fees are reduced because there is less preparation and completion time. Indeed, companies may in some instances proceed without attorneys. Second, because expert witnesses seldom testify in most ADR processes, the expense incurred by retaining them is limited or avoided. Third, in cases involving potential substantial economic exposure, it is common for litigants to expend considerable sums on jury selection assistance. Virtually all ADR processes deem this expense unnecessary because juries either are not used or are only used in an advisory capacity. Finally, pretrial motion practice and discovery may both be curtailed in these processes, due to the focus on negotiated outcomes over evidentiary decisions.

Productive Outcomes

Many alternative dispute resolution processes provide negotiated outcomes that can enhance business relationships in a fashion not possible in an adversarial trial setting. Most ADR processes are without the level of acrimony and confrontation that the trial is likely to produce. In addition, the substance of negotiated resolutions is more likely to meet the individual needs and interests of the parties than the "one size fits all" approach taken in litigation. Indeed, negotiated settings can address types of compensation unavailable through a trial. Consider the following two examples of nontraditional remedies reached in real cases settled through mediation.

1. Faced with a possible substantial punitive damages judgment in a products liability case, a company agreed in mediation to pay a sizable sum of money to a charity chosen by an injured customer. The remedy was attractive to both parties. The company benefited by avoiding damages that could have been much greater than those calculated to compensate the plaintiff for actual losses. Such damages are among the most vigorously contested at trial. In addition, the company realized a potential tax benefit that would not have accrued through the payment of punitive damages to the plaintiff. Finally, the company had an obvious altruistic advantage in this sort of settlement. The plaintiff benefited as well. Payment of compensatory damages was quick and comparatively generous. The difficulty and risk of a trial was avoided. The deterrence associated with punitive damages was largely accomplished by the additional payment to the charity. The plaintiff also engaged in a sort of philanthropy.

2. After lengthy negotiations, an insurance company opted to cover college expenses of a high school senior injured in a facility covered by the company rather than to pay any direct damages to the plaintiff. Among the agreement's stipulations were the following: (1) payment was to be made only upon successful completion of each full year of education, (2) the education must take place in four successive years, (3) the education must be provided by a college or university agreed upon and listed in the mediation agreement, and (4) no further payment was required if the plaintiff failed out of or voluntarily left the college or university. Again, both sides gained through the use of ADR. The plaintiff recovered, without a trial, in excess of the probable value of the case if the four-year degree is completed. The insurance company was able to earn interest on the money reserved for payment by structuring payments over four years. In addition, the company was freed of any obligation if the plaintiff did not successfully complete each year of college. Finally, opportunity exists for very favorable public relations for the company.

Privacy

ADR processes are often confidential, which allows businesses to resolve disputes without creation of a public record or response. A company concerned about eroding public confidence in its product or services will be attracted to processes that allow it to negotiate an outcome without a public trial. Similarly, companies concerned about revealing trade secrets or proprietary information during litigation will welcome a process that avoids such disclosure. Finally, companies seeking to evade the creation of legal precedent that may later harm them will be eager to avail themselves of a process following which no appeal through which legal precedent could be established and generalized is permitted or possible.

Flexibility

Most alternative dispute resolution processes can be customized by the parties. For example, arbitration can be advisory or binding, by panel or by individual arbitrator, and with limited or unlimited evidence. Mediation can be done in a single session or a series of conferences with one or two mediators. In short, while several broadly defined processes exist, they can be refined to meet the needs of the participants. Conversely, the trial is governed in all state and federal courts by inflexible rules of procedure, providing parties with a high level of certainty relative to process but virtually no flexibility.

Internationalization

Businesses are competing on an international level with increasing regularity. As a result, they are often involved in disputes with companies from foreign countries. These sorts of disputes are among the most difficult and expensive to resolve because of jurisdiction issues. Jurisdiction is the law regarding which court has power to hear the case and render a judgment. In addition, companies in other countries often have negative perceptions of the American court system and regard defending a suit in the courts as a profoundly unpleasant experience. Moreover, the individuals managing foreign companies may have cultural orientations that suggest that negotiation, rather than litigation, is not simply the preferable fashion for resolving business disputes, but the only way, if a business relationship is to be continued. In resolving international disputes, ADR offers many of the same advantages listed above: speed, economy, flexibility, etc. It also enables American businesses to resolve disputes in a manner consistent with the cultural expectations of many foreign business managers.

ADR IN ACTION

The National Association of Manufacturers Builds a Dispute Resolution Problem

The National Association of Manufacturers (NAM) offers its members the opportunity to mediate business disputes through a joint project with the CPR Institute for Dispute Resolution. NAM is the old-

http://
For further information on the NAM, see this site: http://www.nam. org

ADR IN ACTION (continued)

http://

For further information on The CPR Institute for Dispute Resolution, see this site:
http://www.cpradr.org/welcome.htm

est industrial trade association in the United States. With fourteen thousand member companies and subsidiaries responsible for 85 percent of all domestically manufactured goods, it is also the largest. The CPR Institute for Dispute Resolution is an international, not-for-profit confederation of corporations, law firms, and academics with a panel of approximately six hundred lawyers, judges, and legally trained executives and scholars to serve as mediators and in other neutral roles.

The new program allows NAM members to submit for mediation any claim involving another NAM member. In addition, nonmembers may participate when one or more parties to the dispute are NAM members. Parties choose from the program roster a neutral to mediate the dispute. The program mediates disputes involving amounts in excess of fifty thousand dollars. Parties may be represented by counsel during the mediation conference, and the process follows a set of rules developed by CPR.

In a recent press release, Jerry Jasinowski, president of NAM, stated that "[t]he Mediation Center for Business Disputes is an excellent way to reduce the problem manufacturers have been fighting for years: excessive litigation." He continued, "[I]f the business community can take the lead in resolving problems without relying on the courts and lawsuits, we will set an example for the rest of the country that there are more productive ways of settling disputes."

The CPR Institute reports an 85 percent settlement rate in mediation. It also finds that companies save an average of three hundred thousand dollars annually by using mediation. Finally, CPR President James Henry believes that "[i]n many cases, [companies] will be able to preserve important business relationships" by using the process.

THE DISADVANTAGES OF ALTERNATIVE DISPUTE RESOLUTION

http://

See the text of the Fifth Amendment as well as annotations at:
http://www.findlaw.com/data/Constitution/amendment05/

Procedural Concerns

Although we have discussed many advantages of ADR processes, there are also some drawbacks. Among the most significant are three constitutional concerns: due process, public access, and equal protection. The civil and criminal court systems at both the state and federal levels are governed by due process requirements rooted in the Fifth and Fourteenth Amendments to the U.S. Constitution. **Due process** is essentially the obligation to create laws and the procedures by which they are applied, including the trial, that are fair and reasonable. To ensure that parties receive due process at trial, carefully constructed rules of civil and criminal procedure have been developed. These rules provide parties with trials that are procedurally fair and consistent. For example, due process prohibits courts in criminal proceedings from requiring self-incriminating statements from a defendant. It provides the right to present evidence, to confront one's adversaries, and to cross-examine hostile witnesses. In short, this bedrock American legal principle assures litigants of consistent and equitable treatment under the law.

It should be noted, however, that due process requirements create longer and more difficult proceedings. In addition, due process, as we know it in the United States, is based upon the adversarial system of evidentiary justice. As a result, parties seeking amicable resolutions to disputes rarely find them through the trial.

Equal protection rights, based on the Fourteenth Amendment of the U.S. Constitution, assure all individuals and businesses of similar, if not identical, treatment at law. Equal protection prohibits governments from closing the courts to the indigent, while allowing access to the wealthy. Likewise, it guarantees the same level of consideration to all litigants once in court. In short, it provides a day in court for all who have a justiciable issue for resolution, irrespective of their social or economic status.

Because alternative dispute resolution processes are informal and private, they are not governed by due process principles in any meaningful way. Parties normally either draft rules of procedure for themselves on a case-by-case basis or rely voluntarily on model rules promulgated by professional associations. As a result, by pursuing an alternative dispute resolution process, parties waive certain due process rights and protections they may have had at trial. Furthermore, because certain claims of minimal economic consequence have become subject to mandatory ADR, the courthouse has been effectively closed to some disputants.

The following two cases consider the variety of constitutional rights affected by alternative dispute resolution. The *State Farm* case, including a dissenting opinion, considers both due process and equal protection rights as they relate to mandatory arbitration of insurance claims. The *Rhea* case explores a right closely associated with due process, the potential violation of the Seventh Amendment right to a jury adjudication of a dispute when mandatory mediation is required prior to a jury trial. These issues are also important in the NLO case, which addresses mandatory participation in a summary jury trial, and which is considered in Chapter 5.

http://

See the text of the Fourteenth Amendment as well as annotations at: http://www.findlaw.com/data/Constitution/amendment14/

STATE FARM MUTUAL AUTOMOBILE INSURANCE COMPANY V. BROADNAX, ET. AL.
827 P.2d 531 (1992)

FACT SUMMARY

State Farm issued an automobile insurance policy to Earle Broadnax. After being involved in two car accidents, Broadnax submitted claims to State Farm for personal injury benefits under his policy. A dispute regarding payment ensued, and Broadnax served State Farm with a Demand for Arbitration. State Farm filed a Petition to Stay Arbitration and sought a declaration that the No Fault Act requiring mandatory arbitration was unconstitutional. Insurers are obligated under the No Fault Act to provide direct benefits to insureds. When an insured is liable for benefits paid by another insurer, the No Fault Act requires insurers to resolve reimbursement issues through mandatory, binding arbitration.

OPINION: *VOLLACK, Justice*

State Farm contends that the No Fault Act requiring mandatory arbitration of certain claims extinguishes its right of access to courts because the section removes State Farm's statutory cause of action for disputes arising under the No Fault Act from a trial to jury before a district court, without providing a right of review by a district court following an adverse arbitration award. After careful consideration of the constitutional guarantee, we find no violation of State Farm's right of access to courts. State Farm's contention posits that the right of access to courts guarantees Colorado litigants a trial to jury before a district court for disputes arising under the No Fault Act.

The United States Constitution does not expressly provide for a right of access to courts. Rather, the federal right of access to courts has been located in the Due Process Clause of the Fourteenth Amendment, in the First Amendment's provision securing the right to petition the government for redress of grievances, and in the Privileges and Immunities Clause of the Fourteenth Amendment.

The United States Supreme Court has noted that the right of access to courts and the guarantees of due process have developed in response to challenges by defendants involuntarily haled into the formal judicial process. Thus, whether litigants are afforded adequate constitutional access to courts often sounds in due process under federal analysis.

Colorado, however, is one of thirty-seven states which diverged from the federal constitutional model by creating an express right of access to courts independent of constitutional due process guarantees.

In evaluating the right of access under the Alabama Constitution, Justice Shores has noted that the origins of the right can be traced back to the Magna Carta. Although its language is broad enough to be subject to varying interpretations, it can generally be said to incorporate into our constitution a fundamental principle of fairness, a perhaps vaguely conceived but important notion of limitation on the power of government to infringe upon individual rights, and to act arbitrarily. What those rights are, what degree of infringement is permitted, and with how much justification, are inquiries which have been the subject of long-standing debate.

Under the Louisiana constitutional guarantee, for example, the legislature is free to allocate access to the formal judicial system using any system or classification which is not totally arbitrary so long as access to the system is not essential to the exercise of a fundamental constitutional right.

The Utah access to courts provision "guarantees access to the courts and a judicial procedure that is based on fairness and equality." Utah courts construe the constitutional right of access to courts by examining its history and plain language, in addition to its functional relationship to other constitutional provisions. The Utah Supreme Court has accordingly noted that the right of access provision and the due process clause "are related both in their historical origins and to some extent in their constitutional functions." The two provisions are thus "complementary and even overlap, but they are not wholly duplicative. Both act to restrict the powers of both the courts and the legislature."

In Colorado, the access to courts provision guarantees that courts will be available to effectuate rights that accrue under law. This court has stated that "generally, a burden on a party's right of access to the courts will be upheld so long as it is reasonable." We have recently observed that the right of access under the Colorado Constitution "protects initial access to the courts."

In the present case, State Farm calls on this court to evaluate its access to the judicial process as set out in the No Fault Act. Disputes arising under the No Fault Act proceed to binding arbitration before resorting to courts. Each party to the arbi-

tration selects an arbitrator, and these two arbitrators select a third. The arbitrators then set a time and place for a hearing, with the mutual consent of the parties. Arbitrators may issue subpoenas for witnesses and compel production of evidence. Arbitrators must file an order with the insurance commissioner within ten days of the hearing. Such orders may be vacated, modified, or corrected pursuant to the Uniform Arbitration Act.

The Uniform Arbitration Act in turn confers jurisdiction on Colorado courts to enforce and enter judgments on arbitration awards. Parties may apply to courts to confirm arbitration. Parties may also apply to courts to vacate awards where the arbitrators exceeded their powers or where an award was procured by fraud, corruption, or other undue means. Parties may also apply to courts to modify or correct arbitration awards where there was an evident mistake or where the award was premised on a matter not submitted to the arbitrators. Finally, parties may appeal such court orders "in the manner and to the same extent as from orders or judgments in civil actions."

In determining whether this dispute resolution scheme secures State Farm's right of access to the judicial process, we are guided by the requirements of due process. The United States Supreme Court has consistently held that due process requires some form of hearing—the opportunity to be heard at a meaningful time, and in a meaningful manner.

Under the statutory scheme, State Farm clearly has the right to a hearing in which State Farm can present all the evidence, and raise all the defenses available to it. State Farm also has the right to resort to the formal judicial system should it find an arbitrator's order adverse to its interest. We thus conclude that State Farm is not

> **http://**
>
> *The American Arbitration Association has placed the Uniform Arbitration Act text on-line at this site:* http://www.adr. org/uniform.html #intro

deprived of its access to the judicial process under the Colorado Constitution.

We are not alone in our determination. The Court of Appeals for the Fourth Circuit has observed that "it is too late in the day to argue that compulsory arbitration, per se, denies due process of law . . . Congress may require arbitration so long as fair procedures are provided and ultimate judicial review is available." Where a party "may come to the district court to enforce, vacate or modify an arbitrator's award, [the party] is not denied meaningful access to the Courts."

We similarly have noted that the No Fault Insurance Act seeks to reduce tort litigation, and that arbitration serves that end. We conclude that State Farm has not been deprived of its right of access.

We have observed that "arbitration provides an efficient, convenient alternative to litigation." We again note that one of the General Assembly's primary purposes in passing the No Fault Act was "to reduce the amount of tort litigation arising out of automobile accidents," and to provide prompt resolution of disputed payments. Were we to adopt State Farm's position, we would be required to overlook both the current demands on the Colorado judicial system and the need for prompt payment of personal injury protection benefits that we have acknowledged when encouraging the use of arbitration as a method of dispute resolution. We decline to take that approach.

State Farm contends that [the No Fault Act] violates its right to equal protection of the laws because the section imposes a restriction on the fundamental right of access to courts.

We have already recognized the state's interest in reducing tort litigation arising out of automobile accidents and in prompt payment of personal injury protection benefits. This state prefers arbitration as a method for resolving disputes because it "promotes quicker resolution of disputes by providing an expedited opportunity for the parties to present their cases before an unbiased third party." By promoting quicker resolution of disputes, arbitration thus reduces the parties' costs. Colorado's dispute resolution scheme is rationally related to legitimate interests in expediting dispute resolution, reducing parties' costs, and securing prompt payment of benefits. We reject State Farm's equal protection challenge.

KIRSHBAUM, Justice dissenting

Because the United States Constitution contains no express right of access guarantee, federal courts have by necessity addressed issues with respect to access to state courts in the framework of due process analysis. The right itself, however, is firmly rooted in the right of petition guaranteed by the First Amendment to the United States Constitution. The right has also been defined as one of the privileges and immunities guaranteed to all citizens by article 4 of the United States Constitution. The right is "one of the fundamental rights protected by the Constitution."

State courts assessing the significance of particular right to access provisions contained in their state constitutions have predictably described the characteristics of the right itself in various ways. Some have emphasized its historical roots in sections of the Magna Carta. In a thorough and thoughtful opinion declaring a portion of a statute of repose for products liability cases to be violative of state constitutional open access guarantees, the Utah Supreme Court articulated a two-part test seeking to balance the legislative authority to alter rights and remedies with the fundamental guarantee of access to courts contained in Utah's constitution.

I find persuasive those decisions that conclude that right to access guarantees must be considered in relationship to the significance of the right advanced by the party seeking such access. If the underlying right is a fundamental right, the right of access itself must be fundamental. Such analysis requires careful evaluation of issues and facts on a case-by-case basis. However, it rejects the conclusion that the right of access guarantee is merely a due process guarantee—a conclusion that in this jurisdiction ignores the separate due process guarantee provided by our constitution and tends to reduce the language of article II, section 6, to a mere statement of principle. That analytical framework also avoids many of the problems perceived to result from a conclusion that the right of access is in all contexts fundamental.

In the context of this case, the interest advanced by State Farm—the right to protect its property interests under particular contracts—must be deemed a fundamental right. We have recently noted that at least some of the inalienable rights enumerated in that section are fundamental in nature. Surely the right to protect one's property interests from conduct by private parties allegedly appropriating those interests is fundamental to our concept of ordered liberty.

Application of strict scrutiny analysis to the circumstances of this case requires the conclusion that the compulsory arbitration provisions violate State Farm's fundamental right of access to the courts for the protection of its property interests. The primary justification advanced for the adoption of these compulsory arbitration provisions is the legislative goal of reducing tort litigation. That policy is not furthered through legislation prohibiting a person alleging a deprivation of property interests by conduct of private parties from pursuing appropriate judicial remedies. No other justification appearing of record, the provisions cannot stand.

Even if the right to protect property interests by access to courts secured by our constitution is not accorded fundamental status, application of due process requires the conclusion that the judicial review provisions contained therein are constitutionally inadequate.

Because the General Assembly has authority to alter established rights and remedies, arguments premised on access to courts provisions are unpersuasive to the extent they are based on a vested rights analysis. This legislative authority is not absolute, however; it must be exercised within constitutional constraints, including the limitations established by article II, section 6. Assuming that the minimal rational relationship standard of due process analysis is applicable, the determination of whether a particular statutory scheme limiting access to the courts is rationally related to a legitimate legislative purpose requires examination of the government interests involved and the procedural alternatives provided, as well as the significance of the affected private interests. At a minimum, the legislation must provide the litigant with a meaningful opportunity to obtain independent judicial analysis of those interests at a meaningful stage of the dispute resolving process.

The right to participate in an arbitration proceeding is not a right to participate in a judicial proceeding. At a minimum, due process analysis requires that abolition of the traditional judicial forum be justified on a quid pro quo basis. As has been noted, the General Assembly did not abolish common law contract remedies by [the No Fault Act.] It rather directed disputes about the availability of such remedy to arbitration processes, thus prohibiting determination of those traditional common-law claims by trial. To the extent the reciprocal benefit is the elimination of tort claims, there is no quid pro quo at all. To the extent the reciprocal benefit is a reduction in delay of payments to insureds, it is far from clear that the procedures established will substantially achieve such results.

Assuming the constitutional validity of the General Assembly's decision to require submission of common-law contract claims to compulsory arbitration, thus insulating such claims from adversarial examination of testimony, exhibits and witness credibility under the procedural and evidentiary rules associated with the trial process, such assumption does not answer the serious questions raised by the legislative decision to restrict judicial review of such proceedings to the narrow standards established by the Uniform Arbitration Act. Those provisions are wholly inadequate to protect the important, if not fundamental, right here involved.

The Uniform Act contains stringent limitations on the scope of judicial review of initial arbitration awards. A reviewing court has authority to vacate an arbitration award only if the award was procured by "corruption, fraud, or other undue means . . . ; if there is evidence that a party's rights were prejudiced because of corruption or misconduct or lack of impartiality by one or more arbitrators; if the arbitrators or one of them acted in excess of the powers granted by the Uniform Act; if the arbitrators failed to postpone a hearing or to hear relevant evidence, to the prejudice

of parties; or, in specified circumstances, if there was no arbitration agreement." A reviewing court may modify or correct an award only if the award contains miscalculations of figures or mistakes in descriptions; if it was made upon a matter not submitted to arbitration and the award may be corrected without affecting the merits of the decision appropriately rendered; or if the award is "imperfect in a matter of form, not affecting the merits of the controversy."

The Uniform Act thus does not permit the reviewing court to review the sufficiency of the evidence or the propriety of procedural rulings. Furthermore, the reviewing court is for all practical purposes precluded from reviewing evidentiary rulings, and in the absence of specific contractual directions may not vacate an arbitration award even if the arbitrator misapplied applicable rules of law. In view of the absence of initial judicial evaluation of evidence and issues and the presence of the inalienable, if not fundamental, right to have meaningful access to the judicial process to resolve contractual disputes involving private property interests, this extraordinarily limited right to judicial review is neither meaningful nor reasonable.

At the very least, the right of access provisions of the Colorado Constitution require the availability of meaningful judicial review of non-judicial determinations of private disputes over property interests. In my view, [the No Fault Act] does not provide such meaningful review of State Farm's property interests.

For the foregoing reasons, I find the compulsory arbitration provisions violative of the Colorado Constitution. I therefore respectfully dissent from the contrary conclusion reached by the majority.

http://

For a more indepth look at dispute resolution in Colorado, see the site of the state office of dispute resolution: http://www.courts.state.co.us/odr/odrcol.htm

RHEA V. MASSEY-FERGUSON, INC.
767 F.2d 266 (6th Cir., 1985)

FACT SUMMARY

Rhea was injured when he inadvertently shifted a Massey-Ferguson 245 tractor into gear while he stood beside it. The tractor began moving forward, although no one had depressed the clutch lever. The tractor's right rear wheel first rolled over Rhea's leg, forcing him under the machine, before it rolled over his shoulder and chest. Rhea suffered numerous fractures and lost part of one ear in the accident. Rhea filed this action in state court alleging that Massey-Ferguson was liable for negligent design and breach of implied warranty. Massey-Ferguson transferred the action to federal district court. The case was then sent to mediation prior to trial, but no settlement was reached.

OPINION: *Per Curiam Decision*

Massey-Ferguson challenges the district court's referral of this case to mediation under the Eastern District of Michigan's Local Rule 32, which provides that a diversity case involving only monetary damages may be referred to mediation before trial. Massey-Ferguson rejected and Rhea accepted the resulting $100,000 proposed award. Therefore, Massey-Ferguson was liable for costs unless the verdict at trial was more than ten percent below the evaluation. The jury returned a verdict that was more than twice the mediation evaluation and the district court awarded $5,400 in actual costs to Rhea.

Massey-Ferguson contends that this procedure violates its Seventh Amend-

ment right to a jury. The Seventh Amendment "was designed to preserve the basic institution of jury trial in only its most fundamental elements, not the great mass of procedural forms and details." At the core of these fundamental elements is the right to have a "jury ultimately determine the issues of fact if they cannot be settled by the parties or determined as a matter of law." Federal courts have repeatedly upheld mandatory arbitration procedures in the face of challenges based on the right to a jury trial. In keeping with the Seventh Amendment's requirements Massey-Ferguson received the jury's determination of the disputed facts in the present action.

Massey-Ferguson also characterizes [the referral to mediation and imposition of costs] as violating numerous Federal Rules of Civil Procedure. Federal Rule of Civil Procedure 83 authorizes district courts to "regulate their practice in any manner not inconsistent with these rules." The challenged local rule is not inconsistent merely because it interposes an additional step between the jury demand and trial. The mediation panel merely issues a settlement evaluation that has no force unless accepted by the parties. In sum, no flaw requiring this Court to intervene in the district court's practice under Local Rule 32 has been raised in the present suit.

http://

See the text of the Seventh Amendment as well as annotations at: http://www. findlaw.com/data /Constitution/ amendment07/

Discussion Questions

1. Does imposing mandatory participation in an alternative dispute resolution process prior to jury adjudication unfairly inflate the cost of resolution for a party unable or unwilling to settle?
2. Is the right to jury adjudication diminished in situations where parties have been given exposure to the case an opponent is prepared to present in litigation?
3. Is a trial a fundamental right? If not, should it be?

Public Policy Issues

See the text of the First Amendment as well as annotations at: http://www.findlaw.com/data/Constitution/amendment01/

Public access and First Amendment questions are often raised by the use of alternative dispute resolution processes. Because virtually all ADR processes are conducted off the record, in private settings, and with no public access, the public and the press have expressed reservations about the processes. The following case addresses the public's right to gain access to information presented during litigation leading to settlement. The case relies on a long-standing, common-law right of access to court proceedings. The dissent is included because it carefully conveys the public policy reasons for supporting settlement by upholding the secrecy of materials used to reach settlement.

BANK OF AMERICA NATIONAL V. HOTEL RITTENHOUSE
800 F.2d 339 (3rd Cir., 1986)

FACT SUMMARY

The dispute that forms the basis for this case arose out of the construction of the Hotel Rittenhouse. In 1981, the Bank of America contracted with Hotel Rittenhouse Associates and other developers to finance the construction of the hotel. FAB III was the concrete contractor on the project. In June 1983, the Bank filed suit against Hotel Rittenhouse Associates, its partners, and some involved individuals, referred to collectively as HRA, in the U.S. District Court in order to foreclose on the Hotel Rittenhouse property and to collect on a loan. HRA counterclaimed on numerous state and federal law grounds. In April 1984, FAB III filed suit in federal court against the Bank, but not against HRA. FAB III was seeking over $800,000 on the basis of an alleged assurance by the Bank of direct payment for FAB III's HRA work. The Bank-HRA action proceeded to trial in January 1985. Before the case could be sent to the jury, the parties reached a settlement, and the jury was discharged. At the parties' request, the settlement agreement was filed under seal. Prior to this, all proceedings in the litigation had been open to the public. Shortly thereafter, the Bank of America and HRA disagreed about the settlement. Release of the documents filed to enforce the settlement would reveal the contents of the settlement agreement.

At this time, FAB III attempted to obtain the settlement agreement and the documents filed in federal court to enforce the settlement. In April 1985, FAB III and other creditors of HRA met with the district court and requested it to unseal the documents. This request was denied. Shortly thereafter, FAB III filed a formal motion with the district court to unseal the settlement documents. Following what FAB III's brief characterizes as "an informal conference in chambers," the court denied the motion to unseal. The court stated that it had weighed "the public interest in access to judicial records," as well as FAB III's interest in access to the settlement, against "the public and private interests in settling disputes" and had found that the latter interest was paramount.

OPINION: *SLOVITER, Circuit Judge*

In this appeal, we are faced with an issue that this court has confronted with increasing frequency in recent years, under what circumstances documents filed in the district court may be sealed from public access.

FAB III bases its claim for access to the documents filed in the district court on the common law right of access, rather than on the First Amendment. The right of the public to inspect and copy judicial records antedates the Constitution. The Supreme Court reaffirmed the common law right of access to judicial records and proceedings in *Nixon v. Warner Communications, Inc.* [435 U.S. 589, 55 L. Ed. 2d 570, 98 S. Ct. 1306 (1978)], where it held that there was a presumption in favor of access to "public records and documents, including judicial records and documents."

This court first considered that right of access in Criden I, where we held that there was a "strong presumption" that the public and the media were entitled to access to tapes played during the criminal trial of two of the Abscam defendants. We have also held that the common law presumption of access encompasses as well all "civil trials and records." More recently, we held that "the common law right of access to judicial records is fully applicable to transcripts of sidebar or chambers conferences in criminal cases at which evidentiary or other substantive rulings have been made."

Other opinions in this court have grounded access to court hearings on the First Amendment. In *United States v. Criden* [675 F.2d 550 (3d Cir. 1982) (Criden II)], we held that there is a First Amendment right of access to pretrial criminal proceedings. We explicitly based our holding that the press and the public could have access to a hearing in a civil proceeding and the transcript thereof on the First Amendment right of access as well as the common law.

Just as the right of access is firmly entrenched, so also is the correlative principle that the right of access, whether grounded on the common law or the First Amendment, is not absolute. Our opinions may be read to suggest that there are somewhat different standards, depending on whether access is sought under the common law presumption or under the First Amendment. In Publicker, we required the party opposing access to show " 'an overriding interest based on findings that closure is narrowly tailored to serve that interest' " [733 F.2d at 1073]. In Criden I, we held the strong common law presumption of access must be balanced against the factors militating against access [648 F.2d at 818]. The burden is on the party who seeks to overcome the presumption of access to show that the interest in secrecy outweighs the presumption.

The district court was cognizant that its decision required it to balance the factors favoring secrecy against the common law presumption of access. In denying FAB III's motion for access to the settlement documents, the court held that the "public and private interests in settling disputes" outweighed the "public interest in access to judicial records" and FAB III's private interest in knowing the terms of the settlement.

The balancing of the factors for and against access is a decision committed to the discretion of the district court. Thus, the issue before us is whether the district court abused its discretion in holding that the judicial policy of promoting the settlement of litigation justifies the denial of public access to records and proceedings to enforce such settlements.

We acknowledge the strong public interest in encouraging settlement of private litigation. Settlements save the parties the substantial cost of litigation and conserve the limited resources of the judiciary. In order to encourage the compromise and settlement of disputes, evidence of settlements or offers of settlement are ordinarily not admissible in federal proceedings. See Fed. R. Evid. 408 and advisory committee note thereto.

Judge Garth [who authored the dissenting opinion that follows] has written an interesting and vigorous essay about the importance of settlement to the overburdened court systems of this country. Since the proposition is self-evident, it is intended to, and undoubtedly will, touch a sympathetic chord in the hearts of all judges who, after all, bear much of the burden of the litigation explosion to which Judge Garth refers.

Noteworthy, however, is the fact that Judge Garth practically ignores the relevant posture of the case before us. This is not like *FDIC v. Ernst & Ernst* [677 F.2d 230 (2d Cir. 1982)], which he relies on, where there was an effort to unseal a settlement agreement made two years earlier. Here, there were motions filed and orders entered that were kept secret, in direct contravention of the open access to judicial records that the common law protects. FAB III began its efforts to unseal the court papers almost immediately after these court documents were filed and sealed.

In the name of encouraging settlements, Judge Garth would have us countenance what are essentially secret judicial proceedings. We cannot permit the expediency of the moment to overturn centuries of tradition of open access to court documents and orders.

Having undertaken to utilize the judicial process to interpret the settlement and enforce it, the parties are no longer entitled to invoke the confidentiality ordinarily accorded settlement agreements. Once a settlement is filed in the district court, it becomes a judicial record, and subject to the access accorded such records.

Such public access serves several of the important interests we identified in our earlier cases. First, it promotes "informed discussion of governmental

A complete version of the Federal Rules of Evidence is provided at: http://www.law.cornell.edu/rules/fre/overview.html

affairs by providing the public with [a] more complete understanding of the judicial system" and the "public perception of fairness which can be achieved only by permitting full public view of the proceedings." Disclosure of settlement documents serves as a check on the integrity of the judicial process. Although FAB III does not allege that the district court engaged in any impropriety, as a general proposition access assures "that the courts are fairly run and judges are honest." [*Crystal Grower's Corp. v. Dennis,* 616 F.2d 458, 461 (10th Cir. 1980)] The applicability and importance of these interests are not lessened because they are asserted by a private party to advance its own interests in pursuing its lawsuits against the Bank and HRA.

We conclude that the district court abused its discretion in denying FAB III's motion to unseal the motions and settlement agreement papers.

GARTH, J., Dissenting

The majority today, totally disregarding the difference between the sealing and the unsealing of an agreement, in an unprecedented decision, holds that the interest in settlement may not outweigh the public's right of access even in private litigation. I cannot agree, and therefore, I dissent.

I believe that the majority misconstrues the issue now before the court. The majority claims the issue before us to be: "under what circumstances [may] documents filed in the district court . . . be sealed from public access." However, that is not the issue this case presents. The question is not whether material which is already public should now be sealed; the question is whether a privately negotiated settlement agreement, agreed to and entered into a court record only on condi-

tion that it remain secret, should now be unsealed because of the district court's supposed abuse of discretion in permitting it to be filed under seal.

The resolution of the correct issue raised here dictates an approach that would protect the reliance interests of the parties absent exceptional circumstances. Moreover, in reviewing the district court's denial of FAB's motion to unseal the Bank-HRA agreement, the majority adopts, for all practical purposes, a per se rule that the interest in settling cases can never outweigh the public's right of access and thereby justify a court in sealing the terms of a voluntary settlement. The majority opinion holds that the generalized interest in encouraging settlements does not rise to the level of interests that we have recognized may outweigh the public's common law right of access. The majority's holding on this point is not compelled by any precedent, and it utterly ignores the importance of, and the practical realities surrounding, the process of settling lawsuits.

Because I believe that the public and private interest in encouraging settlement is entitled to significant weight, and because the majority's analysis and holding cannot help but impair seriously the efficacy of judicial efforts to encourage settlement of many cases, I cannot join in this result.

As the majority recognizes, in deciding whether the common law right of access compels the disclosure of materials before the court, the district court must "weigh the interests advanced by the parties in light of the public interest and duty of the courts." [*Nixon v. Warner Communications,* 435 U.S. 589, 602, 55 L. Ed. 2d 570, 98 S. Ct. 1306 (1978)] This court has held that the common law right of access creates a presumption of access to all judicial records and documents. I therefore agree that, as a general matter, the common law right of access applies to settlement agreements when such agreements are filed with the court and become a part of the public record.

However, a settlement agreement that has never been disclosed to the public, but which was only entered into the record by the parties with the understanding that it would remain secret, presents a situation different from any situation that this court has addressed before. Although a presumption of access certainly arises when a court seals the transcript of a sidebar conference that has already taken place on the record in open court, or when a party seeks access to material already entered into evidence and provided to the jury, this case involves material and information that was never public, giving rise to a new and different factor: the reliance of the parties on the initial and continuing secrecy of the settlement agreement.

Although this court has not apparently addressed this precise situation, the Second Circuit has held that, "once a confidentiality order has been entered and relied upon, it can only be modified if an 'extraordinary circumstance' or 'compelling need' warrants the requested modification." [*FDIC v. Ernst & Ernst,* 677 F.2d 230, 232 (2d Cir. 1982)] The Second Circuit therefore affirmed the denial of a motion to lift a protective order sealing a settlement agreement.

The *Ernst & Ernst* case presents what I regard as a sensible standard and a sensible result. Although the common law right of access must be given due regard, a court cannot operate in a vacuum. To apply mechanistically the same test no matter what the factual circumstances, is to risk doing injustice to parties before the court. Therefore, I agree that when a document or item of evidence has been entered into the public record without any reliance on secrecy, the interests of the parties seeking to seal or unseal such material must be weighed in light of a presumption of openness. However, when a document has only been entered into the record in reliance on an order keeping it under seal, and when time has passed and the parties have acted in reliance on the terms of that settlement remaining under seal, I would hold with the Second Circuit that the presumption must shift. While the public interest in openness of court records must nevertheless be factored into the balance, I think it is appropriate that a protective order or seal order which itself induced the production or entry of the contested material be presumed to remain in effect, absent a showing of an "extraordinary circumstance" or "compelling need" by a third party seeking to unseal that information.

Even if I were to accept (which I do not) the majority's holding that the presumption in favor of access to judicial records still applies when a third party seeks to unseal a settlement agreement entered under seal and in reliance upon secrecy, I still could not agree to the majority's rule of law that the interest in settling cases cannot serve to rebut the presumption of access and therefore cannot justify the sealing of a settlement agreement. I believe that such a rule is completely out of touch with the reality of running a trial court docket—a reality with which our district court judges must wrestle every day—and if permitted to remain as the law of our circuit will wreak havoc with judicial efforts to encourage settlement of appropriate cases.

Although I believe the matter to be self-evident, the majority's out-of-hand rejection of the encouragement of settlement as a relevant factor in the decision to seal a settlement agreement requires me to explain both why I believe that fostering voluntary settlements of civil disputes is desirable and necessary, and why this goal will be unavoidably subverted by the majority's holding in this case.

It is impossible to gainsay that we have experienced a litigation explosion in the United States during the last twenty years and that developing techniques for managing the increased caseloads and for otherwise stemming the burgeoning tide of litigation costs has become a subject of intense interest and debate. Between 1973 and 1983, new filings of civil cases in the federal district courts rose from 98,560 to 241,842, an increase of 145 percent. Perhaps more importantly, the number of long, complex, and difficult-to-try cases has also increased dramatically. The federal courts held 213 trials lasting 20 days or more in 1973. The figure doubled to 426 by 1983.

To cope with the increasing volume of litigation, many commentators have advocated an active, "managerial" role for judges in supervising the course of litigation—a role that includes the encouragement of a variety of alternate means of resolving disputes short of full-dress trials.

Although arbitration, mediation, mini-trials, and other forms of alternative dispute resolution have gained prominence in recent years as potent weapons in the war against litigation glut, the key component of every rational approach to reducing the burden on our clogged court dockets has been and remains settlement. With very rare exceptions, commentators and judges who may concur on little else, agree on the value and necessity of a vigorous policy of encouraging fair and reasonable settlement of civil claims whenever possible. Indeed, the literature

on the settlement of civil suits focuses not on whether settlement is desirable, but on how best to achieve it and how far a judge should go to encourage it.

This court, too, has recognized the overwhelming importance of settling civil suits and avoiding the wasted resources and institutional burden of trying every case.

> Voluntary settlement of civil controversies is in high judicial favor. Judges and lawyers alike strive assiduously to promote amicable adjustments of matters in dispute, as for the most wholesome of reasons they certainly should. When the effort is successful, the parties avoid the expense and delay incidental to litigation of the issues; the court is spared the burdens of a trial and the preparation and proceedings that must forerun it. [*Pennwalt Corp. v. Plough, Inc.,* 676 F.2d 77, 80 (3d Cir. 1982)]

Indeed, recognition of the desirability of settlement has even found its way into the Federal Rules of Civil Procedure. Rule 16 was amended in 1983 to include the pursuit of settlement as an express goal of the pretrial conference. Thus, an activist role for judges in managing cases—and encouraging their settlement—has expressly been provided for under the federal rules.

As any trial judge knows, the settlement of civil cases is not just a permissible and desirable goal, but a practical necessity. In one study of cases filed in ten courts, fully 88 percent were settled; only 9 percent went to trial.

While the importance of settlement would seem to be self-evident, I believe it is equally obvious that confidentiality is often a key ingredient in a settlement agreement—and that many settlements would not be reached if the secrecy of their terms could not be safeguarded.

Both courts and commentators have recognized the crucial role of confidentiality in facilitating settlement of civil cases. In addition, the need to keep secret the terms of a settlement has been recognized as a justification for imposing a protective order guaranteeing confidentiality of certain discovery material exchanged prior to settlement.

While few cases address the question of the sealing of settlement agreements, I suspect that this is because many trial judges regard it as self-evident that secrecy is often necessary, and they therefore order settlement agreements filed under seal as a matter of course. This conclusion is supported by the frequent references to such sealings made without comment or challenge in reported cases.

Parties may have many reasons for desiring secrecy for the terms of their settlements. Settlement agreements may include trade secrets or information that threaten the privacy of the parties. While this kind of information would itself justify a seal order, parties may in good faith be concerned about releasing a far wider range of information, including information which would not itself entitle the parties to a protective order, but which might stand in the way of settlement if required to be disclosed.

The necessity for confidentiality may be particularly acute in the mass tort area, where a defendant must look beyond the parameters of a settlement with a single plaintiff and anticipate the impact of its settlement on innumerable future cases. As Edward A. Dauer, Associate Dean of Yale Law School, explained in a Second Circuit Judicial Conference discussion on alternative dispute resolution.

> There are legitimate, good faith reasons for the parties who are trying to work out a solution to something like this toxic tort case to want their discussions to be

private, immune both from later admission and immune from discovery by other potential plaintiffs' lawyers later down the road, maybe even from competitors, and I think there are good faith reasons for wanting that privacy. That confidentiality is a very large advantage that will, if it can be guaranteed, make these kinds of [alternative] procedures even more useful as adjuncts to the judicial process than they already are.

For example, if a defendant facing multiple plaintiffs seeks to settle a meritorious claim for a certain sum of money, it may be deterred from doing so if it knows that the terms of such a settlement would have to be made public. The defendant may reasonably assume that disclosure of the comparatively favorable settlement terms would interfere with its ability to settle other cases for smaller amounts. I have no doubt that if all such settlement details were by rule of law always public, many settlements would never take place at all. Many defendants would almost certainly proceed to trial rather than broadcast to all potential plaintiffs how much they might be willing to pay.

Moreover, it is precisely in the context of mass torts with multiple plaintiffs—such matters as air disasters, toxic injuries, and product liability claims—that the interest in settlement is particularly strong. Such cases are characteristically long, complex, and costly to try, and the savings in public and private resources achieved by settling them are immense. As one judge familiar with the trial of mass tort cases noted:

> Even saving one week of judicial time per case would, as most trial judges know, be substantial. For example, in the Dalkon Shield litigation, the record disclosed that, if the usual percentage (90) of the 1000 members statewide class settled their cases, the savings of judicial resources in the trial of the remaining 100 would amount to

400 weeks, or, roughly eight years of trial time. In addition, there would be an estimated savings of $26 million in litigation expense to the parties and $7 million of court expenses.

The rule announced today by the majority flies in the face of this reality. By holding that settlement agreements may not be sealed to serve the interest of encouraging settlements, I believe the majority has removed from the discretion of our district courts an important technique for encouraging settlement. It is my belief that district court judges in this circuit will read the majority's opinion to the same effect.

Under the majority's rule, a district court judge faced with the prospect of a six month, 12 month or longer trial, who is told by the parties that they would settle the case if the terms of settlement could be filed with the court under seal, would have only one choice—to reject the settlement and proceed to trial. The judge would have no discretion to accept the settlement under seal even if the proposed settlement contained little information of public interest and the interests of both sides of the dispute would be furthered by the settlement.

With all due respect to my colleagues in the majority, theirs is an illogical and impractical result. We are dealing here not with a constitutional right, but with a flexible common-law rule that has historically been applied subject to the discretion of the district court. Moreover, decisions regarding the management of its docket and the expediting of case resolutions would seem to lie at the core of the district court's discretionary powers. Therefore, assuming that a district court judge correctly weighs the public and private interests involved in deciding whether to order a settlement admitted under seal, I can see no reason why the interest in encouraging settlement should not be entitled to due weight. Indeed, any other rule would improperly abridge the traditional discretion of the district judge and seriously impair the ability of judges to expedite settlement.

In this case, the district court acknowledged the correct standards and concluded in its order that "FAB III's asserted interest in access to the sealed information does not outweigh the public and private interests in favor of settling disputes." Although I believe that the district court thereby satisfied its duty to weigh the relevant factors, I could nevertheless understand how others might prefer a more detailed and particularized discussion of how the various asserted interests were, and were not, served on the facts before the court. In such a situation, however, the indicated resolution would have involved no more than a remand to the district court for a fuller statement of its reasons in denying FAB's motion to unseal. Unfortunately, the majority holds instead that the interest in settling cases cannot justify sealing a settlement agreement. Consistent with that holding the majority reverses the district court's order.

I believe the adoption of such a rule can only be counterproductive and must necessarily have the effect of discouraging settlement in many cases that would otherwise be routinely ended by the parties' agreement. This, in turn, will undoubtedly force costly and ultimately unnecessary trials. Accordingly, I respectfully dissent from the majority's judgment, and, rather than reverse, I would affirm the district court's order which refused to unseal the Bank-HRA settlement agreement.

Discussion Questions

1. What interest does the public have regarding "access to judicial records," and why is it a foundational legal concept?
2. Could the district court have found a middle ground that supported access and settlement not only by unsealing the records for FAB III but also by retaining the seal as to other parties and the public?
3. The dissent essentially makes an economic argument: more settlement results from more secrecy, which equals dramatic savings in court resources. Is this argument persuasive? Is it a dangerous way to assess public rights relative to the court system?
4. Without public access to judicial records, what safeguards exist against settlements that violate public interest?

Enforcement Concerns

In addition to constitutional concerns, parties in an alternative dispute resolution process are often justifiably troubled by questions regarding an agreement's finality and enforceability. While arbitration decisions normally are accorded great judicial deference, other processes do not have so well-defined a sense of certainty. Generally, the agreements reached in negotiated processes are treated as contracts. They are therefore subject to defenses and subsequent judicial scrutiny for deficiencies. Parties may demand contract performance, but the agreements they reach in ADR do not have the effect of a rapidly enforceable legal judgment. The following case illustrates the sort of analysis possible in such circumstances.

D.R., BY HIS PARENTS AND V. EAST BRUNSWICK BD. OF EDUCATION
109 F.3d 896 (3rd. Cir., 1996)

FACT SUMMARY

D.R. is a multiple-handicapped individual classified by the New Jersey Board of Education as in need of special education. He was diagnosed at age two with athetoid ataxic cerebral palsy and moderate retardation. D.R. is now twenty-one years old, but his adaptive behavior is considered to be at the preschool level. The parties agree that D.R. has difficulty performing simple daily tasks by himself. He has trouble walking, dressing, and toileting without assistance. In the classroom, he often regresses into a hypnotic rocking behavior and must be constantly monitored by an assistant in order to engage him in classroom activity.

At age four, D.R. began attending day school at the Cerebral Palsy Center (CPC) in New Jersey, where he remained until January 1992. While at CPC, D.R. resided with his parents in East Brunswick, New Jersey. During the first semester of the 1991–92 school year, D.R.'s parents became convinced that he was not progressing at CPC and should be enrolled in a residential program. In December 1991, D.R.'s parents filed a petition with the New Jersey Department of Education requesting a due process hearing under the IDEA. The petition alleged that the CPC program was not appropriate for D.R. and that he would benefit from a transfer to the Benedictine School, an out-of-state residential school in Ridgely, Maryland.

The Board, however, disagreed that residential placement was necessary for D.R. His parents proceeded in early January 1992 to unilaterally place him at the Benedictine School. The Benedictine School subsequently informed D.R.'s parents that their son's acceptance in the program would be on a five-week "trial basis." They were told that the proposed program might be modified depending on D.R.'s adaptation to his new circumstances. The Board now complains that it was never informed of the "trial" nature of D.R.'s acceptance at Benedictine, nor that the program in which he was placed was subject to modification.

Before D.R.'s trial period was complete, his parents and the Board met at a mediation conference and entered a settlement agreement. The parties agreed to these three conditions.

1. The East Brunswick Board of Education will compensate placement costs for D.R. at the Benedictine School at an annual rate of $27,500, prorated for the balance of the 1991–92 school year including the summer of 1992 and beginning January 1, 1992.
2. For the 1992–93 school year, the Board will contribute 90 percent of any increase over the 1991–92 rate.
3. The Board will be absolved of any further costs based upon this placement, related service, or transportation in connection therewith.

During D.R.'s first semester at Benedictine, the school "practically" provided one-to-one assistance. Classes were small in size, with a high ratio of assistants and teachers to students; weekend and residential staff were able to provide the personal help that D.R. needed with daily functions. Later in the adaptation process, however, the school felt that it could not continue to expend such resources on D.R. without neglecting its other students. The school informed D.R.'s parents that D.R. would not be allowed to re-enroll for the 1992–93 school year unless personal aides were provided.

In April 1992, the Board received a cost estimate from the Benedictine School for the 1992–93 school year. The tuition totaled $62,487—more than double the amount provided by the settlement agreement. In addition to the amount that the Board had agreed to pay in 1992–93, the estimate charged the Board for the services of a special classroom aide and a special residential aide, each at a cost of $16,640.

The Board refused to pay any portion of the cost of the personal aides. It asserted that, under paragraph 3 of the settlement agreement, the cost of the aides was a "related service" for which the Board was not liable. D.R.'s parents disagreed and requested a hearing before a New Jersey administrative law judge. They sought an order that D.R. was in need of residential placement, that personal aides were necessary, that the current placement at Benedictine was appropriate, and that the Board was required to pay for the cost of the placement and the necessary aides.

At the hearing, the Board moved for dismissal on grounds that the settlement agreement was binding and that under the agreement the Board was not liable for the cost of the aides. The administrative law judge (ALJ) agreed. She dismissed D.R.'s petition, finding the settlement agreement to be binding and determinative.

On the basis of the pleadings and briefs submitted, the court concluded that the settlement agreement was binding. It found that the language of the agreement was unambiguous and required only that the Board pay for 90 percent of any increase in the cost of an array of services provided the previous year. Because personal aides were not within the array of services previously provided, the district court held that the Board would not be liable for the cost of the aides under the terms of the settlement agreement, unless D.R.'s personal circumstances had changed since the parties entered the agreement.

The district court therefore remanded the case to an ALJ to determine whether D.R.'s personal circumstances changed following the closing of the agreement. If the ALJ found that D.R.'s circumstances had changed such that the services provided by the agreement no longer satisfied the requirements of the IDEA, the court instructed that the agreement could not bind the parties and should be invalidated. The Board would then be liable, under the IDEA, for the cost of the personal aides for the 1992–93 school year.

On remand, the ALJ first concluded that during the 1992–93 school year, one-to-one assistance was effectively provided by Benedictine and was "educationally necessary and consistent with the IDEA." She then found that because D.R.'s disability had not changed, his "personal circumstances" had not changed. As a result, the ALJ again ruled in favor of the Board, holding that the settlement agreement was binding and that the Board was not liable for the cost of the additional aides.

D.R.'s parents appealed this decision to the district court, seeking reversal of the ALJ's order. Again, both parties moved for summary judgment. The district court concluded that the record supported the ALJ's finding that a one-to-one aide was "educationally necessary and consistent with the IDEA." It held that this finding dictated the outcome of the case. Applying the Supreme Court's interpretation of the IDEA, the district court concluded that states receiving federal funds under the Act must provide services that are "necessary to permit the child 'to benefit' from the instruction." The district court thus concluded that New Jersey could not refuse to provide educationally necessary services. Such essential services are the right of the disabled individual and cannot be waived by a contract to provide something less.

As a result, the district court held the Board liable for the cost of the personal aides for the 1992–93 school year, which amount was to be established by agreement between the parties. Following the judgment, D.R.'s parents moved for an award of attorneys' fees and related costs as "prevailing parties" in the litigation. A few days later, the Board filed a notice of appeal. The Board then moved to stay the motion for attorneys' fees filed by D.R.'s parents, pending the outcome of this appeal. D.R.'s parents did not oppose the Board's motion, and the court granted a stay on the matter of attorneys' fees and related costs.

The district court set aside the settlement agreement based on its finding that D.R.'s circumstances had changed since the parties entered the agreement. In finding changed circumstances, the district court rejected the conclusions of the state administrative law judge. The court held that, because D.R.'s circumstances had changed, the personal aides had become "educationally necessary" for him to obtain an appropriate education as guaranteed by the IDEA. The court found that the settlement agreement improperly excused the Board from its duty to provide educationally necessary services, and it therefore concluded that the agreement did not meet the IDEA's mandatory standards. As a result, the district court invalidated the agreement and placed liability for the cost of the personal aides on the Board.

OPINION: *ROTH, Circuit Judge*

This action was brought before the United States District Court for the District of New Jersey pursuant to the Individuals with Disabilities Education Act ("the IDEA" or "the Act") [20 U.S.C. Section(s) 1401 et seq]. It raises an important question regarding the enforceability of settlement agreements made between parents and school boards with the intent of enforcing the IDEA. We conclude that the settlement agreement was improperly

voided by the district court. On the facts of this particular case, the settlement agreement was voluntarily and willingly entered by the parties. It is therefore a binding contract between the parties and should have been enforced as written.

We believe that the district court erred when it found that D.R.'s circumstances changed following settlement. Instead, we find that the only change that occurred in this case appeared on the bill sent by the Benedictine School to the Board. There was no change in D.R.'s individual circumstances; he continued to need individual assistance in toileting, dressing, grooming, and eating. The only circumstance that changed was that Benedictine decided that its staff could not maintain the level of individualized attention that D.R. was receiving at the negotiated price. The School decided that additional help was needed to deal with D.R.'s unchanged condition, increasing the total cost of services provided by the School.

Once a school board and the parents of a disabled child finalize a settlement agreement and the board agrees to pay a certain portion of the school fees, the parents should not be allowed to void the agreement merely because the total cost of the program subsequently increases. A party enters a settlement agreement, at least in part, to avoid unpredictable costs of litigation in favor of agreeing to known costs. Government entities have additional interests in settling disputes in order to increase the predictability of costs for budgetary purposes.

We are concerned that a decision that would allow parents to void settlement agreements when they become unpalatable would work a significant deterrence contrary to the federal policy of encouraging settlement agreements. Settlement agreements are encouraged as a matter of public policy because they promote the amicable resolution of disputes and lighten the increasing load of litigation faced by courts. In this case, public policy plainly favors upholding the settlement agreement entered between D.R.'s parents and the Board.

We agree that reaching a settlement agreement during mediation, rather than during litigation, does not lessen the binding nature of the agreement on the parties. When the parties entered the settlement agreement at issue in this case, they entered a contract. [*Columbia Gas System, Inc.,* 50 F.3d 233, 238 (3d Cir. 1995)] We will therefore enforce the agreement as a binding contract voluntarily entered by both parties.

When D.R.'s parents appealed the ALJ's decision to dismiss on grounds of res judicata, the district court noted that, if D.R.'s circumstances had not changed since settlement, the settlement agreement was binding on the parties. It also held that, if the contract was to be enforced as

binding, the terms of the agreement were "clear and unambiguous." Under the agreement and as a matter of law, for the 1992–93 school year, the Board was responsible for 90 percent of any increase in the cost of services provided during the 1991–92 school year. The additional services of personal aides were not provided during the 1991–92 term. Nor was the cost of personal aides contemplated by the parties in negotiating the agreement. Thus, the district court held that, if enforced, the contract clearly required that D.R.'s parents pay the cost of the aides' services provided during the 1992–93 school year.

We agree that this is the proper reading of the settlement. Because we conclude that D.R.'s circumstances have not changed and that the settlement agreement is therefore binding on the parties, we hold that the district court reading of the "clear and unambiguous" terms of the agreement applies.

Discussion Questions

1. Does the rule enunciated in this case seem overly harsh? Should parties be permitted to revisit agreements previously concluded in an ADR process?

2. Under what circumstances, if any, should a court substitute its judgment for that of the parties where a settlement agreement is at issue?

CHAPTER CONCLUSION

Alternative dispute resolution processes offer businesses a range of settlement and private adjudication options that provide rapid, inexpensive, private, and customized methods for resolution. While not appropriate in all cases and subject to constitutional and practical limitations, ADR processes can be used advantageously in many disputes. Courts welcome the considerable reduction to docket size these processes offer. Business managers should be thoroughly schooled in their application.

BEST BUSINESS PRACTICES

Here are some practical tips for managers on using alternative dispute resolution.

- Strongly consider using alternative dispute resolution to resolve business cases unless your attorney feels the specifics of your case don't warrant it. Attorneys resist use of alternative dispute resolution for many reasons, some appropriate, some not. If an ADR process can be beneficial in solving your business dispute, pursue it.

- Implement alternative dispute resolution in your company policies to resolve disputes before they become legal matters. Consider employee handbook provisions and managerial training in dispute resolution as a way to increase the bottom line by preemptively addressing conflict.

- Carefully draft settlement agreements reached through alternative dispute resolution, with input from counsel to avoid subsequent enforcement difficulties. Thoughtful parties will provide for payment of legal expenses incurred if enforcement actions become necessary.

- While accounting for the statute of limitations, parties desiring complete confidentiality should consider submitting their case to a private practitioner before filing with a court. Such a decision avoids the possibility of mandated participation in a court-annexed, and therefore less private, setting.

- Because participation in ADR may be mandated, companies should establish relationships with law firms conversant in the various ADR processes before their legal services become a necessity.

http://
The Rand Institute for Civil Justice provides research data on the use of ADR. Their home page is at: http://www.rand. org

http://
The American Arbitration Association provides a site devoted to forms and rules at: http://www.adr. org/rules/rules. html

KEY TERMS

ETHICAL AND LEGAL REVIEW

Consider the following questions as you analyze the cases provided: Is alternative dispute resolution appropriate in this matter? If so, is it preferable to litigation? Why? Finally, which ADR process is best suited to the dispute, if one is to be used?

1. Acme Inc. faces a breach of contract case brought by its principal supplier, Imperial Corp. The case involves an ambiguity in their long-term sales contract relating to delivery of component parts by Imperial to Acme. The highly successful parts are integral elements of Acme's product line and are potentially highly profitable. Loss of Imperial as a supplier would be devastating to Acme as the nature and quality of the parts make them difficult to find elsewhere. However, Acme believes that it represents a sizable portion of Imperial's business and, therefore, is unwilling to simply capitulate.

2. Hightech, Ltd., a software design company, is involved in a copyright infringement matter with a competitor, Megasoft Inc. The case involves several highly complex legal and technical questions that a jury is unlikely to fully understand. Moreover, the companies both possess what they regard to be trade secrets which they are reluctant to reveal to one another or the rest of the industry through a public trial.

3. Empire Corporation has been sued by a male employee for sexual harassment by a male supervisor. This is a question of first impression in the jurisdiction where the case has been filed. Empire is reluctant to admit responsibility for the conduct of its manager, but is also concerned about losing a trial and thereby creating new laws that may disadvantage them in future litigation. The conduct of the supervisor was reprehensible but, under the current law, probably not illegal.

4. A class action suit has been filed against the manufacturer of a prosthetic device used by thousands of consumers internationally. While the injuries on an individual basis are fairly minimal, even if taken at face value, the company is deeply concerned about how such a case could impact consumer confidence in its new version of the same device. Moreover, the opposing lawyers are absolutely intractable, insisting that the facts and law are clear and unarguably supportive of their claim. They have tendered what the company regards as an outrageous settlement demand and have refused to negotiate because they believe that their case is airtight.

SUGGESTED ADDITIONAL READINGS

Goldberg, S., E. Green, and F. Sander. *Dispute Resolution*. Little, Brown & Company, 1992.

Harr, J. *A Civil Action*. Random House, 1996.

Kanowitz, L. *Alternative Dispute Resolution: Cases and Materials*. West, 1986.

Lebedoff, D. *Cleaning Up: The Story Behind the Biggest Legal Bonanza of Our Time*. Free Press, 1997.

Murray, J., A. Rau, and E. Sherman. *Processes of Dispute Resolution: The Role of Lawyers*. The Foundation Press, 1989.

Nolan-Haley, J. *Alternative Dispute Resolution in a Nutshell.* West Publishing Company, 1992.

Riskin, L., and J. Westbrook. *Dispute Resolution and Lawyers.* American Casebook Series, West, 1988.

Trachte-Huber, E., and S. Huber. *Alternative Dispute Resolution: Strategies for Law and Business.* Anderson Publishing Company, 1996.

Ury, W., J. Brett, and S. Goldberg. *Getting Disputes Resolved: Designing Systems to Cut the Costs of Conflict.* Jossey-Bass, 1988.

Part II

ADR SETTLEMENT MECHANISMS

The ADR processes described in Part II of this text are facilitative settlement processes. By this we mean processes that are structured to create negotiated outcomes and in which the role of the third party, if one is present, is to assist in those negotiations. Chapter 3 describes the process of negotiation from both theoretical and skills perspectives—teaching the reader to negotiate well and exploring the legal and ethical issues attendant to negotiation as a method of conflict resolution. Chapter 4 describes mediation, likely the fastest growing form of alternative dispute resolution. In Chapter 4 the reader is introduced to the stages and timing of the process as well as the legal and ethical questions associated with mediating business disputes. Finally, in Chapter 5, we describe the minitrial and summary jury trial—two semiformal, evidentiary processes still built around settlement negotiation.

3

NEGOTIATION

CHAPTER HIGHLIGHTS

In this chapter, you will read and learn about the following:

1. The two major dispute resolution negotiation paradigms.
2. The principal skills required for effective negotiation in either paradigm.
3. The relationship of private negotiation to the public legal process.
4. Several significant ethical issues involved in negotiation.
5. International and cross-cultural negotiation.

Negotiation is the most flexible approach to the resolution of business disputes and thus the most common. Most experts agree that approximately 90 percent of all cases filed in state and federal courts are settled through some form of negotiation or alternative dispute resolution. This estimate may be on the low side, when one considers that many disputes are resolved without filing a lawsuit or formal action.

This chapter considers both the theories and the skills associated with the process of negotiation. We will define and assess the prevailing models for negotiation and give an overview of crucial skills employed by effective negotiators. The ethics of negotiation will be addressed as well as international and cross-cultural negotiation.

Perhaps more than any other area of alternative dispute resolution, negotiation is represented in a body of literature from a wide variety of perspectives. This chapter draws from these resources to provide a general primer on effective negotiation. While this chapter emphasizes the negotiation of business disputes, these ideas may also apply when no conflict is involved, such as in the creation of a business contract.

http://

Information about the Harvard Negotiation Project is at:
http://www.law.harvard.edu/Programs/PON

DEFINING NEGOTIATION

Negotiation is a process of balancing one's own needs against the competing needs of another and arriving at an agreement that is mutually satisfying. Because negotiation involves asserting one's needs while accounting for another's, it can lead to very unproductive responses to conflict. Some people are unable or unwilling to assert their own needs and are unwilling to satisfy those of their counterpart; they *avoid* negotiating altogether. Others vigorously assert their own needs and ignore those of the opponent; they see negotiation as a setting in which to *compete*. Still others capitulate to the demands of the opponent without asserting their own needs; in short, they *accommodate*.

Two common models of negotiation balance the needs of all parties against one another. They are competitive-compromise and interest-based collaboration. The competitive-compromise model normally allocates a fixed set of resources in a way that either produces a winner who receives more than the other or a draw in which an equal division is made. Conversely, the interest-based collaborative model seeks to enlarge the pool of resources, to satisfy to a realistic degree all party interests, and to create a result from which all involved draw maximum results.

Negotiation can be a challenging and daunting process for many people, since it is often done without representation and for significant stakes. It is unlike the wide range of dispute resolution processes that involve negotiation, but normally also involve third parties as either decision makers or facilitators. While negotiation is a fundamental skill in business dispute resolution, those uncomfortable with or unskilled in direct negotiation will find attractive negotiation-based alternatives in mediation, the minitrial, and the summary jury trial (Chapters 4 and 5).

Negotiation is the basis for much of what follows in this text. For example, mediation is a process built entirely upon cooperative and effective negotiation facilitated by a third party. However, direct negotiation differs in several significant ways from the processes described in the following chapters. For example, it is less formal, excludes third-party intervention, and can be more confidential. Finally, it likely involves a less adversarial exchange of information, rather than structured presentation of evidence as may be the case in many negotiation-oriented, as well as all of the adjudicative ADR processes.

TABLE 3.1   Direct Negotiation v. Other ADR

Direct Negotiation	**Other Forms of ADR**
Unrepresented	Represented
Unstructured	Structured
No neutral third party	Neutral third party
Information exchange	Evidence presentation

Negotiation can be defined as a three-step process.

1. *It establishes the parameters of the dispute* by identifying party interests and needs through the exchange of information. In other words, it clarifies the facts and issues that bring the parties to the table and the results they seek.
2. *It creates a variety of options to resolve the dispute* by considering all of the resources and alternatives available to the parties.
3. *It refines and secures agreement to those options* by specifying the terms of the agreement.

NEGOTIATION MODELS

As stated previously, there are two general models of dispute resolution negotiation. These models have been widely discussed in both teaching materials and research, and though they represent two very different approaches, each has proponents.

The first model is commonly called distributive or competitive negotiation, but we will refer to it as the **competitive-compromise model.** We do so because this model normally places the parties in opposition to one another so that outcomes are measured comparatively or in a win-lose fashion. It emphasizes maximizing gains in a way that may, concomitantly, maximize the opponent's losses. Parties using this adversarial model may engage in puffery, deception, or coercion to achieve these often unilaterally satisfactory outcomes. Even when practiced in a principled, honest manner, this model stresses the assertion of one's own needs and the diminishment of the opponent's needs. It is a model based in substantial part on negotiating power, rights, and ability.

The second model is variously known as *interest-based, principled, cooperative, integrative,* or *collaborative negotiation,* but we will refer to it as the **collaborative model.** This approach stresses a process that leads to mutually satisfactory outcomes resulting from a nonadversarial, problem-solving approach. It seeks to establish—through truthful and reasonably complete disclosure from each party— a set of genuine interests and needs and to create settlement options to address these needs. Collaborative negotiation requires the parties to negotiate objectively and cooperatively and seeks to maximize the outcomes achieved for both parties. It is a model that strives to *avoid* win-lose outcomes.

Both models have strengths and weaknesses. The competitive approach allows the skillful advocate to achieve maximum advantage in a negotiation setting irrespective of the needs and interests of the other side. It can therefore result in sizable and highly advantageous recoveries. When involving negotiators of equal skill, it may result in agreements consistent with the relative merits of the case. In other words, the competitive model works toward settlements that are consistent with the strengths and weaknesses of a case, assuming the advocates are effective representatives of their respective positions.

However, the competitive model has at least three significant drawbacks. First, the model stresses achieving maximum advantage through power and bargaining tactics and often results in one party or the other perceiving the outcome to be less than desirable. Therefore, it is not a model upon which amicable long-term business relationships are regularly built. Second, it is a model in which unethical conduct may be more common, if not expected. It can be a process in which the end justifies the means. Lawyers, for example, speak of zealously representing clients in negotiation, while being less than forthcoming with information that is not specifically requested. In addition, they may rely on threats of litigation and discovery abuse to achieve high-dollar value agreements. Whether it is ethical to prevail under these circumstances is a difficult question, and one far more likely to be raised by competitive-compromise negotiation than in collaborative negotiation. Finally, if the negotiators are not of equal ability, competitive negotiation may result in agreements that are unfair and inconsistent with the merits of the underlying case. In short, a very good negotiator may obtain an agreement that exceeds the value of the case if the opposing negotiator is less skilled or less well-prepared.

ADR IN ACTION

Competitive Negotiation Training

The competitive-compromise model is the approach taught at many business negotiation seminars and workshops, because of the ease in developing tactics to be employed at different stages of a negotiation or against various opponents. In addition, this model is popular because most people expect to excel in it when they negotiate. But outrageous claims and suggestions can result. Consider the following scenario from an actual seminar delivered by a well-known negotiation training firm.

After concluding a seminar on negotiation that focused on a "winner's approach," the trainer offered the following advice to a group of men who inquired about tips and skills to effectively employ when negotiating with women. "The key is to be tough. So, try the following: First, because women have larger personal space needs than men, get close, lean in, invade her space. Doing so will put her on the defensive and distract her from thinking about the case. Second, women do not gesticulate, so you should slap the table, point fingers, do something to intimidate that doesn't cross any legal lines. Also, women are threatened by vulgarity, so sprinkle some into your delivery. I'm not talking about sexual words, but I am suggesting the use of words that continue your strategy of focusing her attention on something other than the

The advantages and disadvantages of the collaborative model are opposite those of the competitive model. One pitfall of this approach is that highly effective negotiators may forfeit the opportunity to win in favor of pursuing bilateral satisfaction and hence dilute what would otherwise be very strong cases. However the collaborative model is very successful in developing, preserving, or rehabilitating important long-term business relationships. Where losers are not an inevitable result of the process, parties are far more comfortable both in the process and with an ongoing business relationship, perhaps a relationship structured through the collaborative negotiation process. Finally, the process is less susceptible to ethical lapses, since it stresses mutually satisfying interests rather than maximum gains. Table 3.2 summarizes the characteristics of each model.

EFFECT OF REPRESENTATION IN NEGOTIATION

Representation in negotiation dramatically changes the tone and content of the process. **Representation** means turning over a matter to an attorney or other third-party advocate for the purpose of having the advocate participate on a party's behalf

TABLE 3.2   Comparing Negotiation Models

Competitive-Compromise Negotiation	Collaborative Negotiation
Win-lose	Win-win
Deceptive	Legitimate
Power	Interests
Rights	Needs
Evidence	Information
Partisan viewpoints	Agreed perceptions
Process	Outcome
Inauthentic style	Genuine style

in the negotiation process. It is unlikely for formal representation to be sought unless the parties are unsuccessful at negotiations. Also, if the case goes to suit, a lawyer will become involved, or if the matter is extremely complicated, a substantive expert may become involved. Representation has the advantage of allowing one to provide input indirectly yet without any face-to-face negotiations. In addition, representation protects unknown interests by bringing expertise to the case. Finally, the representative is in some ways responsible for the outcome of the case. Should a mistake or miscalculation be made, there is someone to blame.

Using a representative to negotiate changes the process in at least three critical ways. First, the process becomes more formal and, as a result, more expensive and time-consuming. The lawyer, for example, will attempt to settle the case in a way that is consistent with the law and, perhaps, the attorney's need to benefit from the transaction or the management of the transaction. Second, the representative's interests may start taking priority, thereby making it difficult to bargain on the basis of real party interests and needs. When a lawyer becomes involved, the tangible issue of maximizing recovery to support fees or an hourly bill may become important. Intangible concerns, like preserving the representative's ego, may also be introduced into the process. It is possible that some or all of these external concerns will be unrelated or even antithetical to the party interests in the case. For example, an attorney confident of the client's case may be more interested in winning than in settling and may encourage a client to take the case to trial. While the trial might be won, the business relationship with the opponent may be lost. Finally, when representatives are used, settlement becomes more difficult. The more interests involved, the less the likelihood of settling.

Several factors should be considered before relinquishing a case to a representative. First, the nature of the relationship that one has or wishes to have with the other party should be addressed. Negotiating through a representative depersonalizes the process and may eliminate the opportunity to build a relationship with the other side. Second, it should be determined whether the case is complicated in legal or substantive ways. Complicated patent claims involving sophisticated science may, for example, be best negotiated by an expert in the field or science at the heart of the claim. Finally, it would be unwise to negotiate directly with the legal or expert representative on the other side unless one possesses both legal and substantive knowledge. As we shall see later in the chapter, courts enforce settlement agreements fairly rigorously. A party should not expect to void an agreement on the grounds that they were unrepresented and faced a lawyer as an opponent, even if doing so deprived them of an important right.

RELATIONSHIP OF NEGOTIATION TO THE LEGAL PROCESS

Negotiation of a legal dispute is generally a legally protected activity in which the judicial rules of evidence may be applicable. The federal rules of evidence, as well as those of most state courts, provide important protection to the party who endeavors to negotiate a resolution to a legal claim. As a general rule, an offer to compromise a claim is not admissible in court as an acknowledgment of the validity or invalidity of the claim. The same applies for a statement made in support of that offer which is not available from other sources and is made in the course of a settlement negotiation. Consequently, an opponent in a failed settlement negotiation will not likely be permitted to argue that willingness to settle should be interpreted by the finder of fact as evidence of liability. Indeed, evidence of such discussions probably never will reach the the trier of fact. The rule applies to both offers of settlement and completed settlements. This latter situation ordinarily will not occur unless a party to the present litigation has also settled through third-person negotiation.

This evidentiary exclusion is based on two arguments. First, evidence of settlement negotiations is arguably irrelevant, since an offer to settle may be motivated by a desire for peace or by purely economic considerations rather than from any concession of weakness. The validity of this argument will depend on how much the offer varies in relation to the size of the claim, and it may also be influenced by the timing of the proposal. Second, public policy favoring compromise and settlement of disputes is supported by protecting efforts to do so in later litigation. In short, the rules of evidence support settlement discussions, whether direct or indirect, as confidential.

ADR IN ACTION

Federal Rule of Evidence 408

Evidence of (1) furnishing or offering or promising to furnish, or (2) accepting or offering or promising to accept, a valuable consideration in compromising or attempting to compromise a claim which was disputed as to either validity or amount, is not admissible to prove liability for or invalidity of the claim or its amount. Evidence of conduct or statements made in compromise negotiations is likewise not admissible. This rule does not require the exclusion of any evidence otherwise discoverable merely because it is presented in the course of compromise negotiations. This rule also does not require exclusion when the evidence is offered for another purpose, such as proving bias or prejudice of a witness, negating a contention of undue delay, or proving an effort to obstruct a criminal investigation or prosecution.

http:// A complete version of the Federal Rules of Evidence is provided at this site: http://www.law.cornell.edu/rules/fre/overview.html

---

The following case illustrates another important relationship between the negotiation process and the law: judges are willing to enforce settlement agreements even when they appear to violate principles of fairness. Participants in settlement discussions are generally bound by the results of those discussions when the existence of a contract can be demonstrated. The case presents an interesting discussion of mistakes made in negotiating an employment discrimination lawsuit.

SHENG V. STARKEY LABORATORIES, INC.
117 F.3d 1081 (8th Cir., 1997)

FACT SUMMARY

The parties to this lawsuit attended a settlement conference without knowing that the district court had handed down a summary judgment decision. This appeal addresses what effect, if any, should be given to the agreement they reached before discovering the court's action.

Sheng sued her former employer, Starkey Laboratories, Inc., alleging it violated Title VII. Starkey moved for summary judgment, and after a hearing, the motion was submitted to the district court. While the request was pending, the district court ordered the parties to attend a mediated settlement conference, scheduled for Monday, December 20, 1993. On Friday, December 17, the district court signed an order granting Starkey's motion for summary judgment. Although copies of the order were mailed to each counsel, it was not immediately entered in the official docket, and the clerk of court did not enter judgment. On Monday morning, not yet aware of the district court's decision, the parties met in the chambers of a U.S. magistrate judge. At this conference, the parties agreed that Sheng would dismiss all claims in exchange for Starkey's payment of $73,500. At the conclusion of the meeting, the attorneys shook hands and began discussing the appropriate tax treatment for the payment.

After the conference, the magistrate judge informed the district court of the agreement. The district court then rescinded its summary judgment order,

directing the clerk of court to enter neither the order nor the judgment in the case docket. That afternoon, counsel for both parties received copies of the December 17 order granting summary judgment and the December 20 order vacating the first order. The next day, the district court dismissed the action on the ground that it had been settled.

Starkey filed a Rule 60(b) motion seeking to vacate the court's orders rescinding the summary judgment and dismissing the case. Starkey argues that there was no settlement, because the parties did not agree on all material terms of the contract. Furthermore, Starkey maintains that the agreement is unenforceable because it was based on mutual mistakes.

OPINION: *BEAM, Circuit Judge*

An enforceable settlement requires the parties to reach agreement on the essential terms of the deal. Settlement agreements that do not expressly resolve ancillary issues can, nevertheless, be enforceable . . . [for example a] binding settlement existed when parties had agreed on payment of damages, but failed to resolve property owners' demand for additional drainage. The fact that the parties left some details for counsel to work out during later negotiations cannot be used to abrogate an otherwise valid agreement.

Here, the district court concluded that the parties had an agreement on all material issues. The court specifically found that the deal hinged neither on the tax treatment of the payment nor on other particulars, such as the wording of clauses regarding confidentiality, disclaimers, and the release of liability.

Starkey argues that even if the parties formed a contract, the agreement was based on a mutual mistake. A mistake is a belief that is not in accord with the facts. Restatement (Second) of Contracts Section(s) 151 (1981). "Mutual mistake" consists of a clear showing that both contracting parties misunderstood the fundamental subject matter or terms of the contract.

The district court first held that both parties assumed that Starkey's summary judgment motion was still pending, and then concluded that this misconception rendered the contract voidable as mutual mistake. The intent of contracting parties is an issue of fact, reviewed only for clear error. However, the effect of a mistaken belief is a legal conclusion, reviewed de novo on appeal.

As an initial matter, we are not convinced that the parties' erroneous assumption regarding the disposition of the summary judgment motion would warrant recision. Before a misconception will render a contract voidable, it must be more than an error about the monetary value of the consideration; it must go to the very nature of the deal. In this case, while entry of summary judgment may have affected how much value Starkey was willing to give in exchange for Sheng's release, both parties would have had reason to bargain had they known of the ruling. Litigants who win summary judgment routinely settle with their opponents to avoid the costs of an appeal, to assure confidentiality, or for a wide range of other reasons.

Even if misapprehension about the pendency of Starkey's motion was a fundamental mistake, however, we hold that Starkey assumed the risk of that error. A party may not avoid a contract on the grounds of mutual mistake when it assumed the risk of that mistake. The Restatement instructs courts to examine the purposes of the parties and its own general knowledge of human behavior in bargain transactions to allocate risk in these situations. Here, Starkey knew it had a dispositive motion pending, and yet chose the certainty of settlement rather than the gamble of a ruling on its motion. Practically every settlement involves the element of chance as to future consequences and developments. There are usually unknown and unknowable conditions that may affect the ultimate recovery or failure of recovery. Mutual ignorance of their existence cannot constitute mutual mistake. Consequently, Starkey cannot avoid the deal it struck with Sheng.

The decision of the district court is affirmed in part and reversed in part.

Discussion Questions

1. Under what circumstances is a binding settlement agreement reached? What potential pitfalls should an effective negotiator avoid?

2. What role does intent play in forming an agreement? It would appear that the parties to the Sheng negotiations disagreed about the presence or absence of intent to settle. Should intent to contract be clearly present? How would you determine whether the parties intended to be bound?

3. Is the Sheng court improperly ignoring the rights of the parties in order to support private, out-of-court settlements?

NEGOTIATION PRACTICE: A SKILLS-ORIENTED OVERVIEW

Successful negotiation requires careful preparation, skillful delivery, and thoughtful planning for implementation following negotiation (see Figure 3.1). Let us review four key thinking skills related to negotiation.

- *Effective negotiators think broadly.* The best negotiators can view a case in the broadest sense so that they can develop outcomes that may be novel yet remain consistent with the needs of the business. As they generate options for settlement, they are able to think beyond the normally established boundaries with a view toward understanding the case and all of its implications.

- *Effective negotiators think creatively.* Most cases involve many elements that can be settled in a variety of ways. The best negotiators are artistic thinkers and are capable of seeing noneconomic and other unconventional options for settlement.

- *Effective negotiators think adaptively.* Successful negotiators are often able to make the offer of a counterpart consistent with their own. They modify, manipulate, and reconfigure the issues and settlement options until agreement on each can be reached.

- *Effective negotiators think critically.* Good negotiators recognize negotiation as a process involving problem solving and not merely resource acquisition. The best negotiators can assess a wide range of options and issues in disinterested but careful and thorough ways.

FIGURE 3.1   Stages of the Negotiation Process

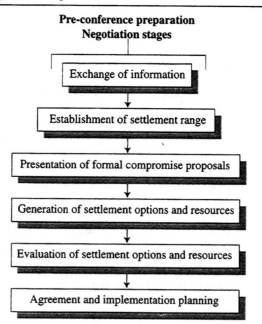

Thorough preparation is essential to effective negotiation. You should perform the following important tasks when *preparing to negotiate.*

- Carefully gather *information* about the matter to be negotiated. Consider all of the necessary parties to the process and all of the facts likely to be addressed at the negotiation so that a final agreement can be reached on all issues. Form a set of broadly framed desired outcomes. In short, effective negotiators begin the process with a clear understanding of the factual background of the case and a set of clear goals and objectives.

- Establish a case value and devise specific settlement options consistent with that value. All aspects of the case must be considered in terms of worth and their resolution possibilities.

- Anticipate the offers and strategies likely to be used by the opposing party, including possible counteroffers and assertions of fact.

Opening the negotiation normally involves exchanging information and making preliminary offers. Fundamental facts should be determined first. While parties need not decide who is responsible for an event, they do need to concur on the basic outline of facts. Without some agreement on what took place, it will be difficult to reach agreement on outcomes. Next, parties should begin to establish the boundaries of the disagreement by disclosing preliminary offers. For example, a plaintiff may initially demand $100,000 and receive a defense counteroffer of $35,000, creating an initial settlement range of $65,000.

Formal initial proposals follow the exchange of information and establishment of a settlement range. Parties often have considered their initial proposal before the negotiation begins and will come armed with a compromise offer or demand. However, it is difficult to persuade an opponent to make the first concession or to decide to concede oneself. Here are several tips for getting first compromise offers on the table for discussion.

- *Start with the old, bring in the new.* Settlement discussion is made easier if there is some history upon which to rely. Parties often make an initial offer by referring to where they left off in previous discussions and where they are now willing to go.

- *Consider convention and expectation.* Parties normally expect the aggrieved party, the one seeking a remedy, to make an initial demand. Otherwise, the nonaggrieved party is required to bargain against him or herself.

- *Allow adequate information exchange.* Because of the difficulty in making an initial offer in negotiation, parties should spend sufficient time agreeing on the facts. Doing so allows each party to become familiar and comfortable with the other and to anticipate their opponent's receptiveness of the offer or demand they plan to make. It is easier to negotiate facts than outcomes, so it is wise to start with the factual matters and move to the more difficult outcome-oriented matters only after some momentum and trust has been established.

- *First proposals are lasting proposals.* Generally, in a competitive negotiation, an inflated initial proposal is likely, while in a cooperative negotiation, a more reasonable initial proposal is expected. Whatever the proposal type, parties work from and stay cognizant of the first set of proposals. Therefore, proposals should not be made until the parties have agreed to the basic facts and are ready to consider outcomes. The party who makes the first offer is likely to set the tone for the remainder of the negotiation.

- *Always seek justification for offers or demands.* Parties are wise to request a complete explanation of the demand or offer that has been made. This minimizes the likelihood of mistake and allows time for consideration of the offer or demand. In addition, it permits time for the opposing party to make the case for the offer. Unexplained demands are far too easily dismissed.

- *Preconditions on negotiation may be problematic.* One dubious technique used in negotiation is the demand for a concession from the other side in exchange for participating in the negotiation. Essentially, the party doing so is negotiating already, only surreptitiously, by asking for a substantive concession outside the negotiation process itself.

ADR IN ACTION

The Israeli-Palestinian Peace Process

http://

The Israeli-Egyptian Peace Agreement is at this address: http://www.jcrc.org/main/isregypt.htm

One of the most intractable international conflicts is the one involving Israel and the Palestinian people. The settlement negotiations between these parties have become highly structured and indirect. An initial obstacle to direct settlement negotiations was an Israeli precondition on participation in the peace negotiations. The Palestinian constitution contains a pledge to abolish Israel as a statement of formal state policy. The Israeli government demanded that this language be stricken from the document and the intention that it embodied be renounced before Israel would begin any form of direct settlement negotiation.

While the language of the Palestinian constitution seems offensive, Israel's demand may be difficult to justify from the standpoint of effective negotiation. The Israelis requested a concession without negotiation and as a precursor to their participation. Parties who make non-negotiable, pre-meeting demands often complicate negotiations, as the subsequent Israeli-Palestinian talks may have demonstrated. In addition, if the pre-conference concession is made, the demanding party may have achieved an advantage that is difficult for the opponent to overcome in later negotiations.

Generating options is the next phase of the negotiation. During this stage, parties move from initial proposals and consideration of the facts toward settlement through modification of party offers and demands. As a preliminary matter, parties must establish a *real* settlement range, which accounts for both the initial and second offer made by each party. Few parties begin a negotiation without an initial offer or demand calculated to set the tone *and* a compromise offer meant to move toward settlement. This second set of offers and demands represents the real settlement range of the case. For example, a plaintiff in a personal injury case may demand $100,000 initially, though this demand is just to set a serious tone in the negotiation, to establish the extent of the injuries, and to appear to be a strong negotiator. While this initial demand will require a response, the plaintiff likely has prepared a compromise position to be made at an appropriate time.

Generating options through negotiation is a difficult process. It requires thoughtful response to offers made, careful reconfiguring of one's own offer, and consistent reference to the facts guiding the negotiation. There are several useful approaches to creating settlement options.

- *Expect incremental movement toward agreement.* Most negotiations move toward compromise in steps. Good negotiators break cases down into small, discrete issues requiring resolution, rather than looking for a complete settlement on the basis of any single offer or demand. Doing so comports with the expectations and the psychological needs of the parties.

- *Expand the resources.* Cases can be settled through structured settlements, annuities, and noneconomic resources as well as lump-sum money payments. Effective negotiators seek to create the largest possible pool of resources and options from which settlements can be crafted. Indeed, in addition to offering more tangible settlement value, they will likely stress the value of the agreement itself to both parties because it ends the cost and distraction presented by the dispute. Parties who think creatively can find settlement options beyond money, and they will settle cases more frequently as a result.

- *Use objective criteria.* Fisher and Ury advocate seeking objective criteria in determining case value and in preparing reasonable offers and demands. There is value in doing so, but only to the extent that additional barriers to settlement are avoided. Objective criteria become detrimental when they are used to defend intransigence. For example, it is not helpful to use the criteria dispositively when it causes a party to refuse to compromise because in a similar case a plaintiff received a certain amount. Instead, effective negotiators use objective criteria late in the negotiation to confirm and solicit agreement to offers, not simply to create them.

- *Prevent early final offer.* The most harmful kind of demand is a "take it or leave it" demand made very early in the negotiation. Such a demand stifles further discussion, creates an artificial settlement range, and unrealistically and unproductively pressures the opposing party. These sorts of offers are rarely legitimate and often force the other party to engage in similar brinkmanship. In addition, because they are usually not true ultimatums, they diminish the credibility of the party who uses them regularly yet has no intention of enforcing them. The response to such final offers should suggest that discussions have not reached the point where such a demand is appropriate or useful.

Evaluating options and reaching agreement is the final phase of negotiation. Parties have substantially narrowed the settlement range and have created pending offers that could successfully conclude the negotiations. It is a point in the process where **impression management** becomes important. Good negotiators realize that allowing the other party to leave with a sense of accomplishment is critical if a long-term relationship is to be established or continued. As a result, agreements should be fully achievable and should give all parties a measure of satisfaction. Negotiators should also carefully consider questions of implementation. Here are some tips for reaching final agreement.

- *Make a grand summary.* Parties respond well to a complete statement of all agreement elements. Even where the parties have summarized discrete issues as they have progressed, it is a good idea to include this summary and the final dispositive elements in the final offer. Doing so takes advantage of the momentum created in the earlier agreements and gives the opponent a sense that the process is nearing conclusion.
- *Articulate the benefits to the parties.* In addition to summarizing all of the elements of the agreement, describing the benefits that each party receives in the deal is a way of enhancing the offer to conclude.
- *Reinforce finality.* Requests for final agreement should include a statement describing and confirming the finality of the agreement. Parties weary of the dispute may compromise considerably just to be finished with it. A concluding summary with a statement of benefits that declares the dispute as fully and finally settled makes for an enticing closing offer.

NEGOTIATING WITH UNCOOPERATIVE PARTIES

Those who negotiate regularly are familiar with the uncooperative party, who agrees to bargain but makes no effort to compromise. Often, they make no substantive offers or demands at all. Because this type of negotiator is rather common, particularly in competitive-compromise negotiation settings, managing the negotiation process with such a difficult party is a crucial skill. Several factors might cause a party to decline to move toward settlement. Competitive irrationality, or the inability to set aside the desire to win, is one possible explanation. Another possibility is that the uncooperative negotiator expected a better initial offer and is hostile at being presented with something less. A third possibility is that the uncooperative party is responding to what they perceive as shoddy treatment in the past. The belligerent party might also be on a "fishing expedition"—doing discovery or considering an opponent's tactics under the guise of negotiation. Finally, some negotiators are simply unwilling to let go. They have a sort of pre-"buyer's remorse" that prohibits them from concluding the dispute.

The effective negotiator should summarize the progress made thus far to remind the aggressive opponent that a settlement is possible. The possibility of a *final* settlement to the dispute can also be presented. A deadline after which no further negotiation will be entertained might also be established. Finally, the overbearing party will likely be asked to reconsider his or her alternatives to agreement, specifically, the time it will take to resolve the dispute in another forum, the cost of doing so, and the risk of an adverse finding.

Here are several additional tips to make the collaborative model work.

- *Create a relationship.* Good negotiators find ways to establish even short-term relationships with the opposing party, because people are far more inclined to agree with someone with whom they have some sort of a favorable connection.

- *Question issues, not people.* Fisher and Ury suggest separating the analysis of the problem from any criticism of the parties. In doing so, placement of blame is avoided. For both legal and personal reasons, parties will rarely agree to settle when one condition of doing so is acceptance of blame. Parties may apologize or otherwise convey feelings of remorse, but they will rarely do so on paper or in response to an unreasonable demand.

- *Make multiple offers simultaneously.* The negotiator who offers multiple options provides an opponent the opportunity to compromise comfortably, to select portions of each offer, and to satisfy a broader set of interests.

- *Encourage parties to respond to their own offers.* Expecting parties to respond to their own offers encourages them to provide a rationale for the offer. It is far easier to agree with an opponent who has rationally supported their offer and "turned the table" to respond to their own offer.

- *Learn to be comfortable with disagreement.* Negotiation is intimidating to many people, partly because it forces them to face disagreement directly. Learning to be comfortable in disagreements allows clear thinking on the issues at hand.

- *Pre-negotiate.* Lay some ground rules and establish the broad issues to be addressed before the negotiating session. Parties who find negotiation awkward might even do some of this preliminary work in written form, so that their actual meeting is a more comfortable and predictable process.

- *Be likable.* It is a myth that the most successful negotiators are the most aggressive and relentless. In fact, functioning in such a way often diminishes the success of a negotiator. It is possible to assert one's needs and appeal to the other side at the same time.

ADR IN ACTION

Decision Analysis Overview: How Much Should You Bet?

Decision analysis is a sophisticated analytic approach to evaluating the options available to a party and the likelihood of achieving them. It allows complicated cases to be valued objectively and therefore negotiated and settled. It can also assist a party in determining whether a settlement exceeds the possible value of the case at trial. In most cases, the options are manifold and the probabilities variable, so that preparing a "decision tree" is fairly complicated. Here is a very simple example of decision analysis.

Assume you have the following wagering opportunity. On a coin flip, you will win $5 if the result is heads and lose $1 if the result is tails. How do you decide on an appropriate bet given those potential outcomes? Decision analysis multiplies possibilities by probabilities and adds the results for a final value. In this case you have two possibilities—heads or tails—the odds of each being 50 percent. Therefore,

$$50\% \times \$5.00 = \$2.50$$
$$50\% \times (\$1.00) = (\$0.50)$$

Your bet: $2.00

http://

To find research at the Harvard Program on Negotiation on Decision Analysis, visit: http://www.hbs.edu/dor/research/SummVG.html

EVALUATING THE OUTCOME

Negotiators should be judged by the results of their work. Fisher and Ury have suggested that in evaluating a negotiation outcome, one needs to consider whether the result is better than the best non-negotiated alternative to the negotiated agreement. They suggest that the negotiation is a success when parties achieve more by bargaining than by refusing to negotiate, by allowing the dispute to remain unresolved, or by allowing it to be adjudicated. This is an important point because it recommends litigation or another form of dispute resolution in some cases. This position is consistent with that taken throughout this text, namely that ADR is appropriate in some cases but not in others. For example, Chapter 4, on mediation, outlines a number of cases inappropriate for privately negotiated outcomes.

Several other indicia can also be considered in measuring negotiation success.

- An agreement that reflects **legitimacy,** one based on truthful and reasonably complete disclosure of material facts in the negotiation process, is successful.

- Agreements should satisfy to a reasonable degree all party interests.
- An agreement that continues or builds good relationships and contains realistic, well-planned commitments is desirable.
- The agreement ought to be **final,** requiring no further negotiation or approval from third parties wherever possible.
- It should be **noncontingent** upon the conduct or decision of an uninvolved party.
- It should be complete and specific, covering all issues addressed by the parties and in ways that are easily interpreted and understood.
- It should be legally enforceable and ethically defensible.

NEGOTIATION ETHICS

Perhaps no other area of ADR offers the number and complexity of ethical difficulties as negotiation. This is a result of the unstructured, unsupervised, and informal nature of the process. Some participants will have professional responsibility codes governing their participation, while others will be bound only by whatever personal moral code they bring to the process. For example, when representing a client, attorneys are bound to a code of professional responsibility. While these codes are created on a state-by-state basis, they generally require the lawyer to balance zealous representation of the client with an obligation to avoid fraud. To most lawyers, this means not making a material affirmative **misrepresentation** to the other party. It may not, however, preclude them from taking advantage of the other party's misunderstanding of the facts if the misunderstanding is not due to any statement made by the attorney or the client. Attorneys are also prohibited from disclosing any fact not made public by the client without the express permission of the client.

Deception is perhaps the most common ethical conundrum faced by negotiators. In the absence of either supervision or regulation, some negotiators view their actions as only being governed by legal requirements, such as avoiding fraud. The following case describes the analysis of a fraud claim in which negotiators deceived buyers in the course of property sale negotiations. It lays out the elements of the fraud case—likely the only recourse available to a party who settles on the basis of deception—and addresses the arguments of the party who engaged in the fraud to achieve the sale. These arguments are very similar to those that are made in any case where one party has taken advantage of another in negotiation through misrepresentation.

DAMON V. SUN COMPANY, INC.
87 F.3d 1467 (1st U.S. Cir., 1996)

FACT SUMMARY

Plaintiffs brought suit in this case claiming misrepresentation. Defendant Sun Oil Company, Inc., built a gasoline station with underground storage tanks on the property in question. An underground pipe leading from the tanks to the pumps leaked roughly 2,000 gallons of gasoline. The spill, caused by a rupture of an elbow joint in the pipe, forced the station to close for approximately six weeks. The plaintiffs, Roy and Eleanor Damon, purchased the property from Sun on the basis of representations from Sun that the property was in good condition. Prior to purchasing the property, Damon inquired of Sun the age of the building and whether Sun had experienced any problems with the station, particularly with the underground tanks. Sun knew of the spill but did not reveal it. Rather, Sun answered that it was a "good station" that just needed to be run by a good operator to be successful. One Sun agent stated, "No, we've had no problems with [the underground storage tank system.] It's all good."

On January 31, 1991, the Damons leased the property to K. Rooney, Inc. In November 1991, Rooney began upgrading the station by installing new pumps and Stage II of a vapor recovery system. As digging commenced, the Abington Fire Department, upon observing petroleum product pooling in the surface excavations, shut down the construction and notified the Massachusetts Department of Environmental Protection, who sent a Notice of Responsibility to the plaintiffs and Rooney. Monitoring wells were installed, and samples of groundwater were taken and analyzed. As a result of the pollution discovery, Rooney refused to pay rent from November 1991 to March 1992. The Damons brought suit against Sun alleging common-law misrepresentation. The district court, after a four-day bench trial, found for the Damons, awarding them $245,000 plus reasonable attorneys' fees and costs.

OPINION: *TORRUELLA, Chief Judge*

The Damons charged Sun with the tort of misrepresentation, also referred to as fraud or deceit. The elements of misrepresentation are well established: in order to recover, plaintiff must allege and prove that the defendant made a false representation of a material fact with knowledge of its falsity for the purpose of inducing the plaintiff to act thereon, and that the plaintiff relied upon the representation as true and acted upon it to his or her damage. The party making the representation need not know that the statement is false if the fact represented is susceptible of actual knowledge. Here, the alleged false represèntations are the statements made by Sun's representatives that it was a "good" station, upon which Damon relied in his purchasing decision. The alleged harm suffered was that the Damons bought a gas station in 1979 that would have been worth more in 1992 if what the defendant's representatives stated had in fact been true. The damages were measured by the difference between the value of the property if it had been uncontaminated, as the defendant represented, and the actual value of the property as contaminated.

Appellant questions the district court's findings related to two of these elements: causation and damages. The causation element requires that the misrepresentation be a substantial factor in the plaintiff's actions, such that it tends along with other factors to produce the plaintiff's harm. The defendant's conduct need not be the sole cause of the injury: It is enough that plaintiffs introduce evidence from which reasonable men and women may conclude that it is more probable that the event was caused by the defendant than that it was not.

Sun first alleges that the alleged representations were opinions and not statements of fact. The distinction is a crucial one, as it is well established that the latter can ordinarily be the basis of a claim of fraud, but the former cannot. The district court held that it should have been clear from Damon's questions to Sun's agents that he was concerned about the past and future integrity of the entire underground gas delivery system; as Damon testified at trial, "the only thing you've got in a gas station is tanks and pumps and the lines. I mean, what else is there?"

Our review of the record leads us to affirm the district court's finding that the statements were factual in nature. The court found that Damon asked if Sun had had any problems with the underground storage tanks, to which Sun responded that it had had "no problems with it. It's all good." Sun further responded to Damon's questions about whether it had any problems with the station, particularly with the underground tanks, by stating "that it was a 'good station' which just needed to be run by a good operator to be successful."

In that context, reading the record in the light most favorable to the Damons, we do not find that the district court erred in finding that the Sun representatives' statements that it was a "good station" were factual. Indeed, we are hard put to see how, where there has been a spill of 2,000 gallons in 1974, which Sun knew of, statements five years later that it was a "good station" and that Sun had had "no problems with it" in reply to a question regarding the underground tanks are not misrepresentations of fact.

Sun's second contention is that the record contains no evidence of the key elements needed to prove fraud. First, Sun asserts that the statements were not misrepresentations of material facts, and thus the first element of the tort has not been shown. We disagree. There can be no doubt that the statements were misrepresentations in terms of the past history of the property: stating that it is a "good station" ignores the fact that there was a 2,000 gallon spill. It may have been a "good station" in 1979, from Sun's perspective: the spill had been cleaned up in accordance with the requirements of the time, and there is no evidence of other problems. Nonetheless, there had been a problem in the past, and to omit that was to misrepresent the situation. The district court found that the fact was material, and it gave credence to Damon's testimony that his affiliation with a car dealership which sold gasoline gave him a general awareness of the growing importance of environmental issues, and that he would not have bought the station had he been aware of the spill. Thus, the statements by the Sun representatives were certainly one of the principal grounds, though not necessarily the sole ground, that caused the plaintiffs to take the particular action that the wrongdoer intended he would take as a result of such representations. Finally, we have already established that these were factual statements. Thus, the statements were misrepresentations of material facts.

Affirm the decision of the district court on all points.

Discussion Questions

1. At what point does puffery, exaggeration, or misrepresentation in negotiation become deception or fraud?
2. When made in defense of a misrepresentation, how much weight should the assertion hold that parties have an independent duty to confirm facts represented at a negotiation?

The use of **coercion** is a second ethical dilemma in negotiation. It is rare, of course, to find circumstances in which an agreement is forced from a party under genuine duress. Coercion can, however, take many forms. A superior position, such as employer relative to employee, can result in tacit coercion in a negotiation. In the interesting case that follows, an employer with dominant bargaining power may have coerced employees into settlement agreements that precluded assertion of their rights under a federal statute.

RONALD H. HOWLETT V. HOLIDAY INNS, INC.
120 F.3d 598 (6th U.S. Cir., 1997)

FACT SUMMARY

Plaintiffs are former upper-level management employees of Holiday Inns, Inc. In 1991, Holiday Inns was acquired by a British corporation, and after a corporate restructuring, plaintiffs lost their jobs. Each plaintiff signed an individual separation and release agreement in exchange for an unspecified sum of money. The agreement provides, in pertinent part:

> Employee forever and unconditionally releases the Released Parties from any and all claims related in any way to anything occurring up to and including the date hereof. Without limiting the generality of the foregoing, this Agreement applies to any and all claims which in any way result from, arise out of, or relate to Employee's employment, termination or resignation from employment with the Company or any of the Released Parties, including but not limited to, any and all claims which could have been asserted under any fair employment, contract or tort laws, ordinance [sic], including Title VII of the Civil Rights Act of 1964, the Tennessee Anti-Discrimination Act, the Employee Retirement Income Security

Act, or under any of the Company's employee benefit, compensation, bonus, performance, award, severance, or vacation pay plans.

Each plaintiff was instructed that he or she had 72 hours to sign and return the agreement in order to be eligible for the incentive. Nowhere does the agreement explicitly refer to ADEA claims.

Under the Older Workers Benefit Protection Act (OWBPA) amendment to the ADEA, there are eight minimum requirements an ADEA release must meet before it can be considered "knowing and voluntary." 29 U.S.C. § 626(f). Paraphrasing, they are:

1. The release must be written in a manner calculated to be understood by the employee signing the release, or the average individual eligible to participate.
2. The release must specifically refer to the ADEA.
3. The release must not purport to encompass claims that may arise after the date of signing.
4. The employer must provide consideration for the ADEA claim above and beyond that to which the employee would otherwise already be entitled.
5. The employee must be advised in writing to consult with an attorney.
6. The employee must be given at least 21 or 45 days to consider signing, depending on whether the incentive is offered to a group.
7. The release must allow the employee to rescind the agreement up to seven days after signing.
8. If the release is offered in connection with an exit incentive or group termination program, the employer must provide information relating to the job titles and ages of those selected (or eligible) for the program, and the corresponding information relating to employees in the same job titles for those who were not selected (or not eligible) for the program.

OPINION: *RYAN, Circuit Judge*

Holiday Inns acknowledges that none of the foregoing requirements were met with respect to the release in question, save possibly the first. Thus, under the terms of the ADEA, the release signed by the plaintiffs was not knowing and voluntary; therefore, it was not valid.

The congressional committee that proposed the OWBPA amendment to the ADEA discussed several of the common-law instances in which a voidable contract could be ratified, such as instances in which the original contract was procured through fraud, duress, coercion, or mistake, thus suggesting that Congress viewed noncompliance with the OWBPA requirements in the same light.

Thus, it is clear from the statute that a former employee could no more assent to the waiver of his or her ADEA claims after having signed the defective release than he or she could at the time of signing it. Although Congress utilized the familiar language of the common law when it deemed that no waiver would be "knowing and voluntary" unless the eight OWBPA requirements were met, it did not stop there; it also provided that an individual may not waive an ADEA claim unless the waiver is knowing and voluntary. 29 U.S.C. § 626(f)(1). Allowing an employee to ratify a release which violates the OWBPA would directly contradict this language.

Congress has purposely interposed an obstacle to application of the traditional ratification doctrine by requiring that a knowing and voluntary waiver of an ADEA claim cannot occur except in cases in which, at a minimum, the eight OWBPA factors are met. The common law would invalidate a contract as not being knowing or voluntary if it were secured through fraud, duress, coercion, or mistake. But, under the common law, such an invalid contract could be ratified by the retention of the consideration once the fraud, duress, coercion, or mistake was uncovered. The rationale for this rule is that, by keeping the consideration after the voidability of the contract is discovered, the promisor makes a new contract, this time knowing all the facts and circumstances. He renews his promise and keeps the consideration, forming a new contract, because the element which made the original contract invalid is no longer present.

But, in this case, the invalidating flaw has not been eliminated. The OWBPA information still has not been supplied. It is as if, under a common-law analysis, the fraud, duress, coercion, or mistake infected the new, supposedly ratified contract as well. Thus, even under this analysis, the employee cannot validate the noncomplying release simply by retaining the consideration.

The overarching purpose of the OWBPA amendment is to provide employees with information giving them the ability to assess the value of the right to sue for a possibly valid discrimination claim. These plaintiffs are in no better position now to make this assessment than they were when they signed the releases.

As a practical matter, we note that the eight OWBPA requirements should not be difficult for an employer to meet. Although questions may arise as to whether the information provided by the employer can be understood by the average individual eligible to participate in the severance program, or as to what constitutes a "job title," courts should read these requirements in a common-sense manner and not dogmatically. When the provided information reasonably assists the employee in determining whether he or she wishes to waive a potential ADEA claim, then summary judgment may be appropriate in favor of the employer. Thus, Holiday Inns can hardly complain about the inequity of losing the benefit of its bargain, when it did not even attempt to comply with the minimal requirements of the OWBPA.

For the foregoing reasons, the district court's order is affirmed.

Discussion Questions

1. How extreme should coercion be before a court orders the recision of a resulting agreement? For what external indicia of coercion should a court look?

2. In the present case, it seems very likely from the relationship of the parties as well as the violation of law that coercion was present. Could coercion be proved in a negotiation between parties of apparently equal status?

3. How might coercion be prevented in a negotiation session? Would representation solve the problem of coercion? If so, how should it be employed in cases like the present one?

A **conflict of interest** poses a third area of ethical uncertainty particularly when representatives are introduced to the negotiation process. The representatives have a fiduciary obligation to those they represent. Consequently, they must scrupulously avoid any conflict of interest, whether real or apparent. In addition, the *duty to bargain in good faith* has been addressed by a number of courts, primarily in the area of labor relations. In short, the negotiator is compelled by duty to put forth a good-faith effort to settle in a way that comports with the interests of the client.

INTERNATIONAL AND CROSS-CULTURAL NEGOTIATION

A **culture,** at its simplest definition, is a group of people who live and work together. More specifically, cultures are based on shared values, laws, and language. As the economy and business have become increasingly global, negotiating across cultures has become a far more important topic. Most businesses receive supplies from a foreign company or depend on foreign consumption of their product. Consequently, understanding the unique aspects presented by cross-cultural negotiation is critical. This text provides only a brief overview of this topic.

Negotiating in cross-cultural settings does not require substantial change to the negotiation models. However, a careful *choice between the models* needs made, consistent with the likely orientation of the opponent. Obviously, it would be detrimental to pursue a competive negotiation model with a negotiator from another culture that values cooperation. Doing so would magnify any weaknesses of the process. Additionally, negotiating across cultures suggests the need to become *conversant in the norms and expectations* of the other culture in terms of both personal comportment and communication. Finally, cross-cultural negotiations present *technical difficulties* beyond language that must be addressed thoroughly during the preparation phase and prior to actual negotiation. For example, a negotiator facing a foreign opponent must understand the economic currency and rate of exchange for that nation before any meaningful monetary settlement can be reached.

The preceding ethical considerations are just as important in this setting as in conventional negotiation. However, cross-cultural negotiation presents an additional important ethical consideration. Much of the popular literature on cross-cultural negotiation stresses the importance of imitating the behaviors of the person with whom one negotiates. This may involve bowing when in Asia, not shaking hands in certain parts of the world, and negotiating over a meal in others. It seems clear that one ought to balance in these contexts authenticity, at both personal and cultural levels, with accommodation of the person and culture with whom one is negotiating. Doing so conveys respect for oneself and one's counterpart in the process, while avoiding manipulation based on fairly superficial criteria.

Finally, cross-cultural negotiation is often successfully done with the aid of a mediator. Such a third-party neutral (not necessarily acting in the same formal role that is discussed later in Chapter 4) acting in an informal, facilitative role can function in several important ways. First, the mediator can act as a buffer, filtering lan-

http://

See The Latin Business Exchange for an example of services available to support cross-cultural negotiation at:
http://www.latinbiz.org/contract.html

guage and conduct so that each side is heard clearly and without distractions related to cultural differences. Second, the mediator may act as an interpreter of culture, providing both sides with insight into one another. Finally, the mediator can be a scapegoat of sorts. When cultural issues become an obstacle, the mediator can take or be given the blame, rather than one of the parties, so that negotiations can continue productively. Use of a mediator in this specialized context can be a very productive approach.

ADR TRENDS IN NEGOTIATION

http://

An example of the training resources available in negotiation can be found at these sites: http://www.negotiationskills.com/speaking.html

http://www.negotiation.com/

http://www.smartbiz.com/sbs/cats/buysell.htm

The trend in ADR is toward the development of processes that integrate negotiation into dispute resolution. These nonadjudicative, negotiation-oriented ADR processes include the minitrial, the summary jury trial, and mediation. At least three reasons exist for the emergence and likely continued viability of such processes. First, such processes empower business executives who seek control over their cases to participate personally and meaningfully in the process. Even when representatives are used, the input into a negotiated process is fairly direct and current. Adjudicative processes rely far more heavily on experts to cover the unfamiliar terrain of the courtroom. Second, negotiation-oriented processes allow parties to retain control over the outcome in their case, rather than relinquishing control to a judge, jury, or arbitrator. This helps preserve the ability to shape a resolution consistent with one's own needs. Finally, negotiated processes are normally cheaper and less time consuming than adjudicative processes.

The trend certainly seems to be toward integrating voluntary, private negotiation into dispute resolution in all areas. Business benefits from such a direction. There also appears to be an inclination, one that will emerge as a central theme in many of the cases covered throughout this text, toward fairly significant judicial deference to and protection of outcomes reached in private ADR settings, including negotiation. Nonadjudicative processes are normally good public policy, so courts fairly consistently honor commitments to use them and commitments made through them.

CHAPTER CONCLUSION

Negotiation forms the basis for all effective nonadjudicative dispute resolution and therefore is a key business skill. The business professional must become comfortable with the process and the many ways in which it is practiced. The business professional should also learn to negotiate in both the competitive and cooperative models and should understand that a crucial test of negotiator effectiveness is the long-term viability of the commercial relationship between the opposing parties following negotiation. Finally, complete preparation is essential to avoiding fraud and coercion and succeeding when negotiating across cultures.

BEST BUSINESS PRACTICES

Here are some practical tips for managers on using alternative dispute resolution.

- Because negotiation is the single ADR process in which the manager may directly resolve a business dispute, it should serve as the preferred method in most cases.

- The cooperative model of negotiation may not maximize the results in any individual case because it stresses compromise and mutual satisfaction; it may, however, create long-term business relationships that more than compensate for the incremental losses it potentially involves.

- Negotiation becomes a completely different process when representatives engage in it; one should carefully consider whether to include them and should have a good substantive or procedural reason to support that decision.

- The most effective way of eliminating the pitfalls presented by an unscrupulous negotiator is to thoroughly understand one's own case. It is very difficult to coerce or deceive a party who understands the facts and law that underpin a case as well as the likely outcomes.

- The best negotiators know that not everything can be settled nor everyone settled with; be prepared to walk away if the deal or the opponent presents sufficiently negative consequences.

- When negotiating across cultures, an informal mediator can bridge some cultural differences; one should consider using an interpreter who has skills as a mediator.

KEY TERMS

Coercion, p. 80
Collaborative model, p. 63
Competitive-compromise model, p. 63
Conflict of interest, p. 82
Culture, p. 83
Deception, p. 77
Final, p. 77

Impression management, p. 74
Legitimacy, p. 76
Misrepresentation, p. 77
Negotiation, p. 62
Noncontingent, p. 77
Representation, p. 65

ETHICAL AND LEGAL REVIEW

1. During the course of a difficult negotiation session involving a commercial dispute, you realize that the other party does not fully understand the facts. More specifically, the other party believes that your losses are greater than they

actually are. You did not create the misapprehension, nor did you obscure facts or evidence in such a way as to encourage it. Moreover, you could greatly benefit from it. Should you correct the mistake and potentially reduce your recovery or settle the case without disclosing the truth and achieve a more significant recovery than is due? Does your answer change if you believe that something you actually said contributed to the other party's misunderstanding? Does your answer change if you represent someone else in the negotiation?

2. Your counterpart in a contract renegotiation is a relatively inexperienced negotiator from a small supplier and is obviously intimidated by you because you represent a large company with considerable resources. You believe that a very aggressive, even threatening approach may allow you to maximize your position by creating contract terms more favorable to your company. Should you assert your case in ways calculated to subdue and defeat your opponent? What are the consequences of doing so? Is it appropriate in this setting to threaten to seek another supplier in order to obtain concessions?

3. You are aware that a competitor is negotiating to purchase a company that would give it a strategic advantage over you. Indeed, as you learn more about the negotiations, you realize that in principle a deal has already been reached. Formal documents have not yet been drafted, but the parties appear to have successfully concluded the negotiation. Hoping to prevent such an alliance, you contact the target company and make them an offer above and beyond that of your rival. In the process of making that proposal, you make some disparaging comments about your competitor. As a result of your offer, the target company declines to complete the negotiated deal and seeks to enter talks with you. Have your actions been illegal or unethical?

4. You are preparing to send a valued colleague to a foreign country to consummate a highly technical deal. She has spent weeks preparing for the negotiation and has mastered several difficult areas of technical expertise. In addition, she has supervised the "number crunching" and is more familiar with the costs of the project than anyone else in the company. During a brief phone call from an employee of the company with whom you are negotiating, you accidentally learn that a male negotiator is expected and that the presence of a woman as the principal negotiator will adversely affect the process and may delay the deal. The employee tells you that as a cultural matter, his company is simply not ready to embrace the more liberal American attitude toward women. Should you send your female colleague anyway, as both a statement of your trust in her and your ethics, or should you delay the process to master the material yourself?

SUGGESTED ADDITIONAL READINGS

Bazerman, M., and M. Neale. *Negotiating Rationally.* The Free Press, 1992.

Cohen, R. *Negotiating Across Cultures.* United States Institute of Peace Press, 1991.

Craver, C. *Effective Legal Negotiation and Settlement.* The Michie Company, 1993.

Fisher, R., and W. Ury. *Getting to Yes: Negotiating Agreement Without Giving In.* 2d ed. Penguin, 1991.

Guernsey, T. *A Practical Guide to Negotiation.* National Institute for Trial Advocacy, 1996.

Kritek, P. *Negotiating at an Uneven Table: Developing Moral Courage in Resolving Our Conflicts.* Jossey-Bass Publishers, 1994.

Lewicki, R., et. al. *Negotiation: Readings, Exercises and Cases.* Richard D. Irwin, Inc., 1993.

Lindley, D. *Making Decisions.* 2d ed. Wiley, 1985.

Thompson, L. *The Mind and Heart of the Negotiator.* Prentice-Hall, Inc., 1998.

Ury, W. *Getting Past No: Negotiating With Difficult People.* Bantam Books, 1991.

Williams, G. *Legal Negotiation and Settlement.* West Publishing Company, 1983.

Zartman, I., ed. *International Multilateral Negotiation.* Jossey-Bass Publishers, 1994.

4

MEDIATION

CHAPTER HIGHLIGHTS
In this chapter, you will read and learn about the following:

1. The development of mediation as an alternative to adversarial dispute resolution models like arbitration and trial.
2. The advantages and disadvantages of voluntary facilitative mediation as a method of ADR.
3. The specific mediation models, including facilitative mediation as well as hybrid mediation processes, such as evaluative mediation and mediation-arbitration.
4. The steps in a typical facilitative mediation conference.
5. The evaluation of cases' suitability for mediation.
6. The selection of the proper mediator and the roles, tasks, and ethical responsibilities of the mediator.

Mediation is perhaps the fastest growing form of alternative dispute resolution (ADR) in business today. Lawyers and clients seeking rapid, economical, and private dispute resolution are using mediation in court-annexed and private, for-fee settings. Mediation allows parties to negotiate outcomes to disputes themselves, rather than relinquish control of the case to a judge, jury, or arbitrator.

THE HISTORICAL DEVELOPMENT OF MEDIATION

Although mediation is a much newer process than trial or arbitration, it has been used to resolve labor and commercial disputes for decades. It is also used successfully in community disputes and divorce cases. It is a process that can be adapted to many different types of cases and parties.

Arbitration has always been the primary means of formally resolving labor difficulties under collective bargaining agreements. Attempts to settle labor disputes through mediation occurred as early as the nineteenth century in both the United States and England. The U.S. government first sponsored labor mediation in 1913, when the Department of Labor made a "commission of conciliators" available to parties involved in labor disputes that were often profoundly contentious, sometimes violent disputes.

In 1947, the commission of conciliators was renamed and rechartered as the **Federal Mediation and Conciliation Service.** The **Labor Management Relations Act of 1947** provided a broad mandate to the Service, allowing it to "proffer its services in any labor dispute in any industry affecting commerce . . . whenever in its judgment such dispute threatens to cause substantial interruption in commerce."[1] Federal Mediation and Conciliation Service mediators have participated in virtually every major labor-management confrontation in recent history, including those involving Caterpillar throughout the 1990s and the Major League Baseball strike that ended the 1994 season. Many states maintain similar agencies.

For at least fifty years mediation has also been used to resolve commercial disputes. Although arbitration is probably the most common ADR mechanism used outside of the courtroom, due to the relatively recent proliferation of arbitration contract clauses, mediation is being used with increasing frequency. Commercial disputes often arise between parties who, out of necessity, must be able to maintain an amicable working relationship. Mediation's nonadversarial approach to dispute resolution is an attractive option. For example, Ford Motor Company provides a dispute resolution process resembling mediation to some customers unsatisfied with Ford products in the hope of avoiding litigation and preserving customer goodwill.

Private commercial mediation is far less well defined than labor mediation, which is normally conducted according to fairly formal rules of procedure. A small number of states have relatively minimal mediator qualification and/or privilege statutes, but the mediation process remains largely unregulated and undefined in most states. As a result, mediation is less widely used in commercial matters than in labor disputes. Nonetheless, it is a viable and growing alternative as both state and federal court dockets become increasingly congested. Further contributing to the use of mediation in commercial cases has been the formulation of model rules for commercial mediation by the American Arbitration Association, the most widely recognized of the national commercial dispute resolution process providers.

http://

Find information on the DOL's Dispute Resolution Program at: http://www.dol. gov/dol/asp/ public/programs/ adr/main.htm

http://

A complete text of the model rules for the American Arbitration Association is available at: http://www.adr. org/rules/ medrules.html

---

1.   29 U.S.C. 171 (a)(b).

Mediation has been used for decades to resolve domestic relations disputes, particularly asset allocation and child custody issues resulting from divorce. Because of the need for the parties involved to be able to maintain an amicable long-term relationship, and because of the emotional costs of an adversarial resolution, mediation can be an ideal mechanism for settlement of these often intractable cases.

The successful use of mediation in labor, commercial, and domestic relations cases has led to the broader use of private mediation to resolve business disputes. Mediation is mandated for certain types of disputes. While parties may not be required to settle, they are occasionally required to participate in a mediation conference. Some jurisdictions, for example, require mediation for entire categories of cases, such as contested divorce cases where child custody is at issue.[2] Certain labor disputes must also be taken to mediation before arbitration or litigation can begin.[3]

Courtroom rules of procedure have also contributed to the development of mediation. The **Federal Rules of Civil Procedure** mandate use of a settlement conference, often presided over by a judge, magistrate, or special master.[4] Because the conference resembles mediation in many significant ways, private mediation is accepted more readily by attorneys as a mechanism for conflict resolution. In fact, attorneys often prefer to use a skilled mediator to resolve the case, rather than the judge who may later be called upon to try the case. Mediation prevents the parties from biasing the judge's impression of the case through his or her participation as a neutral advisor during the pretrial settlement conference. Finally, the rules empower a judge to consider the "possibility of the use of extrajudicial procedures to resolve the dispute."[5]

Another factor contributing to the increased popularity of mediation is Federal Rule of Evidence 408. This rule allows parties to offer compromises and disclosures in a mediation conference that will not be admissible in court should their case go to trial.[6] The federal rule is limited in scope and subject to differing interpretations. Therefore, parties are still somewhat cautious about the disclosures they make at a mediation conference. Most states have similar rules covering the admissibility of the contents of settlement negotiations in state courts. All of the rules have the intent and effect of encouraging parties to consider settlement prior to commencing a more formal proceeding.

Finally, attorneys are being called on by courts and state licensing bodies to explore the use of nonlitigation alternatives, like mediation, to resolve disputes. The following case illustrates the need for mediation. It concerns a complicated patent infringement matter, and the court addresses the obligation of the attorney to discuss the costs attendant to litigation and the alternatives available to the client to reduce those costs. The decision is rooted in the **Civil Justice Reform Act**, a

http://

The text of Rule 408 is at:
http://www.law.cornell.edu/rules/fre/408.html

http://

A searchable database containing the U.S. Code and the Civil Justice Reform Act is at:
http://www.gpo.ucop.edu

---

2. See, for example, the Cook County Rules of the Circuit Court, Section 13.4(g)(C).
3. 29 U.S.C. 173 allows a Federal Mediation and Conciliation Service mediator to intervene even without party consent.
4. F.R.C.P. 16.
5. F.R.C.P. 16 (c)(7).
6. F.R.E. 408.

The
Administrative
Dispute
Resolution Act of
1996 can be
found at:
http://www.adr.
org/adminlaw.
html

federal law designed to reduce federal court dockets. Under this act all federal courts must adopt measures that incorporate ADR mechanisms.[7] Pursuant to the Act, trial court judges may require counsel to educate their clients as to the costs and time of litigation and alternatives to it.

7.   23 U.S.C. sec. 471 ff.

SCHWARZKOPF TECHNOLOGIES CORPORATION V. INGERSOLL CUTTING TOOL COMPANY
142 F.R.D. 420 (D. Del., 1992)

FACT SUMMARY

Schwarzkopf brought this patent infringement action against Ingersoll. The patents in suit concern a coating designed to improve certain industrial tools. Ingersoll's Answer contains eleven affirmative defenses relating to patent unenforceability and invalidity.

OPINION: *FARNAN, District Judge*
C. The Civil Justice Reform Act

Section 471 of the Civil Justice Reform Act (CJRA) requires that each United States district court implement a civil justice expense and delay reduction plan:

> to facilitate deliberate adjudication of civil cases on the merits, monitor discovery, improve litigation management, and ensure just, speedy, and inexpensive resolutions of civil disputes. 28 U.S.C. § 471.

The mandate of the CJRA is clear. Federal trial courts are now required, by statute, to implement techniques and strategies designed to dispose of cases in an efficient and inexpensive manner. District courts may employ various methods to achieve the goal of delay and expense reduction, depending on the character of the court's caseload, geography, volume and a myriad of other factors. In this district, patent cases represent a statistically significant portion of the caseload and a significant challenge with regard to delay and expense reduction methods. The judges of the district have adopted a Plan under the CJRA, which incorporates measures to foster a reduction in the disposition time of all cases filed in the district.

Although the Plan relies principally upon the reduction in time delays as the catalyst for cost reduction, the Court is convinced that additional efforts are necessary to accomplish the CJRA's goal of expense reduction. In this regard, the Court is persuaded that courts must entrust the task of expense reduction to attorneys and their clients with courts acting in a supportive role.

In particular, courts should facilitate dialogue between an attorney and client regarding the cost of litigation. A meaningful discussion on the subject of litigation expense should include, at a minimum, the attorney's estimation of costs and fees vis-á-vis the anticipated result, as well as consideration of the alternative means available to the client for dispute resolution. With these principles in mind, the Court will require counsel to certify to the Court that they have discussed with their clients the estimated costs of this litigation, the anticipated result, and alternative means of dispute resolution. The certification shall be signed by counsel and the client.

The Court will require counsel to certify to the Court that they have discussed with their respective clients the anticipated costs and fees of this litigation and the alternatives to litigation. An appropriate Order will be entered.

Discussion Questions

1. Is there any way to accurately determine whether attorneys have meaningfully advised their clients on the costs and expected outcomes of litigation?

2. Can an attorney or client be reasonably expected to predict with any certainty the results of a trial by jury?

3. Will rulings like this one deter litigants with meritorious claims from requesting a trial? Should this decision have a prohibitive effect on litigants?

INTRODUCTION TO THE MEDIATION PROCESS

Mediation is defined as a private, voluntary negotiation process using a trained neutral third party to facilitate a final, contractually binding settlement between parties involved in a dispute. Unlike litigation and arbitration, which consist of a formal evidentiary hearing, mediation is a semiformal negotiation between the parties without the use of evidence or witnesses. While litigation and arbitration are presided over by a judge who renders a decision in the case, mediation is facilitated by a specially trained neutral advisor who is not empowered to decide the case, only to assist the parties in negotiating effectively. Mediation is also unlike litigation in that it is non-adversarial. Indeed, the most effective mediators build a process in which parties understand their role as active participants and collaborate to resolve the dispute. Unlike a trial or arbitration, mediation often results in a mutually agreeable outcome.

http://
Information on the Federal Mediation and Conciliation Service's efforts is at: http://www.fmcs.gov

Advantages of Mediation

Mediation, now readily available throughout the United States, has several advantages over traditional adversarial forms of dispute resolution. First, it is less costly than evidentiary processes. Mediation is normally completed in a matter of hours through a series of one to three conferences. It may occur much earlier and with much less preparation in a dispute than in a trial or an arbitration. Furthermore, mediation is not a formal evidentiary process requiring extensive use of expert witnesses or demonstrative proof. Indeed, the process is most effectively accomplished without introduction of evidence or witnesses, relying instead on the parties to negotiate in good faith. As a result, the costs associated with the use of expert witnesses, trial counsel, and case preparation are substantially reduced or even eliminated. Costs are further controlled because parties traditionally share the comparatively minimal fees of hiring a mediator.

Second, the process is more efficient than most evidentiary processes. One of the principle attractions of mediation is the speed with which parties can resolve their disputes. Because mediators are present to manage negotiation, not to represent a party or render a legal decision, they need not prepare extensively to conduct the conference. As a result, one can retain a mediator on relatively short notice. In addition, mediation requires less preparation by the parties than formal processes, so they are able to participate sooner. Finally, overcrowded court dockets throughout the United States often delay trials for years. Private mediation can be accomplished virtually on demand.

Third, the process offers a range of settlement options limited only by the creativity of the parties and the mediator. Judicial processes and arbitration are largely tailored to create economic outcomes. Although certain forms of injunctive relief are possible through litigation, most judges and juries think of the resolution of a civil case in dollar terms. Conversely, mediation allows parties to consider a far wider range of remedies. Long-term structured payment schedules and annuities allow parties to treat economic outcomes more creatively. In addition, noneconomic remedies like provisions for service, public statements of apology, and charitable gifts or gifts in kind are possible. In short, parties can create outcomes custom designed for their particular situation. Parties can also craft outcomes likely to sustain important business relationships by avoiding the confrontation and acrimony associated with a trial.

Fourth, the process does not preclude the use of further, more formal dispute resolution mechanisms such as arbitration or litigation. Parties are therefore free to strive for a settlement without jeopardizing their chances for or in a trial if mediation is unsuccessful. Parties do not formally waive their right to litigate or arbitrate in the event they cannot settle, nor are they bound to legal arguments made in mediation. Indeed, mediation is often a process of weighing the costs and benefits of a formal process against those of a settlement. Parties can, and sometimes do, decline to settle, and will move on to more formal proceedings. For those parties able to settle, the time and expense saved can be substantial. For those who cannot settle, the cost of mediation has likely been minimal relative to the total costs associated with the continuing litigation. They may even settle some portion of the case, reducing the issues remaining for trial or arbitration.

Fifth, as noted earlier, the parties control the outcome of the case. Mediation does not create the risk of outright loss associated with trial, because the parties do not transfer the power to decide the case to someone else. This is invaluable to those who are able to negotiate, want to be involved in the resolution of the dispute, and seek outcomes tailored to their particular case.

Disadvantages of Mediation

Mediation is not without its disadvantages. Principal among them is the absence of due process protections for the participants. The formalized procedural and evidentiary rules of due process designed to protect parties and associated with the trial or arbitration of a lawsuit are lacking in mediation. This lack of formality is a disadvantage in the eyes of those who believe it may permit mediator bias, coercion, or party bad-faith. For others, it affirms the need for an attorney to assist in preparation before mediating and to participate during the process to ensure that important legal rights are not being waived without informed consent and that the agreement reached is legally enforceable. It also underscores the need for a mediator who is neutral and experienced in creating and managing a process that is fundamentally fair.

A second concern for some parties and attorneys is the absence of an appeal process in the event that the privately negotiated agreement is later determined by one of the parties to be flawed in some way. Because mediation is a highly confidential process, it is never performed on the record or recorded by a court reporter. In addition, it precedes trial and does not involve an official legal judgment by a third party. Thus, unlike arbitration, mediation agreements are virtually impossible to appeal. As a result, parties are generally bound by the agreements they reach in mediation. It is possible to argue that an agreement was tainted by fraud, duress, or some other legal defense to a contract, but this is much different from formally appealing a court's judgment or an arbitrator's decision.

Finally, the lack of standardized rules and the tremendous flexibility of the process sometimes make it inconsistent, haphazard, unpredictable, or unreliable. In fact, the process is entirely within the discretion of the individual mediator, though parties unsatisfied with the proceedings may withdraw from them at any time. Parties should therefore ask mediators specific questions on how they intend to conduct the process.

ADR IN ACTION

Delaware's ADR Program

Delaware, a state where a substantial number of major American businesses are incorporated, recently adopted an innovative state ADR law. Entitled the Delaware Voluntary Alternative Dispute Resolution Act, the law encourages individuals and businesses to voluntarily file with the state a certificate of agreement to submit disputes to ADR.[8] An entity that files this certificate is bound to participate in an ADR procedure in all cases in which it becomes involved, and which a court

8.   77 Delaware Laws sec. 7701 ff.

ADR IN ACTION Continued

designates as suitable for such a process. The entity may later file a certificate of revocation and pay an additional fee to be released from this agreement.

The Delaware program is noteworthy for at least three reasons. First, it binds parties to participate in an ADR process in all disputes in which they are involved, rather than encouraging parties to select some of the cases they may have pending for an alternative dispute resolution process. Although the cases are designated for ADR by a judge with party input, the law is designed to move cases out of the courthouse. In fact, a party involved in a dispute with an opponent who has not filed the certificate of agreement is permitted to request that the other party submit to ADR. Enabling parties to agree to ADR before they are actually involved in a dispute results in more reasoned and prudent consideration of the value of ADR procedures.

Second, the official Delaware ADR process to which these cases are subjected is a form of mediation provided by a trained ADR practitioner rather than arbitration. Many states have adopted mandatory arbitration provisions to alleviate court overcrowding. These provisions send parties to a panel of arbitrators for an abbreviated evidentiary hearing that resembles a trial in both procedure and outcome, rather than to a courtroom for a genuine trial. Such programs generally arbitrate cases with relatively minimal dollar values. Delaware has elected instead to employ a negotiated process to resolve all suitable disputes regardless of dollar value. The state will allow a trial if the case cannot be settled amicably or if the case is determined to be unsuitable for mediation at the outset.

Third, the Delaware provision carefully describes the qualifications of the ADR professionals permitted to resolve cases under the statute. The law permits either currently licensed and experienced attorneys or nonattorneys with state-approved mediation training to provide the services. In addition, because the statute provides those practitioners with a clear and complete testimonial privilege with respect to all matters introduced at the mediation conference, confidentiality is guaranteed. The statute even includes a fee provision allowing mediators to charge prevailing rates for the services provided.

FORMS OF MEDIATION

Mediation is normally an informal process to which the parties voluntarily submit their cases. As a result, they are free to tailor the process, with input from the mediator selected, to meet their needs. Three major forms of mediation exist: facilitative mediation, evaluative mediation, and mediation-arbitration. In the first and most prominent, **facilitative mediation,** the mediator manages the process by which the parties negotiate their case. The mediator rarely offers direct assessment of the merits of the cases, nor appraises the outcomes the parties suggest. Instead, he or she constructs a process that allows the parties to negotiate effectively, offering procedural assistance and nonbinding substantive input.

Evaluative mediation or mediation-recommendation is a hybrid form of facilitative mediation. Here, the role of the mediator changes significantly. Unlike facilitative mediation, in which the mediator provides few, if any, judgments on the case, the evaluative mediator is often an expert in the area of law or controversy confronting the parties and is called on to provide input from that perspective after hearing the case from both parties. The mediator does not provide legal counsel, as the attorneys representing the parties do, but does provide a neutral and informed evaluation of the merits and demerits of the positions and options offered to and by each party. The object of such mediation is to move the parties toward an objectively defensible resolution of the case based on the estimate provided by the mediator.

In **mediation-arbitration,** a less common, hybrid form of mediation, the initial step is conventional facilitative mediation. However, in this process, the mediator assumes the role of arbitrator in the event that the parties cannot negotiate a resolution to all aspects of the case. In that capacity, the mediator renders a final and legally enforceable judgment for the parties. Parties must, of course, consent to this process before it begins at the first stage.

Mediation-arbitration blends elements of negotiation, mediation, and arbitration by strongly encouraging parties to create their own best settlement because of the threat of the binding settlement the mediator will otherwise impose. This process has the advantage of being highly efficient because it guarantees a final resolution of the case during the conference. However, it may reduce the level of disclosure from the parties during the mediation phase because they will be aware that the mediator may later use this statement to their disadvantage in the arbitration phase. In response to these concerns, occasionally parties will substitute a different neutral to act as arbitrator in the event that a mediated settlement is not reached.

OVERVIEW OF THE MEDIATION PROCESS

Mediation is most frequently initiated when one party contacts a mediator and requests the mediator to solicit the participation of other parties to the dispute in a mediation conference. When such a request is made, the mediator will typically begin by confirming that no conflicts of interest exist between him or herself and the parties. **Conflicts of interest** exist when the mediator has a personal stake in the outcome of the case or appears to have such a stake. If no conflicts exist, the mediator will contact the remaining parties and explain the process of mediation in an effort to secure their agreement to participate.

Fees will likely be arranged at this point as well. Private mediators typically charge on an hourly or flat conference fee basis, which includes minimal preparation time. Some mediators levy an additional payment if they settle the case. Parties normally are expected to share the expenses of the mediator. Although some mediators will allow one party to pay the entire fee, this may create the appearance of partiality toward that party. In addition, the nonpaying party arguably has a diminished incentive to participate actively in the settlement of the case.

In the event that both parties agree to mediate, the mediator has several additional preconference responsibilities beyond scheduling duties. The mediator will send and explain a formal document entitled the **agreement to mediate,** which lays out the expectations of the parties and the mediator when the conference begins. The agreement is normally in contractual form and contains, among other things, guarantees regarding the confidentiality of the process, the finality of any agreement reached, and the authority to settle. The parties will be expected to sign the document at the mediation conference. In addition, the mediator will ask the parties to consider who must be present to settle the case so that a final agreement may be reached. Finally, the mediator will confirm that all parties participating agree to do so with full authority to settle the case. **Authority to settle** does not mean that a party agrees to settle but that it agrees to participate with intent to settle if a satisfactory offer is made. Authority to settle also implies that a lawyer or agent representing the party at the mediation is authorized to resolve disputed issues in a binding fashion for the principal.

Mediators often do not familiarize themselves with the details of the dispute before commencing the conference. For a variety of reasons, they may avoid reviewing pleadings and discovery documents as well as discussing the facts of the case with the parties. First, discussions of the case outside of the mediation conference may bias the mediator or create the appearance of bias. Second, mediation is not an adversarial or evidentiary process. Therefore, reviewing the documents used in litigation sends an inappropriate signal to the parties that the mediator seeks or expects argument of the case, rather than negotiation leading to settlement. Third, parties often find that at the heart of their dispute is a miscommunication. When a mediator forces the parties to completely describe the case at the start of the mediation conference, he or she allows for the possibility that parties may view the case differently than they did while discussing it in the context of litigation.

The mediation process itself consists of several stages. The mediation conference begins with a brief, relatively informal **mediator opening statement.** The mediator's statement has at least three objectives. The opening statement describes the process and the role of the mediator. The opening statement also establishes the tone of the proceedings. The mediator will want the parties to understand that, unlike an adversarial process, mediation is a process that seeks cooperative approaches and mutually satisfactory resolutions. Both the tone and the language of the mediator opening statement are important in setting the stage for this to happen. Finally, the mediator seeks to establish his or her credibility, as well as that of the process, by describing both thoughtfully and professionally.

Following the mediator opening statement, the **party opening statements** will be delivered. Typically, each party's opening statement is directed to the mediator and summarizes all of the facts, issues, and desired outcomes. Most mediators ask that the party opening statements be uninterrupted and provide a complete description of the facts that lead to the dispute as well as the outcomes each party seeks. The party opening statements allow the mediator to assess the negotiation skills and approaches of the parties and to understand the facts of the case so that negotiations may proceed in a productive manner. The party statements offer the mediator a chance to establish a settlement range for the case, acclimate the parties to the process, and set the stage for the parties to begin to negotiate effectively.

The heart of the mediation process is the **facilitated negotiation** that takes place next. During this period, the mediator will assist the parties in articulating their respective cases to one another in more productive ways than they may have used previously. The mediator will summarize positions, ask questions calculated to elicit additional information, and suggest approaches not yet considered by the parties.

Throughout the negotiation period, the mediator will attempt to facilitate incremental compromise from both parties toward settlement. This is accomplished most significantly by helping the parties to expand the resources by identifying assets not previously described by the parties, by redefining or reconfiguring certain assets, or by looking for noneconomic assets that may be of some value to the parties.

Most mediators understand the value of allowing parties to speak fully on their case, perhaps to vent frustration and emotion and to foster an environment that permits such free expression. Often mediators will use objective criteria to change the perceptions of the parties with respect to the offers and demands on the table. The mediator will always structure the process carefully by selecting useful issues and addressing them in a productive order, by moderating the tempo and tone of the negotiations, and by allowing the parties time to think through the options presented to them.

At some point in virtually all mediation conferences, the mediator will caucus with each party. The **caucus** is a private meeting taken separately with each party to allow the parties to address issues not suitable for open session coverage, such as strengths and weaknesses of a particular aspect of the case. Caucuses, when used, are always taken with each party involved and are always strictly confidential. Many mediators will hold several sets of caucuses during the mediation conference. In addition to allowing the mediator to address and be addressed by the parties more candidly, the caucus can serve to overcome a negotiating impasse, a point at which the parties refuse or are unable to bargain. The caucus is also a useful mechanism for addressing an emotional outburst by a party who interrupts the process. Finally, it is a point in the process at which the mediator may assist a party struggling to negotiate effectively.

The caucus fulfills several additional objectives from the mediator's standpoint. It provides an opportunity to confirm his or her understanding of the information and settlement options offered by each party. It allows him or her to collect any additional information the parties are willing to provide in a more private setting. Finally, it serves as an opening for parties to create and evaluate new settlement options in a less threatening forum than directly in front of the opposing party.

When the parties have negotiated to a point of agreement, the mediator will assist them with **closure.** At this point, the mediator will assume two roles. First, the mediator will function as a catalyst, helping the parties to reach a point of final, formal acceptance of the settlement. For example, the mediator may set a deadline for agreement, effectively signaling to the parties that they have reached a point at which the mediator deems settlement advisable. The mediator may ask the parties to consider the costs saved through settlement compared with the costs associated with moving to a more formal process. In addition, the mediator will likely remind the parties of the finality of any agreement reached, in an effort to make settlement appear more attractive. Finally, the mediator will summarize the positions and offers of the parties in such a way as to elicit an unequivocally favorable response.

As the mediator works to move the parties to agreement, he or she will also likely assist the parties in evaluating and clarifying the agreement they have crafted. The most successful mediation conference results in an agreement that is final, permanent, and immediate. It should be, as well, noncontingent. This means it does not depend on the approval of an absent and uninformed third party. It should, of course, also be complete in the sense that all issues described during the party opening statements as essential to settlement are fully resolved. In addition, it should be realistic and specific. Finally, most mediators would argue that they must avoid illegal or unethical agreements.

Once the agreement is reached, the mediator may assist the parties in implementation planning. As a final measure, in some cases, though far less often when lawyers are involved, the mediator will write a settlement agreement for the parties. In all cases, the mediator will seek to gain the parties' agreement that they will return to mediation in the event that the settlement agreement becomes impossible to perform. Parties are often asked to evaluate both the process and the mediator prior to leaving the conference. See Figure 4.1 for a summary of the steps involved in a typical mediation conference.

Evaluating the success of mediation as an ADR mechanism in business is difficult. The most obvious indicator of success is the total number of cases settled and therefore moved out of the litigation system. A second, perhaps more meaningful measure for business is dollars saved by mediating versus litigating or arbitrating. An accurate measure of dollar savings is difficult to obtain, but certainly would include not only legal expenses but also any potential judgment rendered against a company.

Participant satisfaction with the process, notwithstanding dollars saved, is another way to measure success. It is likely that in some cases parties will be principally interested in whether, regardless of cost, they achieve an outcome consistent with their mutual needs. One might also consider the fairness of the outcome, as well as the rate of compliance with agreements reached in mediation.

FIGURE 4.1 Steps in the Typical Facilitative Mediation Conference

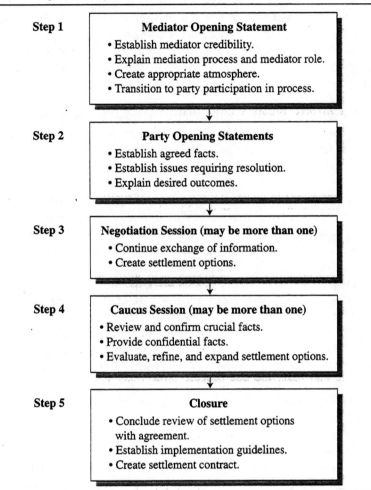

Step 1

Mediator Opening Statement
- Establish mediator credibility.
- Explain mediation process and mediator role.
- Create appropriate atmosphere.
- Transition to party participation in process.

Step 2

Party Opening Statements
- Establish agreed facts.
- Establish issues requiring resolution.
- Explain desired outcomes.

Step 3

Negotiation Session (may be more than one)
- Continue exchange of information.
- Create settlement options.

Step 4

Caucus Session (may be more than one)
- Review and confirm crucial facts.
- Provide confidential facts.
- Evaluate, refine, and expand settlement options.

Step 5

Closure
- Conclude review of settlement options with agreement.
- Establish implementation guidelines.
- Create settlement contract.

SELECTING CASES APPROPRIATE FOR MEDIATION

Virtually all disputes can be resolved through some form of mediation as both a legal and a practical matter. Some cases, however, are particularly well suited to the mediation process. Perhaps the most significant indicator of appropriateness for mediation is the presence of an important ongoing or potential business relationship. Mediation is, arguably, the only ADR process that offers parties the opportunity to resolve their dispute without disrupting their relationship, and in a way that may in fact strengthen it over time.

Cases involving parties who desire but fail to reach settlement are also well suited for mediation. The addition of the third-party neutral advisor, trained to move intransigent or incapable parties to a point of compromise, may remove impediments to a desirable settlement. A mediator may serve as an intermediary, allowing the parties to talk to one another through the mediator in cases where they are reluctant to meet with one another directly. An example of this would be a case involving sexual harassment allegations.

Cases that involve highly confidential or proprietary information are well addressed in mediation as the parties will likely be attracted to the complete privacy afforded them. Cases that involve trade secrets or that involve conduct that may not reflect well on an individual or company may also be addressed best through mediation.

When the economics of a case require a rapid resolution to avoid further harm to one or both parties, mediation can provide a forum for an expeditious settlement. Companies that are dependent on one another for economic viability, and unable to wait for a trial to address their disputes, may find mediation to be an advantageous process.

The proper selection of a case for mediation is, therefore, less a matter of determining whether a case is suitable for mediation than of determining whether it has factors indicating that mediation is inappropriate. One case type that is arguably better litigated than mediated is that which should receive significant due process protections. When information important for meaningful negotiation is being withheld, but could be obtained through a judicial process, or when a party has consistently acted in bad faith, the due process protections available in court may be necessary to achieve a suitable outcome. In addition, when it is important, either for a legal or a personal reason, to place blame on a party, such as a criminal or intentional tort case, litigation may be a more effective process than mediation because it results in a finding of liability or guilt.

Similarly, cases in which the establishment of important legal rights or responsibilities is a central issue are often best managed by formal litigation. Consider the case of a creditor who forgoes participation in a bankruptcy proceeding and reaches agreement with a debtor through mediation. Such a course of action may prevent the creditor from establishing formal creditor status and therefore deny him or her the right to recover later from the bankruptcy estate.

Cases likely to create important legal precèdent may be better resolved through a legal judgment. For example, the Americans with Disabilities Act continues to present courts with cases involving unique facts subject to judicial interpretation, including whether certain conditions should be classified as disabilities and, if so, what accommodations must made for those afflicted. In addition, many aspects of sexual harassment law continue to require judicial interpretation. Without it, the parties themselves and the broader business community are deprived of any clarifying law on the novel questions presented.

It is important to note that there is no legal obligation to litigate a **case of first impression,** one that may set legal precedent. In consultation with their attorneys, parties must decide if there is some substantial benefit in such litigation that outweighs the costs and risks associated with that course of action. Although a case may present new and interesting legal questions, it is not necessarily a case that may be litigated to the best interests of the parties involved. Indeed, some parties may wish to avoid the creation of a new legal precedent.

Finally, judges may decide that particular cases present such costs and difficulties to the court that mediation is warranted. The following case describes such a decision and the factors that might lead a judge to refer a case on this basis.

SAUK COUNTY V. GREDE FOUNDRIES, INC. AND TEEL PLASTICS, INC. V. WILLIAM BEARD, ET AL.
145 F.R.D. 88 (E.D. Wis., 1992)

FACT SUMMARY

The complaint in this case regarding alleged or threatened release of hazardous substances from a landfill was filed on December 18, 1990. When the case arrived in court, the names of 48 parties appeared on the varied and numerous pleadings, and the docket sheet contained 311 entries. Of immediate concern to the court was the pending motion of the defendant, Teel Plastics, Inc., to refer the matter to a special mediator for settlement discussions. To facilitate this procedure, Teel Plastics and Sauk County jointly submitted a discovery agreement which would provide for a standstill on discovery.

OPINION: *GOODSTEIN, United States Magistrate Judge*

By letter dated October 16, 1992, this court sent a questionnaire to each party requesting that it identify its status in the case and list all parties who have filed a claim against the responding party. More importantly for purposes of the pending motion, the questionnaire asked the party whether it would be willing to participate in mediation at this time, and whether it would consent to a limited further extension of the discovery stay and a modification of the scheduling order so as to facilitate settlement proceedings. Although the court recognizes that it does not need the consent of the parties in order to initiate and compel their attendance at settlement proceedings . . . it is preferable to proceed on the basis of a consensus when exploring settlement.

The questionnaires have been returned and the results have been tabulated. Ninety-two percent of those responding indicate a willingness to participate in mediation. The other respondents simply rejected mediation out of hand. An identical percentage responded affirmatively to staying discovery and modifying the scheduling order, but here certain qualifications were voiced based upon the length of any extension; the concern was that any extension not be unduly long and that the present trial dates remain. Questions were also raised regarding depositions now scheduled for November and discovery responses due during November.

This court concurs with the overwhelming majority that this case is a prime candidate for mediation proceedings. This is a civil action brought under the Comprehensive Environmental Response, Compensation and Liability Act (CERCLA) in regard to the alleged release or threatened release of hazardous substances from a property known as the Sauk County landfill. It is alleged that during a ten-year period, the defendants deposited hazardous substances at this site which has since been closed. As stated earlier, numerous parties have been brought into this action and based upon some of the questionnaire responses, more parties may be on the way. The factual and legal issues are complex. With the plethora of parties and attorneys, the logistics alone of conducting discovery and holding a trial are extremely cumbersome. It is estimated that a trial to the court would last at least two weeks. This has been, and will continue to be, a very costly and time-consuming case.

This district's local rule 7.12, which was enacted as part of the Civil Justice Expense and Delay Reduction Plan, adopted pursuant to the Civil Justice Reform Act, authorizes a judicial officer to invoke one of several settlement options when appropriate. Section 7.12(3) authorizes the court to refer the case "for neutral evaluation, mediation, arbitration, or some other form of alternate dispute resolution." The section goes on to provide that a referral is to be made to persons who have the requisite abilities and skills, and that the reasonable fees and expenses of such person shall be borne by the parties as directed by the court.

This court will enter an order referring the case for mediation. This order will be entered as soon as possible, but the court is still in the process of considering an appropriate person to act as a mediator and the terms and conditions under which such person shall act.

In order that the parties are able to devote their full efforts to mediation, and in order to prevent discovery costs from escalating at an exponential rate as a result of the number of claims, counterclaims and cross-claims, the entry of a discovery order along the lines jointly proposed by Sauk County and Teel Plastics is warranted. Accordingly, the motion of Teel Plastics, Inc. to refer this case to a special mediator for purposes of settlement is GRANTED.

Discussion Questions

1. Is a party forced to participate in mediation likely to participate in good faith?
2. What factors should be considered by a judge prior to referring a case for an ADR process?
3. If the parties fail to settle, is it likely that the referring judge will be prejudiced against them during a subsequent trial?

ADR IN ACTION

What Do Lawyers Think of ADR?

The litigation services group of the accounting firm of Deloitte and Touche conducts surveys to determine whether corporate and outside counsel prefer mediation or arbitration to resolve company disputes. (See Table 4.1 for a comparison of mediation and arbitration.) The 1997 survey was completed by 62 corporate in-house counsel and 77 private law firms. The survey results show for the first time that in-house corporate counsel prefer mediation to arbitration, and by a sizable percentage. Indeed, the number of in-house attorneys who prefer mediation has increased substantially, while those opting for arbitration has declined dramatically since the same data were collected in a 1993 survey.

The 1997 survey found that 65% of in-house counsel prefer mediation, while only 28% prefer arbitration. By way of comparison, in a 1993 survey, 51% of in-house counsel preferred arbitration with only 41% listing mediation as their process of choice. The preferences of outside counsel changed very little from one survey to the next; in 1993, 57% pre-ferred mediation and in 1997, a slight decline to 54% was revealed. There was 34% of outside counsel who preferred arbitration in 1993, and 38% preferred it in 1997. Perhaps most significantly, 71% of all respondents indicated that they believe that ADR processes, whether mediation or arbitration, make solving disputes easier than trial.

In-house counsel indicated that they preferred mediation for many reasons, including cost or time savings, better potential results, and superior qualifications of the neutral advisor. However, respondents indicated concern with the enforcement of ADR solutions, the absence of an appropriate court-annexed process, and the opposing party's lack of commitment to ADR processes as reasons to avoid mediation and arbitration. Despite these concerns, the survey results show that ADR is used most often in cases with dollar values over $500,000 (46% of all cases) and by some very large companies (35% with $1 billion–$4 billion in revenue and 22% with $4 billion–$9 billion in revenue).

TABLE 4.1   Comparison of Mediation and Arbitration

	Mediation	**Arbitration**
Nature of process	Facilitative Negotiated Informal Flexible procedures	Adjudicative Evidentiary Formal Set by parties or administering agency chosen by parties
Witnesses	Rarely	Usually
Documentary evidence	Rarely	Usually
Nature of third party intervenor	Expert in process Unregulated Individual Neutral	Expert in subject matter of dispute Unregulated to semiregulated Individual or panel Neutral or representative
Nature of participation	Virtually always voluntary Direct with legal assistance permitted	Voluntary or mandatory • By contract term/party agreement • Court-annexed • Applicable statute Through legal representative or pro se
Cost	Low to moderate	Moderate to high
Timing	Presuit to post-discovery Virtually always single session	After limited discovery Single or multi-session
Party preparation	Minimal to moderate	Moderate to extensive
Nature of decision	Party controlled Uncertain Binding	Third-party controlled Certain Advisory or binding
Nature of remedies	Broad range Economic and noneconomic	Narrower range Limited primarily to economic
Nature of enforcement	Contract	Valid arbitral agreements enforceable as court judgment
Confidentiality	Complete (by agreement)	Proceedings and awards may be confidential
Right of appeal	None	Limited

http://

The Mediation Information and Resource Center, including a full national mediator directory, can be found at: http://www.mediate.com/resolution.cfm

SELECTION OF THE MEDIATOR

Mediators are often attorneys possessing training and expertise in the mediation process. In addition to legally trained mediators, a wide range of nonattorney mediators is available. This group comprises professionals typically possessing social science or business backgrounds. Parties seeking to retain a mediator consider many factors when doing so. The most significant, of course, is the training and experience of the mediator, as well as any related professional training. Another important factor in mediator selection is the role the mediator is to assume in the process. All mediators do not provide all types of mediation services. Consequently, parties seeking conventional facilitative mediation, for example, should look for mediators trained in that type of mediation.

Parties often look for a mediator with substantive expertise in the area of dispute. This approach often yields mixed results, particularly in facilitative mediation in which process, rather than substantive expertise, is important. The mediator with substantive expertise can help parties grasp the facts of the case quickly, understand the points that need resolution efficiently and accurately, and explore useful settlement options. However, such a mediator may appear biased toward one side or another, or appear to work toward a settlement that is consistent with his or her own views. Although the best choice for evaluative mediation is a person whose expertise is primarily within the scope of the dispute, the best choice for facilitative mediation is a person whose expertise is primarily in the procedural aspects of assisted negotiation.

In either situation, it is helpful to use a mediator experienced in the resolution of the type of case under dispute, whether environmental, product liability, or contractual. This sort of mediator may not be a technical expert in the area of law but will have developed a sense of the approaches taken by other parties to similar problems and of options available that the parties may not have considered.

In addition, parties are often interested in the professional affiliations of the mediators they consider. Membership in the Society of Professionals in Dispute Resolution or the Academy of Family Mediators is an indicator of meaningful professional development in mediation practice.

Finally, when selecting a mediator, parties should be aware that there are circumstances under which they may surrender their right to sue the mediator for malpractice. The following case presents the question of whether a court-appointed mediator or neutral case evaluator, performing tasks within the scope of his or her official duties, is entitled to absolute immunity from damages in a suit brought by a disappointed litigant.

The home page for The Society of Professionals in Dispute Resolution is at: http://www.igc.apc.org/spidr

Find The Academy of Family Mediators home page at: http://www.igc.apc.org/afm

---

JEROME S. WAGSHAL V. MARK W. FOSTER
28 F. 3d 1249 (D.C. Cir., 1994)

FACT SUMMARY

Jerome S. Wagshal filed suit against Charles E. Sheetz, the manager of real property owned by Wagshal. The assigned judge, Judge Richard A. Levie, referred the case to alternative dispute resolution pursuant to Superior Court Civil Rule 16 and the Superior Court's alternative dispute resolution (ADR) program. Although the program does not bind the parties (except when they agree to binding arbitration), participation is mandatory.

Judge Levie chose "neutral case

evaluation" from among the available ADR options and appointed Mark W. Foster as case evaluator. Pursuant to the order of appointment, the parties signed a "statement of understanding" providing (among other things) that the proceedings would be confidential and privileged, and that the evaluator would serve as a "neutral party." Moreover, the parties were not allowed to subpoena the evaluator or any documents submitted in the course of evaluation, and "[i]n no event [could the] mediator or evaluator voluntarily testify on behalf of a party." Wagshal signed in January 1992 (under protest, he alleges).

After Foster held his first session with the parties, Wagshal questioned his neutrality. Foster then asked that Wagshal either waive his objection or pursue it: If Wagshal made no response to waiving the objection, Foster would treat it as a definite objection. Receiving no response by the deadline set, and later receiving a communication that he regarded as equivocal, Foster wrote to Judge Levie in February 1992 with copies to counsel, recusing himself. The letter also reported to the judge on his efforts in the case and recommended continuation of ADR proceedings. In particular, Foster said that the case was one "that can and should be settled if the parties are willing to act reasonably," and urged the court to order Wagshal, "as a precondition to any further proceedings in his case, to engage in a good-faith attempt at mediation." He also urged Judge Levie to "consider who should bear the defendant's costs in participating" in the mediation to date.

Judge Levie then conducted a telephone conference call hearing in which he excused Foster from the case. Wagshal's counsel voiced the claim that underlies this suit—that he thought Foster's withdrawal letter "indicates that he had certain feelings about the case. Now, I'm not

familiar with the mediation process but as I understood, the mediator is not supposed to say, give his opinion as to where the merits are." On that subject, Judge Levie said, "I don't know what his opinions are, and I'm not going to ask him because that's part of the confidentiality of the process." Neither Wagshal nor his counsel made any objection or motion for Judge Levie's own recusal.

Judge Levie soon after appointed another case evaluator, and Wagshal and the other parties settled the *Sheetz* case in June 1992. In September 1992, however, Wagshal sued Foster and sixteen others (whom he identified as members of Foster's law firm) in federal district court. Wagshal claimed that Foster's behavior as mediator had violated his rights to due process and to a jury trial under the Fifth and Seventh Amendments and sought injunctive relief and damages under 42 U.S.C. § 1983. Besides the federal claims, Wagshal added a variety of local law theories such as defamation, invasion of privacy, and intentional infliction of emotional distress. His theory is that Foster's conduct as case evaluator forced him to settle the case against his will, resulting in a far lower recovery than if he had pursued the claim.

OPINION: *WILLIAMS, Judge*

Foster's first line of defense against the damages claim was the assertion of **quasi-judicial immunity**. The immunity will block the suit if it extends to case evaluators and mediators, so long as Foster's alleged actions were taken within the scope of his duties as a case evaluator.

Courts have extended absolute immunity to a wide range of persons playing a role in the judicial process. These have included prosecutors, law clerks, . . . probation officers, . . . a court-appointed committee monitoring the unauthorized practice of law, . . . a psychiatrist who interviewed a criminal defendant to assist a trial judge, . . . persons performing binding arbitration, . . . and a psychologist performing dispute resolution services in connection with a lawsuit over custody and visitation rights. On the other hand, the Supreme Court has rejected absolute immunity for judges acting in an administrative capacity, . . . court reporters charged with creating a verbatim transcript of trial proceedings, . . . and prosecutors in relation to legal advice they may give state police. The official claiming the immunity "bears the burden of showing that such immunity is justified for the function in question."

We have distilled the Supreme Court's approach to quasi-judicial immunity into a consideration of three main factors: (1) whether the functions of the official in question are comparable to those of a judge; (2) whether the nature of the controversy is intense enough that future harassment or intimidation by litigants is a realistic prospect; and (3) whether the system contains safeguards which are adequate to justify dispensing with private damage suits to control unconstitutional conduct.

In certain respects it seems plain that a case evaluator in the Superior Court's system performs judicial functions. Foster's assigned tasks included identifying factual and legal issues, scheduling discovery and motions with the parties, and coordinating settlement efforts. These obviously involve substantial discretion, a key feature of the tasks sheltered by judicial immunity. . . . Further, viewed as mental activities, the tasks appear precisely the same as those judges perform [when] going about the business of adjudication and case management.

Wagshal protests, however, that mediation is altogether different from authorita-

tive adjudication, citing observations to that effect in radically dissimilar contexts. However true his point may be as an abstract matter, the general process of encouraging settlement is a natural, almost inevitable, concomitant of adjudication. Rule 16 of the Federal Rules of Civil Procedure, for example, institutionalizes the relation, designating as subjects for pretrial conferences a series of issues that appear to encompass all the tasks of a case evaluator in the Superior Court system: "formulation and simplification of the issues," "the possibility of obtaining admissions of fact and of documents," "the control and scheduling of discovery," and a catch-all, "such other matters as facilitate the just, speedy, and inexpensive disposition of the action." Fed.R.Civ.P. 16(c) Wagshal points to nothing in Foster's role that a Superior Court judge might not have performed under Superior Court Rule 16(c), which substantially tracks the federal model. Although practice appears to vary widely, and some variations raise very serious issues, it is quite apparent that intensive involvement in settlement is now by no means uncommon among federal district judges.

Wagshal does not assert that a case evaluator is performing a purely administrative task, such as the personnel decisions—demotion and discharge of a probation officer—at issue in *Forrester v. White*. Because the sort of pretrial tasks performed by a case evaluator are so integrally related to adjudication proper, we do not think that their somewhat managerial character renders them administrative for these purposes.

Conduct of pretrial case evaluation and mediation also seems likely to inspire efforts by disappointed litigants to recoup their losses, or at any rate harass the mediator, in a second forum. . . . Although a mediator or case evaluator makes no final adjudication, he must often be the bearer of unpleasant news—that a claim or defense may be far weaker than the party supposed. Especially as the losing party will be blocked by judicial immunity from suing the judge, there may be great temptation to sue the messenger whose words foreshadowed the final loss.

The third of the Supreme Court's criteria, the existence of adequate safeguards to control unconstitutional conduct where absolute immunity is granted, is also present. Here, Wagshal was free to seek relief from any misconduct by Foster by applying to Judge Levie. Alternatively, if he thought Foster's communications might prejudice Judge Levie, he could have sought Levie's recusal under Superior Court R.Civ.P. 63-I, Bias or Prejudice of a Judge. The avenues of relief institutionalized in the ADR program and its judicial context provide adequate safeguards.

Wagshal claims that even if mediators may be generally entitled to absolute immunity, Foster may not invoke the immunity because his action was not taken in a judicial capacity, . . . and because he acted in complete absence of jurisdition. . . . Neither exception applies.

Wagshal's argument that the acts for which he has sued Foster are not judicial (apart from the claim against mediators generally) rests simply on his claim that Foster's letter to Judge Levie, stating that he felt he "must recuse" himself and giving his thoughts on possible further mediation efforts and allocation of costs, breached Foster's obligations of neutrality and confidentiality. We assume such a breach for purposes of analysis. But "if judicial immunity means anything, it means that a judge will not be deprived of immunity because the action he took was in error . . . or was in excess of his authority." . . . Accordingly "we look to the particular act's relation to a general function normally performed by a judge." Applying the same principle to case evaluators, we have no doubt that Foster's announcing his recusal, reporting in a general way on the past course of mediation, and making suggestions for future mediation were the sort of things that case evaluators would properly do.

We hold that absolute quasi-judicial immunity extends to mediators and case evaluators in the Superior Court's ADR process, and that Foster's actions were taken within the scope of his official duties.

Discussion Questions

1. Should a private mediator retained by parties *without* judicial assistance be immune from suit?
2. Under what circumstances should a party be permitted to recover from a private, nonjudicially appointed mediator?
3. If parties participate in mediation and settle voluntarily, should the mediator be immune from suit if the parties later regret the terms of the agreement?

ROLES AND ETHICS OF THE MEDIATOR

The mediator plays several roles during the mediation process. It is important to note again that the mediator does not have the authority to force the parties to settle, or to decide the case for the parties in matters not addressed in mediation-arbitration. Consequently, parties are free to speak candidly and completely about their cases, describing both strengths and weaknesses to the mediator who will try to satisfy the following roles and tasks.

The paramount mediator role is that of **facilitator** of party communications. To that end, mediators structure a process that permits all parties to fully recount the facts of the dispute and to describe completely the outcomes they seek. In doing so, the mediator will assist the parties in uncovering or clarifying their real needs and interests. The mediator will also frequently summarize the positions and offers of the parties, providing new, more productive language for them. Good facilitators also set a careful agenda for the settlement discussions. To do so, they will break down the issues to be resolved into discrete and manageable units and arrange them in a way likely to build momentum toward settlement. Throughout all of this, they will address emotions and allow parties to express them, but only in ways and to the extent that doing so increases the possibility of settlement.

The mediator also controls the process by moving the parties deliberately toward agreement. Without forcing the parties to settle, the mediator intervenes in the negotiations with the intention of securing an agreement. This can be done by asking questions of the parties calculated to clarify issues or to elicit potential settlement options. It can also be done by altering the format of the mediation, by separating the parties, or by suspending mediation pending further preparation by one or both parties.

In addition, the mediator is a resource for the parties, offering settlement options, assessing the options offered by the parties, and perhaps linking the parties with outside experts to assist in the evaluation and resolution of the case. The most capable mediators are skilled at crafting settlement options that include ideas generated by the parties as well as by the mediator into a package that advances the interests of all parties. In addition to generating settlement options for the parties to consider, the mediator should assist the parties in assessing the settlement options they have generated and comparing the outcomes available through negotiation with the outcomes likely at trial or through arbitration. Finally, the mediator will guide the parties in a discussion of implementation of the settlement agreement and draft a written memorandum of agreement if requested.

Mediators have ethical responsibilities as they carry out these tasks. They are obliged to maintain the **confidences** of the participants involved in the mediation and to maintain **impartiality.** Although some states certify mediators and establish minimal rules governing the practice, no uniform set of ethical rules or responsibilities exists. Furthermore, disciplinary actions against mediators are virtually unknown, largely because no formal bodies are empowered to move against mediators who act unethically. In addition, because the process of mediation is one in which the outcomes are controlled by the parties, they, not the mediator, normally are considered responsible for the settlements they reach voluntarily. The following case describes the application of the ethical obligations of a lawyer acting as a mediator.

POLY SOFTWARE INTERNATIONAL, INC., ET AL. V. YU SU, DATAMOST CORPORATION, ET. AL.

880 F. Supp. 1487 (D. Utah, 1995)

FACT SUMMARY

Su was employed as a software engineer by Micromath, Inc., a company specializing in the development and marketing of mathematical software. Wang later joined him in the same capacity. They left Micromath, formed Polysoft Partnership, and began producing their own line of mathematical software. Micromath subsequently sued Polysoft Partnership for copyright infringement. The focus of the litigation was a Polysoft Partnership product entitled "Techplot," later renamed "PS-Plot," and then "PSI-Plot." Micromath claimed that Wang and Su had obtained user's handbooks and computer source codes while working for Micromath, and had illegally used that information in their development of Techplot.

Soon after the complaint was filed, the parties agreed to submit their dispute to mediation and chose Berne S. Broadbent to serve as mediator. Broadbent conducted a series of intensive meetings, conferring with the parties both individually and together. During Broadbent's private caucuses with the Polysoft Partnership, both Wang and Su were present and openly discussed confidential aspects of their case, including a detailed analysis of their source codes and handbook comparisons. At the conclusion of the mediation process, Micromath and the Polysoft Partnership successfully negotiated a settlement of their dispute.

Subsequent to the settlement of the Micromath litigation, Polysoft Partnership continued to market PSI-Plot, and began developing new programs. Two of these were "PSI-Stat" and "PSI-Math." However, in December 1993, Wang and Su dissolved the partnership. Under the terms of the dissolution, Su surrendered his ownership interest in Polysoft Partnership to Wang, and received the rights to the PSI-Stat software. Wang retained the rights to the PSI-Plot and PSI-Math programs. Subsequently, Wang restructured the business as Poly Software International, Inc., and Su formed Datamost Corporation.

The present litigation was commenced when Poly Software filed an action asserting copyright infringement and other related claims against Su and Datamost. These claims asserted that "Statmost for DOS," Datamost's version of the program PSI-Stat (the rights to which had passed to Su upon dissolution of the Polysoft Partnership), illegally duplicated significant portions of the PSI-Plot user's handbook and incorporated source codes unique to PSI-Plot. Prior to commencing suit, Wang interviewed a number of attorneys for the purpose of finding a law firm to pursue his claim against Su and Datamost. Wang ultimately retained Broadbent to represent him and his company. Su and Datamost brought a motion to disqualify Broadbent.

OPINION: *WINDER, Chief Judge*

" 'The control of attorneys' conduct in trial litigation is within the supervisory powers of the trial judge,' and is thus a matter of judicial discretion." . . . When a federal district court is presented with a motion to disqualify, it relies on two sources of authority to guide the exercise of its discretion. The first source is "the local rules of the court in which [attorneys] appear." . . . Additionally, "because motions to disqualify counsel in federal proceedings are substantive motions affecting the rights of the parties, they are decided by applying standards developed under federal law [and are thus] governed by the ethical rules announced by the national profession and considered in light of the public interest and the litigants' rights."

That motion is based on Broadbent's previous role as a mediator in the Micromath litigation. With respect to the appropriate rule governing mediators, this case is one of first impression. In making their arguments on this issue, both parties have cited to the *Utah Prof. Conduct Rules,* Rule 1.12(a). That provision states that "a lawyer shall not represent anyone in connection with a matter in which the lawyer participated personally and substantially as a judge or other adjudicative officer, arbitrator or law clerk to such a person, unless all parties to the proceeding consent after disclosure." Su also cites Nancy H. Rogers & Craig A. McEwen, *Mediation: Law, Policy Practice* (2d Ed., 1994), and its proposed code of ethics for mediators, which provides that "[w]ithout the consent of all parties, a mediator shall not subsequently establish a professional relationship with one of the parties in a related matter." . . . In substance, this proposal is analogous to Model Rule 1.9's proscription of subsequent employment on a "substantially related matter."

Thus, Rules 1.9 and 1.12 promulgate a significant distinction in the scope of prohibited subsequent representation. This distinction becomes important in this case

because the Micromath litigation mediated by Broadbent and the present lawsuit possess a common actual nexus but are distinct legal disputes. With respect to "matter" as that term is employed by Rule 1.12, there is virtually no case law or other comments. Commentary has observed that the same lawsuit or litigation is the same matter. The same issue of fact involving the same parties and the same situation or conduct is the same matter. The same matter is not involved when there is lacking the discrete identifiable transaction of conduct involving a particular situation and specific parties.

A substantially related matter on the other hand is not defined by any particular, discrete legal proceeding. By its terms, it includes aspects of past controversies which are similar, but not necessarily identical to those encompassed within a present dispute. So long as there are substantial factual threads connecting the two matters, the criteria of Rule 1.9 are met.

In this case the lawsuit between Su and Wang is legally distinct from the earlier Micromath litigation because it involves a separate dispute between differing parties, and thereby "lack[s] the discrete, identifiable transaction of conduct involving a particular situation and specific parties." Thus, it is not the same "matter" as that term is understood in Rule 1.12 or 1.11.

The present litigation is, however, "substantially factually related" to the Micromath litigation. Poly Software accuses Su and Datamost of impermissibly copying source code and handbook information from the PSI-Plot program. Micromath accused Wang and Su of pirating source code and handbook information to formulate an earlier version of the very same program. The complaints filed in the two cases are virtually identical in many respects, at times employing precisely the same phrasing. Moreover, as a mediator in the Micromath litigation, Broadbent examined in detail the disputed source code and elicited frank discussions in private caucus with Wang and Su as to which of them might be responsible for alleged illegal copying. Therefore, the determinative question on the issue of the ethical status of Broadbent's current representation of Poly Software is whether mediators should be governed by a same "matter" standard similar to that enunciated in Rule 1.12 and 1.11, or by a "substantially factually related" standard similar to that employed by Rule 1.9.

Preliminary to answering that question a brief discussion of the definition of "mediator" is necessary. For the purposes of this opinion, a mediator is an attorney who agrees to assist parties in settling a legal dispute, and in the course of assisting those parties undertakes a confidential relationship with them. Such mediation may often occur in the context of a court-supervised Alternative Dispute Resolution ("ADR") program. Mediator in this particular context does not apply to circumstances already covered by the *Utah Prof. Conduct Rules,* Rule 2.2, where attorneys take on the role of intermediary between two or more clients with potentially conflicting interests. Rather, it applies to situations where litigation has already commenced, the parties subsequently agree to suspend their litigation, and also agree to the appointment of an attorney to facilitate settlement. The attorney who thus serves as mediator is a neutral individual who confers with each party in private caucus, learning what results are acceptable to each of them and assessing in confidence the strengths and weaknesses of their cases. The mediator also meets with all parties together to facilitate settlement of the case. In this regard,

mediation may well be the most valuable ADR option. "Unlike the litigation and arbitration processes, mediation does not necessarily cast the parties in an adversarial relationship. Nor do parties emerge from the mediation process as clearly defined winners and losers." *Utah District Court ADR Manual.*

These characteristics of mediation demonstrate that it differs significantly from more formal adversarial proceedings at which an adjudicative officer presides. Most importantly, the mediator is not merely charged with being impartial, but with receiving and preserving confidences in much the same manner as the client's attorney. In fact, the success of mediation depends largely on the willingness of the parties to freely disclose their intentions, desires, and the strengths and weaknesses of their case; and upon the ability of the mediator to maintain a neutral position while carefully preserving the confidences that have been revealed. The *Utah District Court ADR Manual,* for instance, encourages the parties to disclose to the mediator (in strict confidence) "[a]ll critical information, whether favorable or unfavorable to the party's position," and recommends that mediators "advise the parties and their attorneys that it is neither helpful nor productive to withhold information with the intent of gaining some tactical advantage."

Adversarial proceedings, on the other hand, are characterized by vigorous attempts to maintain confidences. Attorneys who have received such confidential information are under a strict duty to avoid, without consent of the client, any disclosures of that information. Because adjudicators do not occupy a relationship of confidence and trust with the parties akin to that occupied by the attorneys, they do not, for the most part, have access to those confidences. Thus, although mediators function in some ways as neutral coordinators of dispute resolution, they also assume the role of a confidant, and it is that aspect of their role that distinguishes them from adjudicators.

As a result, the appropriate ethical rule for mediators differs somewhat from the text of the *Utah Prof. Conduct Rules,* Rule 1.12. Where a mediator has received confidential information in the course of mediation, that mediator should not thereafter represent anyone in connection with the same or a substantially factually related matter unless all parties to the mediation proceeding consent after disclosure. This rule also takes into account some important policy considerations. If parties to mediation know that their mediator could someday be an attorney on the opposing side in a substantially related matter, they will be discouraged from freely disclosing their position in the mediation, which may severely diminish the opportunity for settlement. If, on the other hand, the disqualification net is thrown too wide, attorneys will be discouraged from becoming mediators. The "substantially factually related" standard best balances those two interests. It encourages parties to freely disclose their positions during mediation by assuring them that the specific information disclosed will not be used against them at a later time. It also limits disqualification to subsequent situations where there is a substantial factual nexus with the previously mediated dispute. Applying the "substantially factually related" standard to the present motion, it is evident that Broadbent received confidential information in the course of the Micromath dispute. It is also undisputed that Su and Datamost did not consent to his subsequent representation of Wang in a sub-

stantially factually related lawsuit. Therefore, his current representation constitutes a violation of the rule established by this opinion.

Nevertheless, because this is a case of first impression, the court wishes to make clear that in one respect this violation assumes a dramatically different posture than an infraction of a more clearly established rule. Given the paucity of literature on the issue and the tendency of many commentators to lump all ADR methods under the same ethical rubric, an attorney could have understandably selected the "same matter" standard . . . , and thereby reasonably assumed that no violation would occur. Thus, imposition of sanctions or criticism of Mr. Broadbent's professional reputation is unwarranted in this case.

In any event, a finding that a violation has occurred does not necessarily end the inquiry. "The sanction of disqualification of counsel in litigation situations should be measured by the facts of each particular case as they bear upon the impact of counsel's conduct upon the trial. . . . The essential issue to be determined in the context of litigation is whether the alleged misconduct taints the lawsuit." . . . Broadbent received a significant amount of confidential information during the mediation of the Micromath litigation. In particular, he was present while Wang and Su conducted heated conversations on the topic of which of them might be responsible for the copying alleged by Micromath. Poly Software argues that, because Wang was present whenever Su revealed anything to Broadbent, Poly Software does not gain access by employing Broadbent in the present litigation to any confidential information that it does not already possess. However, this argument ignores the fact that Broadbent's professional expertise afforded him a perspective on the legal significance of the confidences that Wang himself could not possibly obtain or communicate to new counsel. In short, his role as a mediator with experience in intellectual property litigation gives him an unfair advantage as an attorney in the present case.

Discussion Questions

1. Should mediators refrain from representing those with whom they have mediated in any subsequent matter, regardless of its relationship to the previously mediated matter?

2. Does the case suggest that courts should prohibit parties from requesting, and mediators from offering, to testify in related litigation?

ADR IN ACTION

Environmental ADR Anticipated by CEOs

http://
JAMS/Endispute,
a private ADR
services
provider, is at:
http://www.
jams-endispute.
com

http://
This site
contains
information on
environmental
mediation:
http://www.
virginia.edu/
~envneg/links.
html

A 1995 joint survey by Coopers & Lybrand and JAMS/Endispute found that a significant percentage of corporate executives, including both chief executive officers and general counsel, expect the use of ADR in environmental matters to increase. The survey, mailed to 2,000 officers at Fortune 1000 companies, was designed to gather data on current and projected ADR use in environmental matters as well as cost information related to environmental litigation. The survey revealed that 74% of those who responded predict increased use of environmental ADR. Respondents particularly favor use of ADR in Superfund matters in which allocation of environmental cleanup costs is an issue.

In addition, 86% of the respondents cited cost savings as the leading reason for using ADR in environmental matters, describing ADR as either "considerably" or "somewhat less" costly than tradi-tional litigation. Approximately 65% of the respondents indicated that costs, primarily legal fees, associated with environmental matters have increased. Indeed, 58% of respondents for those companies with $5 billion or more in revenue stated that costs related to litigating environmental matters exceed $500,000 annually.

Citing a lack of experience and training in ADR, respondents reported fairly sparse use of ADR in the past. A mere 19% of those responding had used ADR in more than 10% of previous environmental matters. In addition, a fairly low percentage of respondents believe that ADR has been or will be used to resolve matters involving local, state, or federal government. Respondents indicated that as they, their counsel, and their opponents become more familiar with the processes, they expect significant increases in use.

MANDATORY MEDIATION

Opinion is divided on whether, and when, mediation should be made **mandatory**. There is, however, pressure from many sources to make mediation mandatory in a wider variety of cases. Judges typically support any opportunity to resolve matters before trial and thereby reduce their dockets. Similarly, legislators faced with mounting public pressure to reform the judicial system are calling more regularly for broader use of mediation and arbitration. However, although most mediators favor wider use of the process, they often disagree on whether mandating mediation is the answer.

When mediation is mandated, parties should be concerned with several factors. First, mandated mediation should be nonbinding; it should not require a party to settle. What distinguishes mediation from other dispute resolution processes is that the parties are free to choose the settlement conditions. Without this freedom, parties would likely resist mediation. Second, the pressure to settle should not be overwhelming. Judges, for example, should be prohibited from penalizing parties who decline to settle with accelerated trial dates or abbreviated discovery periods. Third, meaningful confidentiality guarantees should be given and enforced to assure the parties that their participation in mandatory mediation will not jeopardize them in subsequent proceedings. Referral guidelines and authority should be made clear to parties. When a case is sent to, rather than volunteered for mediation, parties should understand why the case was sent and on whose authority. Finally, a right to review the outcome should be provided. When cases are forced into the process, parties should have the right to independent judicial review of the outcome if they believe the case was inappropriately referred or improperly mediated.

The following case illustrates the power a federal court has to compel parties to participate in settlement discussions and the reasons for that power.

G. HEILEMAN BREWING COMPANY V. JOSEPH OAT CORPORATION
871 F. 2d 648 (7th Cir., 1989)

FACT SUMMARY

A federal magistrate ordered Joseph Oat Corporation to send a "corporate representative with authority to settle" to a pretrial conference to discuss disputed factual and legal issues and the possibility of settlement. Although counsel for Oat Corporation appeared with another attorney who was authorized to speak on behalf of the principals of the corporation, no principal or corporate representative personally attended the conference. The court determined that Oat Corporation's failure to send a principal of the corporation to the pretrial conference violated its order. Consequently, the district court imposed a sanction of $5,860.01 on Oat Corporation pursuant to *Federal Rule of Civil Procedure* 16(f). This amount

http://

The text of Rule 16 can be found at:
http://www.law.cornell.edu/rules/frcp/rule16.htm

represented the costs and attorneys' fees of the opposing parties attending the conference. Oat Corporation appealed the sanction, claiming that the district court did not have the authority to order litigants represented by counsel to appear at the pretrial settlement conference.

OPINION: *KANNE, Circuit Judge*

In this case, we are required to determine whether a court's power to order the pretrial appearance of litigants who are represented by counsel is inconsistent with, or in derogation of, Rule 16. We must remember that Rule 1 states, with unmistakable clarity, that the Federal Rules of Civil Procedure "shall be construed to secure the just, speedy, and inexpensive determination of every action." This language explicitly indicates that the federal rules are to be liberally construed. . . . There is no place [in] the federal civil procedural system for the proposition that rules having the force of statute, though in derogation of the common law, are to be strictly construed.

"[The] spirit, intent, and purpose [of Rule 16] is . . . broadly remedial, allowing courts to actively manage the preparation of cases for trial." *In re Baker.* 744 F. 2d 1438, 1440 (10th Cir., 1984). Rule 16 is not designed as a device to restrict or limit the authority of the district judge in the conduct of pretrial conferences. As the Tenth Circuit Court of Appeals sitting en banc stated, "the spirit and purpose of the amendments to Rule 16 always have been within the inherent power of the courts to manage their affairs as an independent constitutional branch of government."

We agree with this interpretation of Rule 16. The wording of the rule and the accompanying commentary make plain that the entire thrust of the amendment to Rule 16 was to urge judges to make wider use of their powers and to manage actively their dockets from an early stage. We therefore conclude that our interpretation of Rule 16 to allow district courts to order represented parties to appear at pretrial settlement conferences merely represents another application of a district judge's inherent authority to preserve the efficiency, and more importantly the integrity, of the judicial process.

To summarize, we simply hold that the action taken by the district court in this case constituted the proper use of inherent authority to aid in accomplishing the purpose and intent of Rule 16. We reaffirm the notion that the inherent power of a district judge—derived from the very nature and existence of his judicial office—is the broad field over which the Federal Rules of Civil Procedure are applied. Inherent authority remains the means by which district judges deal with circumstances not proscribed or specifically addressed by rule or statute, but which must be addressed to promote the just, speedy, and inexpensive determination of every action.

Having determined that the district court possessed the power and authority to order the represented litigants to appear at the pretrial settlement conference, we now must examine whether the court abused its discretion to issue such an order.

At the outset, it is important to note that a district court cannot coerce settlement. *Kothe v. Smith,* 771 F. 2d 667, 669 (2d Cir., 1985). In this case, considerable concern has been generated because the court ordered "corporate representatives with authority to settle" to attend the conference. In our view, "authority to settle," when used in the context of this case, means that the "corporate representative" attending the pretrial conference was required to hold a position within the corporate entity allowing him to speak definitively and to commit the corporation to a particular position in the litigation. We do not view "authority to settle" as a requirement that corporate representatives must come to court willing to settle on someone else's terms, but only that they come to court in order to consider the possibility of settlement.

As Chief Judge Crabb set forth in her decision which we now review: "There is no indication . . . that the magistrate's order contemplated requiring Joseph Oat . . . to agree to any particular form of settlement or even to agree to settlement at all. The only requirement imposed by the magistrate was that the representative [of Oat Corporation] be present with full authority to settle, should terms for settlement be proposed that were acceptable to [Oat Corporation]." *G. Heileman Brewing Co., Inc. v. Joseph Oat Corporation,* 107 F.R.D. 275, 276-77 (1985).

If this case represented a situation where Oat Corporation had sent a corporate representative and was sanctioned because that person refused to make an offer to pay money—that is, refused to submit to settlement coercion—we would be faced with a decidedly different issue—a situation we would not countenance.

The Advisory Committee Notes to Rule 16 state that "[a]lthough it is not the purpose of Rule 16(b)(7) to impose settlement negotiations on unwilling litigants, it is believed that providing a neutral forum for discussing [settlement] might foster it." Fed.R.Civ.P. 16 advisory committee's note, subdivision (c) (1983). These Notes clearly draw a distinction between being required to attend a settlement conference and being required to participate in settlement negotiations. Thus, under the scheme of pretrial settlement conferences, the corporate representative remains free, on behalf of the corporate entity, to propose terms of settlement independently—but he may be required to state those terms in a pretrial conference before a judge or magistrate.

As an alternative position, Oat Corporation argues that the court abused its discretion to order corporate representatives of the litigants to attend the pretrial settlement conference. . . . Oat Corporation determined that because its business was a "going concern." Consequently, Oat Corporation believes that the district court abused its authority. We recognize, as did the district court, that circumstances could arise in which requiring a corporate representative (or any litigant) to appear at a pretrial settlement conference would be so onerous, so clearly unproductive, or so expensive in relation to the size, value, and complexity of the case that it might be an abuse of discretion. Moreover, "[b]ecause inherent powers are shielded from direct democratic controls, they must be exercised with restraint and discretion." *Roadway Express, Inc. v. Piper,* 447 U.S. 752, 764, 100 S.Ct. 2455, 2463, 65 L.Ed. 2d 488 (1980) (citation omitted). However, the facts and circumstances of this case clearly support the court's actions to require the corporate representatives of the litigants to attend the pretrial conference personally.

This litigation involved a claim for $4 million—a claim which turned upon the resolution of complex factual and legal issues. The litigants expected the trial to last from one to three months and all parties stood to incur substantial legal fees and trial expenses. This trial also would have preempted a large segment of Judicial time—not an insignificant factor. Thus, because the stakes were high, we do not believe that the burden of requiring a corporate representative to attend a pretrial settlement conference was out of proportion to the benefits to be gained, not only by the litigants but also by the court.

Additionally, the corporation did send an attorney, Mr. Fitzpatrick, from Philadelphia, Pennsylvania to Madison, Wisconsin to "speak for" the principals of the corporation. It is difficult to see how the expenses involved in sending Mr. Fitzpatrick from Philadelphia to Madison would have greatly exceeded the expenses involved in sending a corporate representative from Camden to Madison. Consequently, we do not think the expenses and distance to be traveled are unreasonable in this case.

Furthermore, no objection to the magistrate's order was made prior to the date the pretrial conference resumed. Oat Corporation contacted the magistrate's office concerning the order's requirements and was advised of the requirements now at issue. However, Oat Corporation never objected to its terms, either when it was issued or when Oat Corporation sought clarification. Consequently, Oat Corporation was left with only one course of action: it had to comply fully with the letter and intent of the order and argue about its reasonableness later. We thus conclude that the court did not abuse its authority and discretion to order a representative of the Oat Corporation to appear for the pretrial settlement conference on December 19.

POSNER, *Circuit Judge, dissenting*

Rule 16(a) of the Federal Rules of Civil Procedure authorizes a district court to "direct the attorneys for the parties and any unrepresented parties to appear before it for a [pretrial] conference."

The main purpose of the pretrial conference is to get ready for trial. For that purpose, only the attorneys need be present, unless a party is acting as his own attorney. The only possible reason for wanting a represented party to be present is to enable the judge or magistrate to explore settlement with the principals rather than with just their agents. Some district judges and magistrates distrust the willingness or ability of attorneys to convey to their clients adequate information bearing on the desirability and terms of settling a case in lieu of pressing forward to trial. The distrust is warranted in some cases, I am sure; but warranted or not, it is what lies behind the concern that the panel opinion had stripped the district courts of a valuable settlement tool—and this at a time of heavy, and growing, federal judicial caseloads. The concern may well be exaggerated, however. The panel opinion may have had little practical significance; it is the rare attorney who will invite a district judge's displeasure by defying a request to produce the client for a pretrial conference.

The question of the district court's power to summon a represented party to a settlement conference is a difficult one. On the one hand, nothing in Rule 16 or in any other rule or statute confers such a power, and there are obvious dangers in too broad an interpretation of the federal courts' inherent power to regulate their procedure. One danger is that it encourages judicial high-handedness ("power corrupts"); several years ago one of the district judges in this circuit ordered Acting Secretary of Labor Brock to appear before him for settlement discussions on the very day Brock was scheduled to appear before the Senate for his confirmation hearing. The broader concern illustrated by the Brock episode is that in their zeal to settle cases judges may ignore the value of other people's time. One reason people hire lawyers is to economize on their own investment of time in resolving disputes. It is pertinent to note in this connection that Oat is a defendant in this case; it didn't want its executives' time occupied with this litigation.

On the other hand, "die Not bricht Eisen" ["necessity breaks iron"]. Attorneys often are imperfect agents of their clients, and the workload of our district courts is so heavy that we should hesitate to deprive them of a potentially useful tool for effecting settlement, even if there is some difficulty in finding a legal basis for the tool. Although few attorneys will defy a district court's request to produce the client, those few cases may be the very ones where the client's presence would be most conducive to settlement. If I am right that Rule 16(a) empowers a district court to summon unrepresented parties to a pretrial conference only because their presence may be necessary to get ready for trial, we need not infer that the draftsmen meant to forbid the summoning of represented parties for purposes of exploring settlement. The draftsmen may have been unaware that district courts were asserting a power to command the presence of a represented party to explore settlement. We should hesitate to infer inadvertent prohibitions.

The narrowly "legal" considerations bearing on the question whether district courts have the power asserted by the magistrate in this case are sufficiently equivocal to authorize—indeed compel—us to consider the practical consequences for settlement before deciding what the answer should be. Unfortunately, we have insufficient information about those consequences to be able to give a confident answer, but fortunately we need not answer the question in this case—so clear is it that the magistrate abused his discretion, which is to say, acted unreasonably, in demanding that Oat Corporation send an executive having full settlement authority to the pretrial conference. This demand, which is different from a demand that a party who has not closed the door to settlement send an executive to discuss possible terms, would be defensible only if litigants had a duty to bargain in good faith over settlement before resorting to trial, and neither Rule 16 nor any other rule, statute, or doctrine imposes such a duty on federal litigants. There is no federal judicial power to coerce settlement. Oat had made clear that it was not prepared to settle the case on any terms that required it to pay money. That was its prerogative, which once exercised made the magistrate's continued insistence on Oat's sending an executive to Madison arbitrary, unreasonable, willful, and indeed petulant. This is apart from the fact that since no one officer of Oat may have had authority to settle the case, compliance with the demand might have required Oat to ship its entire board of directors to Madison. Ultimately Oat did make a money settlement, but there is no indication that it would have settled sooner if only it had complied with the magistrate's demand for the dispatch of an executive possessing "full settlement authority."

Discussion Questions

1. Does mandatory mediation deprive a party of a constitutional right to jury adjudication of a dispute?

2. Is there any adequate safeguard against improper judicial pressure to settle in mandatory mediation settings?

3. On what basis should judges select and refer cases for mandatory mediation?

CHAPTER CONCLUSION

Mediation, in all its available forms, offers parties in certain cases an opportunity to resolve disputes quickly, cheaply, privately, and in a fashion consistent with their real needs and interests. The ready availability of mediators, combined with the finality of agreements reached in mediation, further enhances its use in resolving business disputes. Mediation does not prejudice parties in future litigation or arbitration if they cannot settle, but does allow parties to preserve important business relationships if they can.

BEST BUSINESS PRACTICES

Here are some practical tips for managers on the use of mediation for the resolution of business disputes.

- Consider including in all contracts and employee handbooks a pre-suit dispute resolution clause mandating a good-faith attempt to use mediation in all disputes between parties to the contract. Such a clause does not preclude subsequent arbitration or litigation, but it does force the parties to attempt to formally negotiate the case with the assistance of a mediator prior to using an adversarial process. Such clauses are generally enforceable.

- In cases where maintaining a long-term continuing relationship is important, mediation is clearly the dispute resolution process of choice. No other process allows so completely for mutually satisfactory outcomes to be created by the parties in a setting that does not diminish the possibility of future commerce.

- Fully prepare your case before mediating. Although mediation is an informal process, with party-controlled outcomes, good settlements are the result of thorough preparation before the conference on both factual and liability issues.

- Select your mediator carefully. Remember that the practice of mediation is largely unregulated, and the competence and training of mediators vary widely. Although confidentiality will prohibit many mediators from giving client references, one should inquire about membership in professional organizations, specialized training, and professional background before hiring a mediator.

- Retain a lawyer and have him or her present for the mediation. Mediation agreements are generally enforceable by courts when properly drafted. Because the agreement is final and binding, you should solicit legal advice during the process of negotiating and drafting it.

- A written and signed **Memorandum of Agreement** created by the parties before they leave the mediation conference will considerably strengthen a later claim that contractual agreement was reached in the mediation. A handshake deal is rather difficult to prove in the absence of testimony from the mediator, who has agreed not to testify under any circumstances. Therefore, being able to show proof of the agreement independent of the mediator is very important.

KEY TERMS

ETHICAL AND LEGAL REVIEW

1. Following the alleged settlement of a matter through mediation, plaintiff engages new attorneys and insists that no agreement was consummated as a result of lengthy and difficult negotiations in mediation. During the mediation session, plaintiff stated that her attorneys would speak for her and that she would not make any statements on her own behalf. Plaintiff approved a settlement offer related to her privately by her attorney, who in turn related plaintiff's agreement to the defendant's counsel. Plaintiff represented to her family members that the case had been settled. Plaintiff did not speak directly to the defendant or the defendant's attorney on the matter. Was an agreement reached and can it be enforced by a court? [*Snyder-Falkingham v. Stockburger,* 457 S.E. 2d 36 (1995); see also *Crain v. Dore,* 578 So. 2d 555 (1991)]

2. In an enforcement proceeding before the National Labor Relations Board, company requests that the Board subpoena the testimony of the Federal Mediation and Conciliation Service mediator who assisted the parties in negotiating the case. Testimony from the mediator was requested on the question of whether an agreement had been reached at the series of mediation conferences over which the mediator presided; company believed no agreement had been reached, while union asserted that one had. Should the Board require the testimony of the mediator? [*NLRB v. Macaluso, Inc.,* 618 F. 2d 51 (1980)]

3. A defendant asbestos manufacturer moved to disqualify a special master appointed by the court to assist the parties in resolving a mass tort litigation case involving asbestos exposure. The company alleged that the appointed special master was not neutral regarding the instant case because he had acted on behalf of another asbestos defendant in a case related to public education and legislative efforts aimed at promoting alternative compensation systems to mass tort

litigation. Should the court disqualify the special master? [*In re Joint Eastern and Southern Districts Asbestos Litigation, 737* F. Supp. 735 (1990)]

4. Plaintiff in a banking case, in which mediation is being used, discloses to a local newspaper that a settlement offer has been made by the defendant in mediation. Plaintiff's attorney is quoted by the paper as saying the defendant made the settlement offer because the defendant regarded the case as "shaky." All parties had signed a mediation agreement promising confidentiality unless all participants waived it. The defendant bank did not waive confidentiality prior to the plaintiff's statements to the newspaper. How should the trial judge respond to this matter? Is dismissal of the plaintiff's case an appropriate solution? [*Paranzino v. Barnett Bank,* 690 So. 2d 725 (1997)]

SUGGESTED ADDITIONAL READINGS

Bush, R., and J. Folger. *The Promise of Mediation: Responding to Conflict Through Empowerment and Recognition.* Jossey-Bass, 1994.

Cooley, J. *Mediation Advocacy: N.I.T.A. Practical Guide Series,* National Institute for Trial Advocacy, 1996.

Folberg, J., and A. Taylor. *Mediation: A Comprehensive Guide to Resolving Conflicts Without Litigation.* Jossey-Bass, 1984.

Golann, D. *Mediating Legal Disputes: Effective Strategies for Lawyers and Mediators,* Little, Brown, 1996.

Kressel, K., and D. Pruitt, et. al. *Mediation Research: The Process and Effectiveness of Third Party Intervention.* Jossey-Bass, 1989.

Lovenheim, P. *How to Mediate Your Dispute.* Nolo Press, 1996.

Marcus, L., et. al. *Renegotiating Health Care: Resolving Conflict to Build Collaboration.* Jossey-Bass, 1995.

Moore, C. *The Mediation Process: Practical Strategies for Resolving Conflict.* Jossey-Bass, 1986.

Rogers, N., and C. McEwen. *Mediation: Law, Policy & Practice.* Lawyers Co-Operative, 1989.

Rothman, J. *Resolving Identity Based Conflict in Nations, Organizations and Communities.* Jossey-Bass, 1997.

Yarbrough, E., and W. Wilmot. *Artful Mediation: Constructive Conflict at Work.* Cairns, 1995.

6

INTRODUCTION TO COMMERCIAL ARBITRATION

CHAPTER HIGHLIGHTS

In this chapter, you will read and learn about the following:

1. The historical development of U.S. statutory and case law on arbitration.
2. Descriptions of voluntary and court-annexed arbitration.
3. The authority and ethical responsibilities of arbitrators.
4. The role of businesspeople and lawyers in arbitration.
5. The main steps in the typical arbitration process.
6. The advantages and disadvantages of voluntary arbitration to resolve a dispute.
7. The major distinctions between court-annexed and voluntary arbitration proceedings.
8. The limitations on a trial de novo or new trial in court-annexed arbitration.

DEFINING ARBITRATION

Arbitration is an adjudicatory ADR mechanism. Parties submit a disagreement to one or more neutral decision makers called arbitrators. Unlike negotiation or mediation, the arbitrator, not the parties, determines the outcome of the dispute along with any applicable remedies. The arbitration process is more formal than other ADR mechanisms and uses abbreviated, trial-like procedures that are adversarial, rather than collaborative, in nature. Although arbitration has just recently become a widely accepted method of dispute resolution in the United States, it has a lengthy history of successful use in other societies.

The Historical Development of Arbitration

http://
Read about the Chartered Institute of Arbitrators at: http://www. arbitrators.org

Arbitration is one of the oldest forms of ADR, dating back to ancient Persian, Sumerian, Egyptian, Greek, and Roman civilizations. For example, Athenians used arbitration as an alternative to the expense and complexity of the Athenian justice system; reasons echoed today by many disputants who use arbitration. Arbitration also played a role in the resolution of mercantile disputes in Europe. Private tribunals of merchants connected to guilds and trading companies or court-supervised panels of merchant referees oversaw the process. Some of this European experience carried over to the American colonies. In the colonial United States, arbitration can be traced primarily to Dutch settlers in New York and Quakers in Pennsylvania. At this time, arbitrators dealt primarily with disputes between merchants. These arbitrators were often untrained in the law but well versed in business customs and practices. Arbitration was also relied on to handle personal matters, as exemplified by an arbitration clause contained in George Washington's will to resolve any challenges to distribution of his assets.

The evolution of the English courts led to a decline in the use of arbitration at the end of the eighteenth century and into the nineteenth century. English judges began to view arbitration with suspicion, concerned that arbitrators were usurping their powers and lacking the requisite legal training to interpret party rights and responsibilities. English courts began to routinely overturn arbitral awards, supplanting their own views for those of the arbitrators. Eventually, disputants moved away from the use of arbitration. Likewise, the U.S. courts disfavored arbitration as treading on their traditional authority to adjudicate disputes.

http://
Find the U.S. Code at: http://law.house. gov/usc.html

However, at the start of the twentieth century, arbitration began to be resurrected as a method for resolving disputes between businesspeople. In 1920, New York passed the first state arbitration statute, which allowed courts to enforce contracts between parties seeking to arbitrate future disputes. The New York statute soon became the model for the first federal arbitration statute, the United States Arbitration Act (now commonly referred to as the Federal Arbitration Act), passed in 1925. The **Federal Arbitration Act (FAA)** was pivotal in the growing acceptance of arbitration to resolve business disputes. The statute promoted the use of arbitration to resolve conflicts involving commercial transactions among businesses in different states or transactions between the United States and foreign countries. The FAA provides parties with the opportunity to resolve their dispute through arbitration rather than the courts. The law also allows parties to seek the assistance of the courts in compelling parties to comply with an arbitration agreement and in enforcing both domestic and foreign arbitral awards.

The **Uniform Arbitration Act** is a state model patterned after the 1920 New York arbitration law. Although some states initially passed statutes antagonistic to arbitration, today nearly all of the states have enacted arbitration acts modeled after the Uniform Arbitration Act. The FAA and state arbitration statutes provide a liberal scheme for the enforcement of arbitration agreements, placing arbitration agreements on an equal footing with other commercial contracts. Under these statutes, a written arbitration agreement, similar to any other written contract, is valid, enforceable, and irrevocable. The only exceptions are those legal or equitable grounds for revocation available for any contract under law.

With the passage of the FAA and applicable state laws, the previous judicial hostility toward arbitration began to dissipate. The heavy backlog of court cases and the successful use of arbitration by many disputants have encouraged the courts, and in particular the Supreme Court, to view arbitration more favorably in recent years. Today arbitration is used in a variety of commercial disputes involving business contracts, intellectual and real property rights, government agencies, construction, finances, health care, insurance, international trade, labor, and employment. Although originally viewed as a method to resolve disputes between two or more businesspeople, arbitration is now also used to resolve conflicts between businesses and their customers. Arbitration was even used to help resolve disputes over athlete disqualifications at the 1996 Olympic Games in Atlanta.

The demand for arbitration has skyrocketed. The American Arbitration Association, a leading nonprofit organization, reported that its arbitration filings were up 34% between 1986 and 1991, with 62,000 cases nationwide totaling more than $4.5 billion in dispute claims. The number of securities arbitration filings has also dramatically risen from about 2,800 in 1987 to nearly 6,000 filings in 1997. The following case illustrates how the FAA may preempt state laws that conflict with its broad acceptance and promotion of arbitration to resolve business disputes.

http://
Learn more about the American Arbitration Association by accessing this site: http://www.adr.org

---

SECURITIES INDUSTRY ASS'N V. CONNOLLY
883 F. 2d 1114 (1st Cir. 1989), cert. denied, 495 U.S. 956 (1990)

FACT SUMMARY

In Massachusetts, the Secretary of State's office has regulatory authority for secured transactions. That office became concerned when investors who opened brokerage accounts were required to give up their right to go to court over investment disputes. In an effort to promote fairness to customers in investment disputes, the Secretary of State's office enacted certain state securities regulations. These regulations indicated, in part, that a mandatory pre-dispute arbitration agreement (PDAA) between investors and brokers was unethical and grounds for revocation of a broker's license. In addition, brokers must provide a complete, written disclosure to investors of the legal impact of agreeing to a PDAA. The Securities Industry Association brought an action against then Secretary of State Michael Connolly, claiming that the regulations were unconstitutional in light of the terms of the FAA. The trial court granted summary judgment for the Securities Industry

Association. The secretary of state's office appealed that decision.

OPINION: *JUDGE SELYA*

Congress passed the Federal Arbitration Act (FAA) . . . to help legitimate arbitration and make it more readily useful to disputants. The hope has long been that the Act could serve as a therapy for the ailment of the crowded docket.

We are asked to decide today if certain regulations . . . are preempted by the FAA.
. . .

The Regulations not only regulate, they do so in a manner patently inhospitable to arbitration. . . .

The Supremacy Clause of Article VI of the federal Constitution prevents the states from impinging overmuch on federal law and policy. Preemption—the vehicle by which the Supremacy Clause is generally enforced—always boils down to a matter of congressional intent. And, because Congress has not expressly delineated the preemptive reach of the FAA, our task is to determine the extent of any implied preemption vis-a-vis the state's regulations.

[It] has been said that implied preemption prospers when Congress intends its enactments "to occupy a given field to the exclusion of state law." That is not the case here: Congress did not want the FAA to occupy the entire field of arbitration. State law may also be preempted "when it actually conflicts with federal law."

Whatever labels may be affixed, the pivot upon which our inquiry turns remains constant: Where Congress has failed explicitly to detail the dimensions of displacement, courts must decide if "the state law disturbs too much the congressionally declared scheme. . . ." Put another way, a state law or regulation cannot take root if it looms as an obstacle to

achievement of the full purposes and ends which Congress has itself set out to accomplish.

Congress, we are told, enacted the FAA to relieve parties from what, even two-thirds of a century ago, was characterized as "the costliness and delays of litigation."

In sum, the legislative history of the FAA, like its text, indicates that the courts must receive the Act hospitably and defend its "mechanisms vigilantly and with some fervor."

Appellants conceded before the district court . . . and on appeal that the regulations apply only to arbitration agreements. They suggest, however, that this bespeaks no unfriendliness. The Commonwealth treats arbitration agreements like other contracts between businesses and consumers; that is, it regulates them as extensively as necessary for the public weal. In our view, that self-congratulatory casuistry will not wash. Indeed, we think it evident that it was precisely this sort of categorization error which Congress sought to cure when it enacted the FAA. The FAA prohibits a state from taking more stringent action addressed specifically, and limited, to arbitration contracts.

That is not to say that a state can do nothing about a perceived problem. The Commonwealth's powers remain great, so long as used evenhandedly. The FAA does not prohibit judicial relief from arbitration contracts which are shown to result from fraud or enormous (unfair) economic imbalance of the sort sufficient to avoid contracts of all types.

Appellants also urge us to find that, notwithstanding the general rule, Congress carved out an exception to the Act by permitting states concurrently to regulate securities transactions.

Simply put, nothing in the Securities Act, the Exchange Act, or the grant of concurrent power to the states to regulate securities manifests a congressional intent to limit or prohibit waiver of a judicial forum for a particular claim, or to abridge the sweep of the FAA.

The long and short of it is that we can find no evidence of a clear congressional command to override the unambiguous proarbitration mandate of the FAA in the securities field.

State law need not clash head on with a federal enactment in order to be pre-empted. If state law "stands as an obstacle to the accomplishment of the full purpose and objectives of Congress," it must topple.

Discussion Questions

1. According to the appeals court, what was the congressional intent behind the passage of the FAA?

2. What are some bases for judicial relief from arbitration agreements that do not offend the FAA?

3. Do you think that states should have the authority to regulate arbitration agreements to protect investors' access to the courts for securities disputes?

MAIN ASPECTS OF VOLUNTARY ARBITRATION

Most arbitrations are voluntary with parties agreeing to submit their disputes to an arbitrator, who renders a final decision or award. **Voluntary arbitrations** are usually binding, with parties agreeing in advance to comply with the terms of the arbitrator's decision. There is little or no opportunity for a judicial appeal, although in some instances, the parties may decide that the award of the arbitrator will be nonbinding or merely advisory. Based on the arbitrator's advisory opinion, the parties may decide whether to negotiate, mediate, or litigate their dispute.

Determining Procedures

As there is no single uniform set of arbitration rules or procedures, numerous community, national, and international entities offer to administer the arbitration process based on their own unique set of procedures. Unlike litigation, the parties can design their own arbitration process, referred to as an **ad hoc proceeding,** or follow the established rules of administering organizations, such as the American Arbitration Association, the International Chamber of Commerce in Paris, or Judicial, Arbitration, and Mediation Services (JAMS)/EnDispute. In some cases, parties may use a number of ADR processes, including arbitration, to handle their conflict. For example, IBM and Fujitsu used a structured ADR process that combined aspects of negotiation, mediation, and arbitration to resolve an intellectual property case concerning operating systems software. A popular hybrid process is called **med-arb.** In med-arb the parties first attempt to mediate the dispute. If unsuccessful, they then have two options: (1) to allow the mediator to take on the

http://
Read about the SEC's securities arbitration regulations at this site: http://www.sec.gov

http://
Find out more about JAMS/EnDispute at: http://www.jams-endispute.com

role of an arbitrator and decide the outcome of the dispute or (2) to dismiss the mediator and select a new third-party neutral advisor to act as arbitrator. In a **rules by reference** proceeding, the disputants elect to follow the established procedures of an administering organization. Although no two arbitrations are identical, most arbitration processes are characterized by an agreement to arbitrate, selection of an arbitrator or arbitral panel, pre-hearing preparation, the arbitration hearing, the arbitration or arbitral award, and post-award actions.

Agreement to Arbitrate

Voluntary arbitration is a creature of contract. A separate arbitration agreement or an arbitration clause within an existing business contract must exist before a disputing party can initiate the arbitration process. In some instances, a court may infer an arbitration agreement based on the business conduct of, or verbal promises made between, the parties. However, to avoid confusion or misunderstanding, it is best to enter into a written agreement to arbitrate. The arbitration agreement will normally outline the types of disputes subject to arbitration, the authority of the arbitrator, the substantive law to be applied to the dispute, and the arbitration rules or procedures to be followed.

There are two types of arbitration agreements: the **pre-dispute arbitration agreement (PDAA)** and the submission agreement. A PDAA is an agreement or clause inserted into a contract *prior to any dispute* that requires the parties to use arbitration if there are any future disagreements. (See Figure 6.1.) For example, the securities industry mandates that customers wishing to open a brokerage account must enter into a PDAA with the brokerage firm. Under the PDAA, the investor and the brokerage house agree that they will use arbitration if they have any future conflicts over trades or other financial dealings.

The second type of written agreement, the **submission agreement,** is a contract to arbitrate that the parties enter into *after a dispute* has already arisen. (See Figure 6.2.) Perhaps two firms have entered into a contract for the purchase of computer hardware and software. The initial sales contract does not contain an arbitration clause. If a dispute arises over the payment terms and warranties for the computers,

FIGURE 6.1 Sample Pre-Dispute Arbitration Agreement (PDAA)

Any controversy, dispute, or claim arising out of, in connection with, or in relation to the interpretation, performance, or breach of this agreement shall be resolved, at the request of either party, by a general reference conducted by a retired judge from the panel of Judicial Arbitration & Mediation Services, Inc. (J*A*M*S), appointed pursuant to the provisions of California Code of Civil Procedure Section 638(1) *et seq.* The parties intend this general reference agreement to be specifically enforceable in accordance with said Section 638(1). If the parties cannot agree upon a member of the J*A*M*S panel, one shall be appointed by the Presiding Judge in the County in which the matter is to be heard.

Source: Reprinted with permission of JAMS/EnDispute.

FIGURE 6.2   Sample Submission Agreement

Structuring the Arbitration Hearing

The Submission Agreement is important in that it sets forth the rights of the parties and the rules and procedures to be followed at the arbitration hearing. The parties must decide whether they prefer to plan a potential arbitration proceeding before a dispute arises or if they would rather postpone those determinations until they actually face an arbitration hearing.

EXHIBIT FUTURE DISPUTE SUBMISSION AGREEMENT

Pre-Hearing Conference

The arbitrator(s) shall schedule a pre-hearing conference to reach agreement on procedural matters, arrange for the exchange of information, obtain stipulations, and attempt to narrow the issues.

Discovery

OPTION 1: The parties will submit a proposed discovery schedule to the arbitrator(s) at the pre-hearing conference. The scope and duration of discovery will be within the sole discretion of the arbitrator(s).

OPTION 2: It is our objective to expedite the arbitration proceedings by placing the following limitations on discovery:

a. Each party may propound only one interrogatory requesting the names and addresses of the witnesses to be called at the arbitration hearing.

b. On a date to be determined at the pre-hearing conference, each party may serve one request for the production of documents. The documents are to be exchanged two weeks later.

c. Each party may depose _____ witnesses. Each deposition must be concluded within four hours and all depositions must be taken within thirty (30) days of the pre-hearing conference. Any party deposing an opponent's expert must pay the expert's fee for attending the deposition.

OPTION 3: It is our objective to expedite the arbitration proceedings by eliminating discovery as provided by the Discovery Act pursuant to CCP §1985, et seq. Instead of discovery, the parties agree to the following exchange of information:

a. Either party can make a written demand for lists of the witnesses to be called or the documents to be introduced at the hearing.

The demand must be received prior to the pre-hearing conference.

b. The lists must be served within fifteen (15) days of the demand.

c. No depositions may be taken for discovery.

The Hearing

I. The parties must file briefs with the arbitrator(s) at least three (3) days before the hearing, specifying the facts each intends to prove and analyzing the applicable law.

II. The parties have the right to representation by legal counsel throughout the arbitration proceedings.

III. Judicial rules of evidence and procedure relating to the conduct at the hearing, examination of witnesses, and presentation of evidence do not apply. Any relevant evidence, including hearsay, shall be admitted by the arbitrator if it is the sort of evidence on which responsible persons are accustomed to rely on in the conduct of serious affairs, regardless of the admissibility of such evidence in a court of law.

IV. Within reasonable limitations, both sides at the hearing may call and examine witnesses for relevant testimony, introduce relevant exhibits or other documents, cross-examine or impeach witnesses who shall have testified orally on any matter relevant to the issues, and otherwise rebut evidence, as long as these rights are exercised in an efficient and expeditious manner.

V. Any party desiring a stenographic record may secure a court reporter to attend the proceedings. The requesting party must notify the other parties of the arrangements in advance of the hearing and must pay for the cost incurred.

The Award

I. The decision shall be based on the evidence introduced at the hearing, including all logical and reasonable inferences therefrom. The arbitrator(s) may grant any remedy or relief which is just and equitable.

II. The award must be made in writing and signed by either the arbitrator or a majority of the arbitrators if a panel is used. It shall contain a concise statement of the reasons in support of the decision.

III. The award must by mailed promptly to the parties, but no later than thirty (30) days from the closing of the hearing.

IV. The award can be judicially enforced (confirmed, corrected, or vacated) pursuant to §1285 et seq. of the Code of Civil Procedure. It is final and binding and there is no direct appeal from the award on the grounds of error in the application of the law.

Fees and Expenses

Unless otherwise agreed, each party must pay its own witness fees.

Unless otherwise agreed, each party must pay its pro rata share of the arbitrator's fees.

OPTION 1: The arbitrator has the authority to award attorney fees to the prevailing party.

OPTION 2: The arbitrator must award attorney fees to the prevailing party.

OPTION 3: Each party must pay its own attorney fees.

Source: Reprinted with permission of JAMS/EnDispute.

the parties may decide to arbitrate their conflict and will enter into a submission agreement. Once a PDAA or submission agreement is in place, either party may demand arbitration pursuant to the terms of the agreement. (See Figures 6.3 and 6.4.)

In some instances, critics of arbitration expressed concern that some PDAAs are being unfairly inserted into standardized or form contracts with consumers (adhesion contracts). In selling goods and services to consumers, many businesses use standardized contracts that do not allow for any meaningful negotiation of terms between the parties. Consumers must either accept the contract as written or forfeit the chance to receive the goods or services. In this situation, consumers do not truly have the opportunity to explore and select conflict resolution methods that best meet their needs. For public policy reasons, courts will sometimes not enforce adhesion contracts that are too burdensome on one of the parties.

Even if a valid agreement to arbitrate exists, a court may be called on to decide the issue of arbitrability. Arbitrability deals with a collection of issues regarding whether a particular dispute was truly intended to be, or should be, resolved through arbitration. There are two types of arbitrability: procedural and substantive. In *AT&T Technologies, Inc., v. Communication Workers of America* [475 U.S. 643 (1986)], the Supreme Court defined these concepts and spelled out the split responsibilities between the courts and arbitrators for arbitrability. Unless otherwise specifically agreed to by the parties, arbitrators determine procedural arbitrability, while courts decide issues of substantive arbitrability.

Specifically, **procedural arbitrability** focuses on whether the party seeking arbitration has fully complied with all procedural prerequisites to arbitration. For example, an arbitration clause might require the initiating party (the claimant) to give thirty days' notice of an intention to seek arbitration to the other party (the respondent) in the conflict. If the claimant fails to provide this notice, the arbitrator can determine that the dispute is not procedurally arbitrable until the claimant has done so.

Courts determine **substantive arbitrability** by answering three basic questions: (1) does an agreement to arbitrate exist? (2) is the dispute within the coverage of the arbitration clause? and (3) are there any legal or equitable limits on the use of arbitration to resolve this dispute?

In deciding whether an agreement to arbitrate exists, the court must look at written or verbal agreements as well as any previous dealings between the parties that

FIGURE 6.3 Sample Demand Form for Arbitration

American Arbitration Association

COMMERCIAL ARBITRATION RULES

To institute proceedings, please send three copies of this demand and the arbitration agreement, with the administrative fee as provided in the rules, to the AAA. Send the original demand to the respondent.

DEMAND FOR ARBITRATION

DATE: _____

TO: Name _____
          (of the Party on Whom the Demand Is Made)

Address _____

City and State _____ ZIP Code _____

Telephone (   ) _____ Fax _____

Name of Representative _____
                                    (if Known)

Name of Firm (if Applicable) _____

Representative's Address _____

City and State _____ ZIP Code _____

Telephone (   ) _____ Fax _____

The named claimant, a party to an arbitration agreement contained in a written contract, dated _____
_____ and providing for arbitration under the
Commercial Arbitration Rules of the American Arbitration Association, hereby demands arbitration thereunder.

THE NATURE OF THE DISPUTE:

THE CLAIM OR RELIEF SOUGHT (the Amount, if Any):

TYPES OF BUSINESS: Claimant _____ Respondent _____

HEARING LOCALE REQUESTED: _____
                                              (City and State)

You are hereby notified that copies of our arbitration agreement and this demand are being filed with the American Arbitration Association at its _____ office, with a request that it commence administration of the arbitration. Under the rules, you may file an answering statement within ten days after notice from the administrator.

Signed _____ Title _____
              (May Be Signed by a Representative)

Name of Claimant _____

Address (to Be Used in Connection with This Case) _____

City and State _____ ZIP Code _____

Telephone (   ) _____ Fax _____

Name of Representative _____

Name of Firm (if Applicable) _____

Representative's Address _____

City and State _____ ZIP Code _____

Telephone (   ) _____ Fax _____

☐ MEDIATION is a nonbinding process. The mediator assists the parties in working out a solution that is acceptable to them. If you wish for the AAA to contact the other parties to ascertain whether they wish to mediate this matter, please check this box (there is no additional administrative fee for this service).   Form C2–6/93

Source: Reprinted with permission of the American Arbitration Association.

FIGURE 6.4 Sample Submission Form for Dispute Resolution

American Arbitration Association
SUBMISSION TO DISPUTE RESOLUTION

Date: _____

The named parties hereby submit the following dispute for resolution under the _____

_____ Rules* of the American Arbitration Association:

Procedure Selected: ☐ Binding arbitration   ☐ Mediation settlement

☐ Other _____
(Describe)

FOR INSURANCE CASES ONLY:

_____   _____ to _____   _____
Policy Number   Effective Dates   Applicable Policy Limits

Date of Incident _____   Location _____

Insured: _____   Claim Number: _____

Name(s) of Claimant(s)	**Check if a Minor**	**Amount Claimed**
_____	☐	_____
_____	☐	_____

Nature of Dispute and/or Injuries Alleged (attach additional sheets if necessary):

Place of Hearing: _____

We agree that, if binding arbitration is selected, we will abide by and perform any award rendered hereunder and that a judgment may be entered on the award.

To Be Completed by the Claimant	*To Be Completed by the Respondent*
Name of Party	Name of Party
Address	Address
City, State, and ZIP Code	City, State, and ZIP Code
( ) ____ Telephone ____ Fax	( ) ____ Telephone ____ Fax
Signature†	Signature†
Name of Party's Attorney or Representative	Name of Party's Attorney or Representative
Address	Address
City, State, and ZIP Code	City, State, and ZIP Code
( ) ____ Telephone ____ Fax	( ) ____ Telephone ____ Fax
Signature†	Signature†

Please file three copies with the AAA.

* *If you have a question as to which rules apply, please contact the AAA.*
† Signatures of all parties are required for arbitration.

Form G1–7/90

Source: Reprinted with permission of the American Arbitration Association.

may show an intention to arbitrate disputes. Often parties may go to court to litigate whether or not an agreement to arbitrate actually exists in their situation. In the following case, the court must decide whether or not the parties have agreed to arbitrate their dispute.

J & C DYEING, INC., V. DRAKON, INC.
93 Civ. 4283, 1994 U.S. Dist. LEXIS 15194 (S.D.N.Y. 1994)

FACT SUMMARY

Between February and June 1992, Drakon, Inc. ("Drakon"), a New Jersey garment manufacturer, submitted purchase orders for yarn to J & C Dyeing, Inc. ("J & C"), a North Carolina yarn dyer and converter. Drakon instructed J & C to ship the yarn directly to Zoltan Toth Knitting Company in Pennsylvania. J & C returned confirmation slips to Drakon, which contained clauses indicating that all disputes between them should be resolved through arbitration in New York City. Drakon never signed the confirmation slips or discussed the use of arbitration with J & C. When problems arose with the yarn, Drakon withheld payment and sued J & C in the Pennsylvania courts in May 1993. J & C then brought a motion to compel arbitration in the New York courts against Drakon, claiming that the parties had an agreement to arbitrate any disputes based on the arbitration clauses contained in the confirmation slips.

OPINION: *JUDGE PIERRE N. LEVAL*

. . . This case presents a classic example of [a] battle of the forms under Section 2–207 of the Uniform Commercial Code. Drakon sent purchase orders to J & C. The shipments of yarn sent by J & C in response to Drakon's orders were accompanied by confirmation slips, all of which contained an arbitration provision. Both parties agree that a contract exists; they disagree as to its terms. The question, then, is whether the arbitration clause contained in the confirmation forms became a term of contract between J & C and Drakon.

U.C.C. § 2-207(2) provides that "additional terms [in an acceptance or confirmation] are to be construed as proposals for addition to the contract." Where, as here, the transaction is between merchants, the additional terms become part of the contract unless (a) the offer expressly limits acceptance to the terms of the offer; (b) they materially alter it; or (c) notification of objection to them has already been given or is given within a reasonable time after notice of them is received. N.Y. U.C.C. § 2-207(2).

Thus, the arbitration clause will be deemed part of the agreement if it falls under one of these three exceptions. Because the parties agree that neither (a) nor (c) apply to their agreement, our analysis is limited to whether the arbitration clause materially alters the contract.

The decision of the New York Court of Appeals in *Marlene Indus. Corp. v. Carnac Textiles, Inc.,* 45 N. Y. 2d 327, 408 N.Y. S. 2d 410, 380 N.E. 2d 239 (N.Y. 1978) is dispositive. (footnote omitted). In *Marlene,* the purchaser placed an oral request for fabrics followed by a written purchase order. An arbitration provision was not mentioned during the oral request and was not included in the purchase order. The seller then sent a confirmation which contained an arbitration clause and instructed the buyer to sign and return a copy of the confirmation. Neither party signed the other's form, and a dispute arose. The seller sought arbitration.

Applying U.C.C. § 2-207(2), the court refused to include the arbitration provision as a term of the parties' agreement. The court explained that "by agreeing to arbitrate a party waives in large part many of his normal rights under substantive and procedural law of the State, and it would be unfair to infer such a significant waiver on the basis of anything less than a clear indication of intent." . . . The court concluded that "it is clear that an arbitration clause is a material addition which can become part of a contract only if it is expressly assented to by both parties." . . .

In certain circumstances, an agreement to arbitrate can be implied from the course of dealing or custom and usage in the trade. However, this must be supported by "evidence which affirmatively establishes that the parties agreed to arbitrate their disputes.". . .

Here, it has not been "affirmatively established" that the parties agreed to arbitrate their disputes. Drakon neither signed any of the confirmation orders, nor otherwise expressly agreed to be bound by the arbitration clause. In addition, the course of dealing between Drakon and J & C does not demonstrate that the parties intended to arbitrate their disputes. Although Drakon did not object to the

arbitration clause, the mere retention of confirmation slips without any additional conduct indicative of a desire to arbitrate cannot bind Drakon, for it does not rise to the level of assent required to bind parties to arbitration provisions. . . .

Nor does the fact that arbitration is a common method of dispute resolution in the textile industry require a different outcome. The prevalence of arbitration in the textile industry "is not an acceptable substitute . . . for finding a specific agreement to arbitrate." . . . We likewise find no merit in the fact that Drakon referred to one of J & C's confirmation slips in correspondence. A single reference to a confirmation number, without more, is not a sufficient basis for inferring an agreement to arbitrate. . . .

The second Circuit's decision in *Pervel Indus., Inc. v. T M Wallcovering, Inc.*, 871 F. 2d 7 (2d Cir. 1989) is also distinguishable. There the court held that a fabric purchaser was required to arbitrate where it manifested its assent to arbitration clauses by signing and returning the order confirmations containing the clauses and retained the other forms without objection. See also *Genesco, Inc. v. T. Kakiuchi & Co., Ltd.*, 815 F. 2d 840, 845-46 (2d Cir. 1987)(arbitration clause binding where buyer returned numerous confirmation forms with signatures of high-ranking officers and as to unsigned forms, where buyer and seller enjoyed a "long standing and on-going relationship").

For the foregoing reasons, J & C's petition to compel arbitration is denied.

Discussion Questions

1. Do you think that Drakon should have been required to arbitrate the breach of contract dispute?
2. Do you agree with the court that an arbitration clause materially alters a commercial contract?
3. What should companies like J & C do to ensure compliance with arbitration clauses contained in their confirmation slips?

The second issue of substantive arbitrability considers whether the conflict between the parties is covered under the terms of the arbitration agreement. In some instances, parties may claim that their arbitration agreement did not intend to use arbitration to resolve a particular type of dispute. For example, two businesses enter into a trademark licensing agreement that contains an arbitration clause. The clause states that any disputes that arise under the terms of the contract will be handled through arbitration. At a later point in time, a conflict develops and one of the parties tries to bring a tort claim against the other in court. The claimant may assert that the agreed-upon arbitration clause was only intended to cover contract claims, not tort actions, and therefore does not cover the dispute in question.

Under the earlier-cited *AT&T* case, the courts are expected to broadly interpret arbitration clauses or agreements under the concept of the **presumption of arbitrability.** Today, if a conflict is arguably covered under the terms of the arbitration agreement, courts will normally find that the parties intended that the dispute be processed through arbitration. In determining whether the dispute is within the terms of an arbitration agreement, courts will favor the use of arbitration. When an agreement to arbitrate exists, parties challenging its use face a heavy presumption in favor of the arbitrability of a dispute.

A party may also try to avoid arbitration by claiming that there are legal or equitable limits on the use of arbitration in a particular dispute. Normally, a party will raise standard contract grounds for rendering the arbitration agreement unenforceable. For example, a consumer may have signed an agreement to borrow money from a lending institution. Later, it may be determined that the lender defrauded the consumer in the lending process. Because the consumer had signed the agreement under a fraud, the arbitration clause in that agreement would be invalid.

In certain situations, a party may argue that under law only the judiciary has jurisdiction to resolve particular disputes. For example, earlier courts once determined that only judges could resolve certain statutory disputes such as Title VII or other federal statutory discrimination claims. These claims were viewed as not susceptible to arbitration (not arbitrable). However, recent judicial decisions have begun to expand the nature of disputes that may be arbitrable, which now include the resolution of many statutory and Title VII disputes.

DEGAETANO V. SMITH BARNEY, INC.
1996 U.S. Dist. LEXIS 1140 (S.D. N.Y. 1996), 70 Fair Empl. Prac. Cas. (BNA) 401

FACT SUMMARY

Plaintiff Alicia DeGaetano filed a gender discrimination and tort suit against defendants Smith Barney, Inc., her former employer, and Frederick Hessler, her former manager at Smith Barney. Plaintiff was hired as a financial analyst for Smith Barney in July 1993. When hired, she signed an agreement entitled "Principles of Employment," which included a dispute resolution clause. The clause allowed employment disputes to be handled initially through an internal grievance process and subsequently through binding arbitration administered through the New York Stock Exchange. The clause explicitly stated that the dispute resolution procedures applied to employment discrimination claims under Title VII of the Civil Rights Act of 1964 and any other federal, state, or local antidiscrimination laws. The agreement advised employees that it was their responsibility to review and understand the dispute resolution procedures and to contact Human Resources if they had any questions. In 1993 and 1994, the plaintiff received updated copies of the employee handbook, which restated these dispute resolution procedures and terms.

In March 1994, the plaintiff was assigned to Smith Barney's Public Finance Division's Healthcare Group under the supervision of defendant Hessler. Between August 1994 and January 1995, plaintiff alleged that her supervisor made unwelcome sexual advances and advised her on numerous occasions that her performance evaluations, promotion, and bonuses would depend on whether or not she submitted to his sexual demands. The plaintiff claims she repeatedly told Hessler that she wanted only a professional business relationship. However, he purportedly persisted in his sexual advances and statements. DeGaetano eventually sought intervention from Smith Barney's Human Resources department, but she was told that no action would be taken against Hessler. In February 1995, the plaintiff alleges she was forced to resign from her position because of the continued pressure from Hessler and Smith Barney's refusal to take any action against him.

In January 1995, the plaintiff filed a complaint with the Equal Employment Opportunity Commission which granted her the right to bring her action in federal court. In March 1995, the plaintiff brought this action based on violations of Title VII of the Civil Rights Act of 1964, as well as New York state and city antidiscrimination laws. She also brought a tort action against defendant Hessler for intentional infliction of emotional distress. The defendants demanded arbitration, and the plaintiff refused to submit to arbitration. The defendants made a motion to compel arbitration under the Federal Arbitration Act.

OPINION: *DISTRICT JUDGE DENISE COTE*

The United States Arbitration Act. . . . "reflects a legislative recognition of the 'desirability of arbitration as an alternative to the complications of litigation,'" and "reversed centuries of judicial hostility to arbitration agreements." . . . The Act was designed to allow parties to avoid the costliness and delays of litigation and to place arbitration agreements upon the same footing as other contracts. . . .

The burden of demonstrating. . . . whether Congress intended to preclude the arbitrability of a claim founded on statutory rights—is on the party opposing arbitration. . . . In order to establish that Congress intended to exclude Title VII claims from arbitration under the Act, the Court must look to the statute's text or legislative history, or infer such an intent "from the inherent conflict between arbitration and the statute's underlying purposes." . . . Throughout this inquiry, the Court must keep in mind that "questions of arbitrability must be addressed with a healthy regard for the federal policy favoring arbitration." . . .

As recent Supreme Court decisions have made it clear, the plaintiff is faced with a difficult task in arguing that Congress must have intended to preclude arbitration when it enacted Title VII because of important public policies behind the statute. See *Gilmer*, 500 U.S. at 23 (Age Discrimination in Employment Act ("ADEA") claims may be subject to compulsory arbitration); *Rodriguez de Quijas,* 490 U.S. at 484 (Securities Act of 1933); McMahon, 482 U.S. at 227-38 (Section 10(b) of the Securities Exchange Act of 1934); *Id.* at 234-42 (civil provisions of Racketeers Influenced and Corrupt Organizations Act ("RICO")); *Mitsubishi,* 473 U.S. at 628-40 (Sherman Antitrust Act). The Second Circuit has extended the above-cited line of cases to claims arising under the Employment Retirement Income Security Act ("ERISA"), see *Bird*, 926 F. 2d at 117, and New York's Court of Appeals has followed suit with respect to claims arising under New York's Human Rights Law. . . . Finally, and although not binding authority, other circuits have held that, in the wake of *Gilmer,* Title VII claims are also subject to compulsory arbitration pursuant to the Act. . . .

. . . The plaintiff does not dispute signing the Agreement, which according to its terms, unambiguously obligates plaintiff to comply with the Arbitration Policy. . . .

The crux of plaintiff's argument pertains to . . . whether Congress intended Title VII claims to be nonarbitrable. Plaintiff argues that, as a matter of law, Smith Barney cannot require employees to prospectively waive "substantive rights" under Title VII, including the right to attorney's fees, punitive damages, and injunctive relief. . . .

In making her argument, plaintiff fails to point out where, either in the text of Title VII or its legislative history, Congress has stated its intent "to preclude a waiver of judicial remedies" by means of arbitration. . . . This is not surprising, however, because the text of Title VII, itself evidences a clear Congressional intent to make arbitration an alternative method of dispute resolution. Section 118 of the 1991 amendments to Title VII states, in relevant part:

> Where appropriate and to the extent authorized by law, the use of alternative means of dispute resolution including. . . . arbitration, is encouraged to resolve disputes arising under the Acts or provisions of federal law amended by this title.
>
> (citation omitted) . . . . Further, plaintiff has not shown, and the Court cannot find any evidence in Title VII's legislative history that Congress intended to preclude the arbitrability of claims under Title VII.

Plaintiff's argument, apparently, is to say that even if arbitration is generally permissible under Title VII, this particular arbitration agreement, which, as stated before, precludes certain remedies (attorney's fees, punitive damages, and injunctive relief) is inherently inconsistent with the purposes of Title VII. . . . The mere fact that these statutory remedies may be unavailable in the arbitral forum does not in itself establish that Title VII claims must be resolved in a court of law. As the Supreme Court in Mitsubishi stated:

> Having made the bargain to arbitrate, the party should be held to it unless Congress itself has evinced an intention to preclude a waiver of judicial remedies for the statutory rights at issue.

. . . [T]here is no inherent conflict between arbitration of plaintiff's complaint against Smith Barney and Title VII's underlying purposes. Although arbitration may not afford the full panoply of remedies otherwise available in a court of law,

> "So long as the prospective litigant effectively may vindicate [his or her] statutory cause of action in the arbitral forum, the statute will continue to serve both its remedial and deterrent function."

. . . For the reasons set forth above, defendants' motion to compel arbitration is granted. Defendants' motion for attorneys' fees is denied. The action is hereby stayed pending arbitration.

Discussion Questions

1. Which party has the burden of proving that the discrimination claim is not arbitrable?
2. Why did the court determine that Congress did not intend to preclude the use of arbitration for Title VII claims?
3. Will a limit on the availability of statutory remedies affect the arbitrability of this dispute?

Selection of an Arbitrator or Arbitral Panel

An important aspect of party control over the arbitration process is the selection of the **arbitrator or arbitral panel.** The disputing parties, usually in consultation with their attorneys, are free to choose the third-party decision maker based on the method of selection they have consented to in their arbitration agreement. Depending on the applicable procedures, the parties may decide to choose one arbitrator or a three-arbitrator panel.

The mutually agreed-upon arbitrator is sometimes named in the initial arbitration agreement. Otherwise, the parties may decide to review lists of qualified arbitrators from administering organizations once a dispute arises. For example, the AAA provides parties with identical lists of potential arbitrators. The parties are given ten days to review the list and cross off the names of arbitrators that are unacceptable to them. If a party does not return the list within the allotted time, it is assumed that all the arbitrators on the list are acceptable. The AAA will then compare the lists to find the names of arbitrators acceptable to both parties. If the parties cannot agree on suitable arbitrators, the AAA may select appropriate neutral arbitrators.

In considering an arbitrator, the disputants will usually review a brief biography provided by the administering organization that outlines the arbitrator's professional background, educational credentials, and industry experience. In addition, parties may address other character traits such as the arbitrator's reputation for attentiveness, objectivity, clear judgment, and integrity. Both parties must trust and respect the chosen arbitrator or arbitral panel to feel that their concerns and issues will be properly evaluated.

An arbitrator may be a lawyer, a retired judge, or an experienced businessperson who is familiar with a particular industry or type of dispute. Businesspeople are used to evaluating complex business problems and can bring vital industry knowledge to the decision-making process. For example, in an intellectual property dispute over rights to a new software program, it may be more useful to select a businessperson with extensive experience in the software industry than a lawyer without it.

The arbitrator's substantive and procedural powers derive from the terms of the arbitration agreement. Arbitrators typically possess certain procedural responsibilities, such as helping the parties to determine hearing dates, issuing subpoenas, ordering discovery, presiding over the arbitration hearing, and determining which evidence to accept or reject in a case.

More important, arbitrators have the substantive authority to decide issues of law and fact in the dispute and to render an **arbitral award.** Typically the parties will agree on a choice-of-law provision that specifies which state's or country's substantive law will apply to the dispute. In interpreting the parties' rights, arbitrators may not add to, delete from, or modify the terms of the parties' contractual obligations.

In addition, the arbitrator must fashion appropriate **arbitration remedies** for the award. The arbitrator has broad authority to determine remedies, provided that the remedies do not violate public policy or exceed the arbitrator's contractual authority. Usually arbitrators have the authority to award equitable remedies, including specific performance and injunctive relief. Arbitrators may also award remedies at law, such as compensatory, consequential, and liquidated damages, as well as interest on such damages.

In some arbitration proceedings, the parties may agree in advance to limit the arbitrator's power to award damages to a mutually agreed-upon range of damages, setting a high and a low figure that is not disclosed to the arbitrator. Under **high-low arbitration,** if the arbitrator's award is below the low figure, the losing party will pay the predetermined low figure. If the award exceeds the high figure, the prevailing party will receive only the preset high figure. Parties use this method when the only real issue between them is the amount of damages to be awarded, not the issue of liability.

In the past, courts have implied that arbitrators cannot award punitive damages for a number of public policy reasons. However, in recent years, court decisions have tended to allow arbitrators to award punitive damages as long as they do not expressly violate the arbitrator's contractual authority.

In addition, the use of commercial arbitration to resolve a wide variety of disputes has grown extensively and forms a significant supplement to the judicial system. Commercial arbitrators therefore undertake serious responsibilities to the public as well as to the parties. Arbitrators are bound by certain ethical **canons** or responsibilities aimed at ensuring the fairness, confidentiality, and impartiality of the proceedings. Violating these ethical duties may result in judicial appeal and a reversal of the arbitration award. The complete text of the Code of Ethics for Arbitrators in Commercial Disputes approved by the American Bar Association and the American Arbitration Association is contained in Appendix 11–B of Chapter 11.

http://
Find the ABA Section on Dispute Resolution at: http://www.abanet.org/dispute

One of the primary ethical duties of arbitrators is to avoid any appearance of bias due to previous or ongoing relationships with the parties, their attorneys, or witnesses. Such relationships would be deemed a conflict of interest. It is essential that arbitrators disclose to the parties any financial, business, professional, social, or familial relationship that may affect their impartiality. If any relationships do exist, arbitrators may withdraw from a case on their own, or upon the request of the parties.

At times, the arbitrator may not become aware of the conflict of interest until after the start of the arbitration hearing. For example, an arbitrator may have carefully reviewed the list of hearing participants and not recognized any conflicts. However, on the day of the hearing, one of the witnesses turns out to be an old college friend who recently married and changed her last name. In this instance, the arbitrator has the ethical duty of **disclosure** as to the prior relationship to the parties, even if the arbitrator believes that he or she can remain objective. The decision concerning whether this earlier relationship affects impartiality should be left up to the disputing parties.

In the following case, an arbitration award was challenged under federal law based on whether an arbitrator had the ethical duty to disclose a prior business relationship.

COMMONWEALTH COATINGS CORP. V. CONTINENTAL CASUALTY CO.
393 U.S. 145 (1968)

FACT SUMMARY

The petitioner, Commonwealth Coatings Corporation (Commonwealth) was a subcontractor that sued the sureties (Continental Casualty Company) on a prime contractor's bond to recover money damages for a painting job. The painting contract included a PDAA to arbitrate controversies under the contract. Under the terms of the PDAA, the subcontractor chose one arbitrator, the prime contractor selected the second arbitrator, and they mutually agreed upon the third arbitrator, Mr. Capacete, who operated an engineering consulting firm in Puerto Rico. The prime contractor was one of the third arbitrator's customers for whom the arbitrator had provided significant and repeated consulting services over the past four to five years. These services included consulting on the same projects as those at issue in this dispute. However, there had been no business dealings between the prime contractor and Mr. Capacete for about a year before the arbitration. Mr. Capacete did not disclose his business relationship with the prime contractor, and the business contacts were unknown to Commonwealth. The outcome of the arbitration hearing was a unanimous decision for the prime contractor. Among other grounds, Commonwealth challenged the award based on bias. The District Court refused to set aside the award, and the Court of Appeals affirmed. The Supreme Court granted certiorari.

OPINION: *MR. JUSTICE BLACK delivered the opinion of the Court*

At issue in this case is the question whether elementary requirements of impartiality taken for granted in every judicial proceeding are suspended when the parties agree to resolve a dispute through arbitration.

. . . .

In 1925, Congress enacted the United States Arbitration Act, 9 U.S.C. sections §§ 1-14, which sets out a comprehensive plan for arbitration of controversies coming under its terms, and both sides here assume that this Federal Act governs this case. Section 10 . . . sets out the conditions upon which awards can be vacated. (footnote omitted) The two counts below held, however, that subsection 10 could not be construed in such a way as to justify vacating the award in this case. We disagree and reverse. Section 10 does authorize vacation of an award where it was "procured by corruption, fraud or undue means" or "[w]here there was evident partiality . . . in the arbitrators." These provisions show a desire of Congress to provide not merely *any* arbitration but an impartial one. It is true that petitioner does not charge before us that the third arbitrator was actually guilty of fraud or bias in deciding this case, and we have no reason, apart from the undisclosed business relationship, to suspect him of any improper motives. But neither this arbitrator nor the prime contractor gave to petitioner any intimation of the close financial relations that had existed between them for a period of years. We have no doubt that if a litigant could show that a foreman of a jury or a judge in a court of justice had, unknown to litigant, any such relationship, the judgment would be subject to challenge. . . . It is true that arbitrators cannot sever all their ties with the business world, since they are not expected to get all their income from their work deciding cases, but we should, if anything, be even more scrupulous to safeguard the impartiality of arbitrators than judges, since the former have completely free rein to decide the law as well as the facts and are not subject to appellate review. We can perceive no way in which the effectiveness of the arbitration process will be hampered by the simple requirement that the arbitrators disclose to the parties any dealings that might create an impression of possible bias. . . .

This rule of arbitration and this canon of judicial ethics rests on the premise that any tribunal permitted by law to try cases and controversies not only must be unbiased but also must avoid even the appearance of bias. We cannot believe that it was the purpose of Congress to authorize litigants to submit their cases and controversies to arbitration boards that might reasonably be thought biased against one litigant and favorable to another.

Reversed.

MR. JUSTICE WHITE, with whom Mr. Justice Marshall joins, concurring.

. . . [A]rbitrators are not automatically disqualified by a business relationship with the parties before them if both parties are informed of the relationship in advance, or if they are unaware of the facts but the relationship is trivial. I see no reason automatically to disqualify the best informed and most capable potential arbitrators.

The arbitration process functions best when an amicable and trusting atmosphere is preserved and there is voluntary compliance with the decree, without need for judicial enforcement. This end is best served by establishing an atmosphere of frankness at the outset, through disclosure by the arbitrator of any financial transactions which he has had or is negotiating with either of the parties. In many cases the arbitrator might believe the business relationship to be so insubstantial that to make a point of revealing it would suggest he is indeed easily swayed, and perhaps a partisan of that party. But if the law requires the disclosure, no such imputation can arise. And it is far better that the relationship be disclosed at the outset, when the parties are free to reject the arbitrator or accept him with knowledge of the relationship and continuing faith in his objectivity, than to have the relationship come to light after the arbitration, when suspicious or disgruntled party can seize on it as a pretext for invalidating the award. The judiciary should minimize its role in arbitration as part of the arbitrator's impartiality. That role is best consigned to the parties, who are architects of their own arbitration process, and are far better informed of the prevailing ethical standards and reputations within their business. . . .

MR. JUSTICE FORTAS, with whom Mr. Justice Harlan and Mr. Justice Stewart join, dissenting.

. . . The Court sets aside the arbitration award despite the fact that the award is unanimous and no claim is made of actual partiality, unfairness, bias or fraud.

. . . .

. . . Both courts below held, and petitioner concedes, that the third arbitrator was innocent of any actual partiality, or bias, or improper motive. There is no suggestion of concealment as distinguished from the innocent failure to volunteer information.

The third arbitrator is a leading and respected consulting engineer who has performed services for "most of the contractors in Puerto Rico." He was well-known to petitioner's counsel and they were personal friends. Petitioner's counsel candidly admitted that if he had been told about the arbitrator's prior relationship, "I don't think I would have objected because I know Mr. Capacete [the arbitrator]."

. . . .

I agree that failure of an arbitrator to volunteer information about business dealings with one party will, prima facie, support a claim of partiality or bias. But where there is no suggestion that the nondisclosure was calculated, and where the complaining party disclaims any imputation of partiality, bias, or misconduct, the presumption is clearly overcome. (footnote omitted.)

. . . .

. . . The Court applies to this process rules applicable to judges and not to a system characterized by dealing on faith and reputation for reliability. Such formalism is not contemplated by the Act nor is it warranted in a case where no claim is made of partiality, of unfairness, or of misconduct in any degree.

Discussion Questions

1. Why is the mere appearance of bias sufficient to overturn the award?
2. What should Mr. Capacete have done to avoid the appearance of bias?
3. Who has the primary responsibility for determining whether a business relationship affects arbitrator impartiality?

Pre-Hearing Preparation

Once the arbitrator has been selected, business representatives normally team with their legal representatives to prepare the case for the hearing. However, due to the informality of the proceedings, businesspeople may choose to represent themselves throughout the arbitration process **(pro se)**. They should carefully evaluate whether an attorney can more thoroughly prepare and present their case, particularly in instances involving complex legal or factual issues.

As in litigation, each party needs to collect and exchange relevant records and documents in the discovery process. However, in arbitration, the arbitrator sets a much more abbreviated schedule of discovery, yielding a savings in both time and costs for the participants. If documents in the other party's possession are needed, the arbitrator may issue subpoenas for the records, if permissible under the arbitration agreement. In addition, relevant witnesses must be interviewed and prepared for cross-examination. Appropriate arrangements should also be made if the arbitrator will need to visit any company or other relevant site in reviewing the case.

The parties may also decide to participate in a **preliminary hearing** to narrow the issues, exchange relevant documents and witness lists, and determine the dates for the upcoming hearing. The preliminary hearing is an important opportunity to clarify and simplify the factual and legal aspects of a dispute. At its best, the preliminary hearing can help the arbitrator and the parties to run more focused hearing sessions.

The Arbitration Hearing

Generally, the **arbitration hearing** is a less formal, abbreviated, trial-like process. To maintain the integrity of the proceedings, the arbitrators should not have any discussions or contact with the parties beforehand. Similar to judges at trial, arbitrators oversee the hearing process. The arbitration hearing should be conducted in a manner that adheres to basic procedural due process requirements. The parties should have an opportunity to be heard and to have their case decided on the basis of the evidence on the record, as well as the right of legal representation for each party. Arbitrators should strive to keep the process moving forward and to stop any harassing or delaying tactics.

To allow each party to fully present his or her case, arbitrators will allow much latitude in the admission of relevant evidence. Parties may offer testimonial evidence through party or other lay witnesses as well as expert witnesses. Participants may also provide documentary evidence, such as company records, or demonstrative evidence, such as charts and graphs, to support their cases. Courtroom rules of evidence do not apply to arbitration procedures. Formal objections, intended to protect juries from making determinations based on unreliable or irrelevant evidence, are discouraged in arbitration as arbitrators are considered to have the experience and judgment necessary to weigh the credibility and relevance of proffered evidence. Note, however, that an arbitrator's refusal to consider relevant evidence may provide the grounds for a judicial appeal.

Unless a party is appearing pro se, lawyers usually present the case to the arbitrators. Following a brief opening statement that summarizes his or her view of the case and requested remedies, the moving party presents its case through direct testimony of witnesses and documentary evidence and other exhibits. The responding party is then allowed to present its defense. Each party is allowed to cross-examine the other's witnesses. Arbitrators may also ask questions to clarify issues under consideration. During the hearing, the arbitral panel should not comment on the merits of the evidence or give any indication of how it will rule on the dispute. At the end of the hearing, each party may sum up its case in a closing statement.

Depending on the agreed-upon procedures, arbitrators may request that the parties submit post-hearing legal briefs or memoranda to further support their claims and demands for relief. Although they are not required to apply substantive law, arbitrators should carefully evaluate any legal briefs provided during the arbitration process. If allowed under the selected procedures, arbitrators may reopen the hearing process to consider additional evidence. Once all the evidence has been heard, the hearing process is formally closed.

The Arbitration or Arbitral Award

Arbitrators possess broad authority to decide issues of law and fact. Typically, there is no required standard of proof in determining the arbitral outcome, unless otherwise agreed to by the parties. Some arbitrators will look at the general persuasiveness of the evidence, while others may borrow standards from the judicial process, such as the preponderance of the evidence or clear and convincing evidence approaches. For example, in instances in which employees have been discharged for sexual harassment (a violation of Title VII), different arbitral awards have used different standards of proof. Some arbitrators use the higher clear and convincing evidence standard because sexual harassment is a serious allegation and they want to be certain of a decision in which a person may lose his or her livelihood. Others use the preponderance of evidence standard because it is the standard a civil court would use in handling the litigation of employment disputes as well as Title VII matters. Many arbitrators will use the general persuasiveness standard in all arbitral matters, regardless of the nature of the conflict. The arbitral award indicates which party has won the case and any applicable remedies. The arbitral panel may split the award on different issues between the parties. The agreed-upon procedures will outline the number of days that the arbitrator has to make the award. Often, arbitrators take 30 to 45 days after the close of the process to draft their award.

No written opinions explaining the reasons for the outcome or detailing findings of law and fact are required. In fact, such opinions are sometimes avoided to prevent subsequent legal challenges to the award. If written opinions are provided, arbitrators need not defend their decision solely on the basis of substantive law.

Post-Award Actions

Generally, parties comply with the terms of the award. Yet the arbitrators cannot enforce the award. If one party refuses to adhere to the terms of the award, the prevailing party must go to court to seek its enforcement. Arbitrators may not disclose information in post-arbitration proceedings unless specifically required to do so by law.

In a few instances, a losing party may seek to vacate (overturn) or **modify an arbitration award** through a court appeal. However, the FAA and state arbitration laws limit severely the grounds for judicial review of arbitral awards. The main statutory grounds for **vacating the arbitration award** are: (1) arbitrator fraud, corruption, or bias; (2) arbitrator failure to comply with procedural due process requirements, including failing to consider relevant evidence; and (3) arbitrator conduct that exceeds arbitrator authority under the terms of the arbitration agreement. These statutes may also allow modifications of arbitration awards for technical errors committed by the arbitrator, including miscalculating amounts, deciding matters not specifically submitted for review, and drafting awards in an improper form that does not affect the substantive issues.

Grounds for Appeal Under the FAA

The Federal Arbitration Act (FAA) provides limited grounds for court review of arbitral awards. The stated bases for appeal seek to balance the need for fairness in the proceedings with the importance of finality in resolving disputes. An excerpt from the applicable provisions of the FAA dealing with appeals to vacate or modify arbitration decisions follows:

Section 10. Same; vacation; grounds; rehearing

(a) In any of the following cases the United States court in and for the district wherein the award was made may make an order vacating the award upon the application of any party to the arbitration:

(1) Where the award was procured by corruption, fraud, or undue means.

(2) Where there was evident partiality or corruption in the arbitrators, or either of them.

(3) Where the arbitrators were guilty of misconduct in refusing to postpone the hearing, upon sufficient cause shown; or in refusing to hear evidence pertinent and material to the controversy; or of any misbehavior by which the rights of any party have been prejudiced.

(4) Where the arbitrators exceeded their powers, or so imperfectly executed them that a mutual, final, and definite award upon the subject matter submitted was not made.

Grounds for Appeal Under the FAA Continued

(5) Where an award is vacated and the time within which the agreement required the award to be made has not expired the court may, in its discretion, direct a rehearing by the arbitrators. . . .

Section 11. Same; modification or correction; grounds; order
In either of the following cases the United States court in and for the district wherein the award was made may make an order modifying or correcting the award upon the application of any party to the arbitration:

(a) Where there was an evident material miscalculation of figures or an evident material mistake in the description of any person, thing, or property referred to in the award.

(b) Where the arbitrators have awarded upon a matter not submitted to them, unless it is a matter not affecting the merits of the decision upon the matter submitted.

(c) Where the award is imperfect in matter of form not affecting the merits of the controversy.

The order may modify and correct the award, so as to effect the intent thereof and promote justice between the parties.

In *United Steelworkers of America v. Enterprise Wheel & Car Corp.* [363 U.S. 593 (1960)], the Supreme Court determined that courts may not vacate the arbitrator's award simply because they would have interpreted the law or facts of the case differently. In that case, the Court recognized the importance of allowing a decision maker selected by the parties to render a decision, based on his knowledge and experience, without the courts second-guessing his determinations of law and fact.

However, courts will refuse to enforce arbitral awards that explicitly violate law or public policy. Public policy challenges are narrowly defined and cannot be based on generalized assertions about the public interest. Such challenges must be based on a well-recognized public policy concern, and the arbitrator's award must be a clear violation of that policy. The following excerpt from a case involves an employer's challenge to the reinstatement of an employee who had threatened to kill her supervisor based on the arbitrator's factual and legal findings as well as public policy grounds.

COLLINS V. BLUE CROSS BLUE SHIELD OF MICHIGAN

916 F. Supp. 638 (E.D. Mich. 1995)

FACT SUMMARY

The plaintiff, Irma Collins, was a nine-year employee of the defendant, Blue Cross Blue Shield of Michigan (BCBSM), with no prior disciplinary record. In 1993, the plaintiff took a medical leave of absence for the psychiatric treatment of stress. Her treating psychiatrist, Dr. Rosalind Griffin, reported to BCBSM that Ms. Collins was mentally disabled from work due to a psychiatric disorder, and she began to receive short-term disability benefits.

To determine whether the plaintiff continued to be disabled from work, a second psychiatrist, Dr. Joyln Welsh Wagner, undertook an evaluation of the plaintiff. In this evaluation process, Ms. Collins made numerous threats against her female supervisor. The plaintiff made statements about her supervisor such as, "She is living on borrowed time and she doesn't know it" and "I have killed her a thousand times in my mind." Neither Dr. Griffin nor Dr. Wagner believed that the plaintiff would act on these threats.

After reviewing Dr. Wagner's report, BCBSM decided to terminate the plaintiff as her threats violated company policy. When Dr. Griffin determined that the plaintiff was no longer mentally disabled, she authorized Ms. Collins's return to work. Upon her return to work, BCBSM terminated Ms. Collins.

Under an arbitration agreement between the plaintiff and BCBSM, Ms. Collins challenged her termination using arbitration. The arbitrator determined that Ms. Collins had been wrongfully discharged in violation of the Americans with Disabilities Act and the Michigan Handicappers' Civil Rights Act. The arbitrator ordered reinstatement of the plaintiff and awarded her back pay and attorneys' fees.

The plaintiff filed a motion in federal court to confirm the arbitrator's award under the Federal Arbitration Act and the Michigan Arbitration Act. The defendant filed a counterclaim seeking to overturn the arbitrator's award on public policy grounds.

OPINION: *JUDGE LAWRENCE P. ZATKOFF*

. . . .

The manner in which a court is to review an arbitration award under the FAA was set forth by the Sixth Circuit in *Federated Department Stores v. J.V.B. Industries, Inc.,* 894 F. 2d 862, 866 (6th Cir. 1990). The court first noted that the party seeking review must prove that "the arbitrators exceeded their powers, or so imperfectly executed them that a mutual, final, and definite award upon the subject matter submitted was not made." . . . The court then reviewed how other courts have interpreted this language, observing that "the standard of review in arbitration decisions is very narrow." *Id.* at 866.

"As long as the arbitrator is even arguably construing or applying the contract and acting within the scope of his authority, that a court is convinced he committed serious error does not suffice to overturn his decision." *Id.* at 866 (quoting *United Paperworkers International Union v. Misco, Inc.,* 484 U.S. 29, 98 L. Ed. 2d 286, 108 S. Ct. 364 (1987)). The *Federated* court concluded that "arbitrators do not exceed their authority unless they show a manifest disregard of the law." *Id.* at 866.

. . . .

Dr. Griffin determined that plaintiff had recovered from her disability and authorized her return to work on February 1, 1994. The arbitrator found that plaintiff was capable of performing her work despite deficiencies in her writing and editing skills, noting that plaintiff had received a well-qualified rating and had not been disciplined for performance deficiencies.

The Court has no authority to disturb the arbitrator's factual findings that the statements were a product of plaintiff's psychiatric disability. Thus, the statements made by the plaintiff did not disqualify her from employment at BCBSM, and terminating her on the basis of the statements was equivalent to terminating her because of her disability.

BCBSM's second argument is that the Arbitration Award is against public policy because it orders the company to reinstate an employee who has threatened to kill her supervisor.

In *Shelby County Health Care Corporation v. American Federation of State, County and Municipal Employees, Local 1733,* 967 F. 2d 1091 (6th Cir. 1992), the Sixth Circuit laid out the manner in which a court may refuse to enforce an arbitration award that violates public policy:

The public policy exception to the general deference afforded arbitration awards is very limited, and may be exercised only where several strict standards are met. First the decision must violate some explicit public policy that is well defined and dominant. *United Paperworkers International Union v. Misco, Inc.,* 484 U.S. 29, 98 L. Ed. 2d 286, 108 S. Ct. 364 (1987). . . . Second, the conflict between the public policy and the arbitration award must be explicit and clearly shown. Misco, 484 U.S. at 43. Further, it is not sufficient that the "grievant's conduct for which he was disciplined violated some public policy or law" rather, the relevant issue is whether the arbitrator's award "requiring reinstatement of the grievant . . . violated some explicit public policy." *Interstate Brands v. Teamsters Local 135,* 909 F. 2d 885, 893 (6th Cir. 1990).

The defendant's counterclaim states "further, the arbitrator, by ordering reinstatement of an employee who threatens to kill her supervisor, violated public policy." Aside from this conclusory statement, the defendant has failed to show that the arbitrator's decision violated "some explicit public policy that is well defined and dominant." Defendant's assertion that "to threaten to kill another employee is a violation of BCBSM policy . . ." simply will not suffice. Thus, the defendant has failed to show that reinstating the plaintiff will violate some explicit public policy.

IV. CONCLUSION

For the above reasons, the Court finds that the arbitrator did not make an error of law and therefore the Arbitration Award shall be confirmed. . . .

Discussion Questions

1. Do you think it is fair to allow Ms. Collins to return to the workplace?
2. What is the district court stating about the responsibility for fact-finding in an arbitration?
3. What must a party do to support an assertion that an award should be overturned based on public policy grounds?

ADVANTAGES OF VOLUNTARY ARBITRATION

Businesspeople do not like to become entangled in disputes, preferring to focus on the daily operation of their companies. Unfortunately, conflict in business is inevitable, making arbitration an attractive and necessary option for resolving it. Although it uses trial-like procedures, arbitration has many advantages over traditional litigation.

Greater Control.   In standard litigation, the parties have no control over the procedures used to resolve their dispute as the courts already have well-established and complex rules of civil procedure and evidence. In addition, parties do not have the opportunity to decide which judge will review their case or when their case will be heard.

Disputants using arbitration exercise greater control over both the type of procedures and the identity of the decision maker. Businesses electing to use arbitration can either create their own set of procedures or select the rules of a preferred administering agency. They can determine the steps the arbitrator must follow and the standards the arbitrator may use in making an arbitral decision. Normally the courtroom rules of evidence are relaxed during arbitration proceedings, allowing for a freer flow of information. The disputants can choose the person who will decide their disagreement. Parties can identify their chosen arbitrator or arbitral panel in their written agreement or select one from a list of qualified decision makers provided by the administering organization. In addition, the parties, with the assistance of the arbitrator, can work out a mutually agreed-upon schedule of pre-hearing activities and set the date for their arbitration hearing. Because the parties maintain greater control over the arbitration process, they are usually more satisfied and more willing to voluntarily comply with the outcome of the dispute.

Confidentiality.   Under the U.S. legal system, court documents and hearings are generally accessible to the public. Although an important freedom, this can be a drawback to disputing parties. Bad publicity from a lawsuit can seriously damage a company's reputation and its relationships with other businesses and customers, even if the lawsuit proves baseless. At times, a party may even seek to use the pressure of bad publicity to secure an unfair settlement. However, arbitration documents and sessions are private and thus, are not open to public scrutiny and resulting bad publicity. The confidentiality of the arbitration process allows the dispute to be decided solely on its merits and not on outside pressures.

Savings of Time and Money.   Due to court backlogs, lawsuits take an average of nineteen months to be tried. A lengthy discovery process can take months and years, further hampering the quick processing of a dispute. Many businesses cannot afford to wait that long. For example, a small equipment business may be teetering on the edge of bankruptcy because its largest customer has not paid for goods the company shipped. The equipment company could sue its customer in court for nonpayment. However, if it takes years to resolve the dispute in court, the small firm may already be out of business.

As with other ADR mechanisms, arbitration can save parties both time and money. The parties can set their own brisk schedule for the handling of their dispute. In addition, discovery, which accounts for about 80% of all legal fees in a dispute, is limited, helping parties reap added savings in both time and money.

Unfortunately, arbitration does not erase the economic disparities between the parties. A wealthier litigant may be able to afford more and better lawyers, investigators, and expert witnesses. However, arbitration proceedings are normally less expensive than standard litigation, so financial differences may at least be reduced or eased.

http://
Access the Society for Professionals in Dispute Resolution at: http://www.spidr.org

Arbitrator Expertise.   A major aspect of the arbitration process is the selection of the arbitrator. Unlike litigation, parties may select a decision maker with the professional experience and industry knowledge vital to understanding the conflict and rendering an appropriate decision. For example, a construction contractor and its subcontractor may have a dispute over whether the subcontractor installed electrical wiring in a commercial building in compliance with government safety codes and architectural drawings. Many judges will not be familiar with the technical aspects of electrical wiring, applicable industry practices, or governmental requirements. The parties may need to spend additional time and money educating the judge about electrical codes, construction practices, and architectural drawings.

Arbitration allows the parties to choose a decision maker who has the necessary construction background. The arbitrator's expertise can speed the arbitration proceedings along, since the decision maker need not be schooled in the business or technical aspects of the case. Consequently, the parties may feel more confident that the arbitrator better understands the nature of the conflict and the peculiarities of the industry and will be better able to render a fair decision.

Finality of the Award.   Matters handled through litigation may become the subject of seemingly endless court appeals on a number of substantive and procedural technicalities. These appeals can waste time and money. In arbitration, the decisions of the arbitrator are normally viewed as final, with no or few opportunities for appeal. The finality of an award means that the parties can anticipate party compliance soon after the award and can return to their normal business activities without fearing appeals.

Socially Valuable.   Arbitration benefits the general public. The heavy backlog of court cases burdens disputing parties and taxpayers, who must support the court system. Businesses that elect arbitration can ease the court docket by privately resolving their disputes. In addition, arbitration resolves conflicts without a financial cost to the public.

As with other alternatives to litigation, arbitration helps to prompt legal reforms in the court system. Some courts have already begun to adopt arbitration programs that have helped to more quickly and cheaply deal with civil complaints.

ADR IN ACTION

Arbitration Keeps Toyota Sales Rolling

In the 1980s, Toyota car sales were brisk, but trouble was brewing. Toyota had established a policy for determining dealer car allotments based on a dealer's level of sales to ultimate retail customers. Car sales between dealers or between car brokers and dealers were not credited toward dealer car allotments.

Some dealers trying to increase their future shares of cars often bought cars from original dealers or car brokers for resale to retail end users. These second dealers, known as reversal requesting dealers, began to demand that Toyota reassign the first dealer's future car allocation credits to them. The first dealers, known as protesting dealers, were angered by attempts to reduce their future car allotments due to their sales to the second dealers.

Bickering soon broke out between dealers, and many dealers directed their hostility toward Toyota. A number of lawsuits followed. Toyota lost hundreds of thousands of dollars in discovery and other pretrial expenses

alone. Toyota knew it had to do something to save time and money on these dealer disputes and to quell unproductive antagonism between Toyota and its dealers.

In 1985, two Toyota attorneys, William A. Ploude, Jr., and David D. Laufer, developed the Reversal Arbitration Board (RAB). The RAB process established a national network of arbitrators to rapidly and simply process these dealer disputes. Parties are still encouraged to negotiate a resolution to their dispute initially, with RAB as a last resort before litigation. The arbitration process is handled by a third-party nonprofit group, with Toyota paying for the administrative expenses. In the first year of the RAB, the administrative expense for all cases was only $80,000—far less than the pretrial costs for just one lawsuit.

The RAB procedure stresses speed, simplicity, and informality. Each dealer is limited to a two-week discovery period after notice of the hearing. The hearing is before a sin-

ADR IN ACTION Continued

gle arbitrator, and each dealer presents his or her own case with neither lawyers nor Toyota representatives present. There are seldom any outside witnesses. The dealer may appear in person or conduct a telephone conference call, which allows for the rapid handling of interstate disputes. Each session tends to take less than a half hour.

The arbitrator provides a written decision to the dealers and Toyota within a week of the hearing. Each decision becomes a form of internal precedent for dealers, who may review and rely on these awards in future disputes. To highlight the fairness of the process and to encourage the participation of dealers, the RAB decision is binding on Toyota but not on the dealers. Dealers may still appeal the outcome.

Despite its nonbinding nature, the RAB process has been a remarkable success. A survey of dealers indicated that eighty percent of the respondents found the procedure to be fair, while ninety-eight percent stated that the arbitrator was objective. Toyota also found that these types of dealer disputes sharply decreased from 178 in 1985 to a mere three cases in 1992.

No longer was Toyota throwing away hundreds of thousands of dollars in legal fees and related costs in court cases over car allotments. More important, the RAB process helped to preserve essential business relationships and to reduce hostility among dealers and between dealers and Toyota.

DISADVANTAGES OF VOLUNTARY ARBITRATION

Although arbitration provides a number of benefits, business disputants should also be aware of some of the limitations. These disadvantages should be weighed by businesspeople in concert with their attorneys to decide whether arbitration is the appropriate option.

Lack of Precedent.   It is important to recognize that arbitral awards, unlike court decisions, do not establish legal precedent. At times, businesses may wish to set a legal precedent to clearly establish their rights or to defend against future claimants on the same matter. For example, a business may want to prove its proprietary rights to a certain product. If a court determines the company's ownership of the product, the business can use the decision to support its position in, or discourage other parties from bringing, future actions on the same issue. An arbitral award on the company's rights is not binding on other future claimants, therefore, the company cannot use it to prevent or to predict the outcome of future lawsuits.

Adversarial Process.   In negotiation and mediation, the parties must collaborate to determine their own outcome. In these processes, the disputants must open up lines of communication to achieve a "win-win" result. The use of these procedures may not only resolve the current conflict, but they can reduce party hostility and promote a more positive working relationship in the future. Conversely, the "win-lose" result and adversarial nature of arbitration may heighten party hostility and seriously harm the business relationship. In addition, the arbitral process fails to teach the parties how to more effectively deal with each other in future conflicts.

Limits on Discovery.   Limiting discovery can clearly save both time and money for the parties. Yet in certain types of disputes, in-depth discovery may be necessary to effectively prosecute or defend against party claims. A dispute requiring lengthy discovery, such as a technically complex dispute or a discrimination claim, may not be well suited for arbitration. With limits on discovery, these cases may become more difficult to prove, even if the claims have merit.

Consent of Parties.   Unlike litigation, all parties to the dispute must agree to arbitration. Many businesspeople unfamiliar with arbitration will be reluctant to go along with their opponent's desire to use it. Without a PDAA or submission agreement, an arbitrator cannot order parties or witnesses to participate in the proceedings. It may be difficult to persuade the other party to consent to arbitration after the conflict has arisen and animosity has built up between the parties.

Constitutional and Policy Concerns.   A number of people have criticized the use of arbitration on both constitutional and social policy grounds. These critics assert that arbitration sets up a dual system of justice—one for the poor and one for the rich—in violation of equal protection guarantees. Some suggest that arbitration allows wealthier litigants to have their conflicts quickly and cheaply resolved, while poorer litigants must rely on the slower, more expensive court system. Without the involvement of richer litigants in the court system, critics of ADR claim that more powerful voices striving for improvements in the current legal system will be lost.

In addition, others argue that the confidentiality of arbitration proceedings violates standards of due process and the First Amendment right of access to proceedings. Public interest groups and media organizations express concern that certain business disputes involving important policy matters that affect the public interest are being resolved behind closed doors. For example, a nuclear power plant may have a dispute regarding the quality of equipment that a company has provided to the plant. The equipment may have an effect on both the efficiency and safety of the plant. If the parties have agreed to use arbitration, the matter may be resolved privately without the public being made aware of safety risks at the plant or allowed any input into the remedy for the problem.

OVERVIEW OF COURT-ANNEXED ARBITRATION

As more disputants clamor for alternatives to standard civil proceedings, some 1,200 state and federal courts have begun offering ADR options including court-supervised or **court-annexed arbitration.** In certain instances, parties may be required to use arbitration under statutory law, local court rules, or court order. State statutes often mandate court-supervised arbitration programs or provide state courts with the authority to develop detailed rules regarding such programs. Federal statutory law directs each U.S. district court to establish a plan to expedite the processing of disputes and to reduce the time and costs of litigation.

Under these plans, federal courts can develop local court rules or criteria for the use of arbitration. State and federal courts using court-annexed arbitration have set standards for the selection of certain types of cases for arbitration. Many of the cases involve simple factual and legal issues with lower monetary levels of damages being sought. Court-annexed arbitration can be distinguished from voluntary arbitration discussed earlier.

Court-annexed arbitration is not voluntary. As a method for diverting cases from overcrowded court dockets, court-annexed arbitration is often required as a nonbinding precondition to a trial. Because the process is involuntary, arbitral awards are not necessarily binding.

Critics of court-annexed arbitration have argued that mandatory arbitration as a precondition to trial violates the Seventh Amendment right to a jury trial. In addition, these critics assert that assigning cases to compulsory arbitration, based primarily on dollar amounts in controversy, deprives only these parties of a right to a jury trial and, therefore, to equal protection of the laws. However, Supreme Court decisions have supported court attempts to increase procedural flexibility under the rules of civil procedure. Court innovation is normally permissible if the change is not **outcome-determinative,** meaning that it does not seriously interfere with or prevent the ultimate determination of the case by a jury. Because court-mandated arbitration is not binding, it is not outcome-determinative. Parties may still request a **trial de novo** or new trial within a specified time period after the arbitration award.

To deter frivolous requests for new trials, some jurisdictions may assess monetary penalties, such as court costs or the other party's arbitration expenses, if the appealing party does not attain a more successful outcome in the new trial. Some critics of court-annexed arbitration contend that these penalties unfairly punish parties for exercising their constitutional right to a jury trial and to equal protection of the laws. Following is a case that challenges a state court-supervised arbitration program as violating both of these rights.

RICHARDSON V. SPORT SHINKO (WAIKIKI CORPORATION)
76 Haw. 494, 880 P. 2d 169 (1994)

FACT SUMMARY

Mrs. Richardson, a disc jockey, was setting up stereo equipment in preparation for a wedding reception at the Queen Kapiolani Hotel in Hawaii. While positioning the equipment and electrical cords, she knelt on the carpet, and a loose carpet staple pierced her left knee through the cartilage and down to the bone. Hotel officials called an ambulance to the scene, and paramedics removed the staple from her knee. She was later treated at a local emergency ward.

Plaintiffs Renee and Thaddeus Richardson brought a negligence action against Sport Shinko, which owned and operated the hotel. Under a Hawaiian law, the case was referred to the state's Court-Annexed Arbitration Program (CAAP). The arbitrator found Sport Shinko liable and awarded the Richardsons $60,441.80 in general and special damages. The Richardsons sought a trial de novo, which was granted. Before the trial, Sport Shinko offered to settle the dispute with the Richardsons for $75,000. The Richardsons rejected the offer, demanding $150,000 in damages.

At trial, the jury determined that Sport Shinko was not negligent and awarded no damages to the Richardsons. Their request for a new trial was rejected. Under a Hawaiian statute (HAR 26), a judge has the discretion to penalize a party that fails to improve its outcome from an arbitration proceeding at the subsequent trial by at least fifteen percent. Sport Shinko then brought an action for sanctions against the

Richardsons and was awarded $5,234.41 in lawyers' fees and court costs. The Richardsons appealed the judgment, which favored Sport Shinko, and the accompanying grant of sanctions. Among a variety of arguments, the Richardsons contended that the referral of their case to the CAAP and the imposition of sanctions violated their right to a jury trial and to equal protection of the laws.

OPINION: *CHIEF JUDGE MOON*

. . . .

A. Right to Trial by Jury in Civil Cases

We deal first with the Richardsons' claim that HAR 26 "impermissibly infringes upon their constitutional right to a jury trial." The resolution of this issue necessarily rests upon the interpretation of state law. . . .

Article I, § 13 of the Hawaii Constitution, as amended in 1978, provides in relevant part: "In suits at common law where the value in controversy shall exceed five thousand dollars, the right of trial by jury shall be preserved." HRCP 38(a)(1990) reaffirms this right providing: "The right of trial by jury as given by the Constitution or a statute of the state or the United States shall be preserved to the parties inviolate." This court acknowledged that article I, § 13 and HRCP 38(a) were patterned after the Seventh Amendment and HRCP 38(a), respectively, and we have therefore deemed the interpretation of those provisions by the federal courts highly persuasive in construing the right to a civil jury trial in Hawaii. . . .

Although trial by jury in civil cases is a "fundamental" right in the State of Hawaii. . . . the right has never been construed so broadly as to prohibit reasonable conditions upon its exercise. Instead, it has been held that "the limitation imposed by the [seventh] amendment is merely that enjoyment of the right of trial by jury be not obstructed, and that the ultimate issues of fact by the jury be not interfered with." . . .

Moreover, in holding that a procedure for non-judicial determinations prior to a jury trial does not violate the seventh amendment, the United States Supreme Court has stated that the seventh amendment "does not prescribe at what stage of an action a trial by jury must, if demanded, be had; or what conditions may be imposed upon the demand of such a trial, consistently with preserving the right to it." . . . This, with regard to mandatory arbitration programs that afford a right to trial de novo, it has been held that the only purpose of the [seventh amendment] is to secure the right of trial by jury before rights of person or property are finally determined. All that it required is that the right of appeal for the purpose of presenting the issue to a jury must not be burdened by the imposition of onerous conditions, restrictions or regulations which would make the right practically unavailable. . . .

Thus, laws, practices, and procedures affecting the right to trial by jury under article I, § 13 are valid as long as they do not significantly burden or impair the right to ultimately have a jury determine issues of fact. In the present case, however, the Richardsons contend that,

although they received a jury trial, the "specter of sanctions" created by HAR 26 impermissibly burdened their exercise of that right. We disagree.

. . . .

. . . HAR 26 serves a necessary and legitimate purpose. Moreover, as we shall discuss, HAR 26 achieves its objectives by reasonable means inasmuch as the authorized sanctions are limited in both amount and application.

First, HAR 26 sanctions are available only if the appealing party does not improve its position, at the present time, by 15% or more, and even then, sanctions are discretionary. Accordingly, every party has the ability to avoid HAR 26 sanctions by undertaking a frank post-arbitration evaluation of the merits of their case.

Second, the potential magnitude of the sanction is not per se unreasonable. Sanctions are presently limited to $5,000.00 in attorneys' fees plus actual "costs" as that term is defined. Many courts have upheld similar or greater potential sanctions as reasonable. . . .

However, although the amount of sanctions authorized by HAR 26 is not per se unconstitutional, "the problem is one of degree rather than kind. . . . The necessity of paying [$75 in arbitrators' fees] as the condition to for the right to appeal [from a mandatory arbitration award] would seemingly operate as a strong deterrent, amounting practically to a denial of that right, if the case should involve only . . . as little as $250.

. . . .

In the present case, the amount in controversy was arguably between $60,441.80 (the arbitration award) and $150,000.00 (the amount the Richardsons demanded in their settlement conference statement filed in the circuit court).

Although no fixed lines can be drawn, we do not believe the $5,234.41 sanction was unreasonable. . . .

When considering the important interests that HAR 26 serves and the limits placed on its use, we cannot say that HAR 26 imposed an unreasonable burden on the Richardsons' right to a civil jury trial. Therefore, we conclude that the sanctions awarded in this case do not violate due process or article I, § 13.

B. Equal Protection of the Laws

Finally, the Richardsons claim that their right to equal protection of the laws under the fourteenth amendment to the United States Constitution was violated "to the extent that [HAR 26] is applied only to a limited class of tort victims exercising their right to a jury trial(.)" Despite their focus on HAR 26, the Richardsons essentially challenge the constitutional validity of the following classifications made by HRS § 601-20(b)(1992), which provides: "All civil actions in tort, having a probable jury award value not reduced by the issue of liability, exclusive of interests and costs, of $150,000 or less, shall be submitted to the [CAAP]." Thus, litigants compelled to participate in the CAAP by HRS § 601-20(b) are subject to HAR 26 sanctions if they exercise their right to a jury trial while other litigants are not. . . .

. . . .

. . . Because mandatory participation in the CAAP by itself does not significantly interfere with a party's constitutional right to a jury trial. . . . we will apply the rational basis test instead.

. . . .

As stated previously, the purpose of the CAAP is "to provide for a procedure to obtain prompt and equitable resolution of certain civil actions in tort through arbitration.". . . We hold that the purpose is a legitimate one. We turn our inquiry then to whether it was reasonable for the legislature to believe that assigning to the CAAP only tort actions having a probable jury award value of $150,000.00 or less would promote its objectives. . . .

First, the legislature could reasonably believe that actions involving more than $150,000.00 would generally require arbitration proceedings of greater length than those intended by the CAAP, and that "the cost of a subsequent trial . . . [would] be very small, relative to the claim itself." . . .

Second, it is fair to presume as a general matter that tort cases will involve only claims for money damages. "In such cases, often the only dispute is over the amount of money owed by one party to the other. In contrast, pleas for equitable relief would probably mean increased complexity and could require continuing supervision of the court. Such cases would be inappropriate for arbitration." . . .

. . . .

Accordingly, we hold that HRS § 601-20(b) does not violate the equal protection clause of the fourteenth amendment.

III. CONCLUSION

Based on the foregoing, we affirm both the judgment and the award of sanctions against the Richardsons.

Discussion Questions

1. Why did the court decide that court-annexed arbitration as a precondition to trial is not overly burdensome? Do you agree with this decision?

2. Would the result of this case be different if court-mandated arbitration was final and binding on parties?

3. Do you think that the sanctions unfairly penalize litigants involved in smaller dollar amount lawsuits?

Unlike voluntary arbitration, court-annexed arbitration rarely gives parties free rein to select the arbitrator or members of the arbitral panel. Arbitrators in court programs are typically individuals certified by the courts, with most being former judges or experienced lawyers. When allowed to choose, the parties are usually limited to court-certified arbitrators; in other instances, the court directly appoints an arbitrator to review the case. Parties are allowed to challenge court-appointed arbitrators on the grounds of bias or lack of impartiality.

Court-annexed arbitration is similar to voluntary arbitration in that there is a limited discovery process. Also, the arbitration hearing tends to be somewhat informal with relaxed procedural rules. However, unlike voluntary arbitrators, court-supervised arbitrators must follow the substantive law of the jurisdiction. In addition, they must apply the standard burden of proof of the preponderance of the evidence rather than one of general persuasiveness.

If the parties do not object to the outcome, the arbitrator's award is entered as a decision of the court. Dissatisfied parties requesting a trial de novo must show that they participated in the court-supervised hearing in good faith. At times, a court may refuse initially to grant an appealing party a new trial if he or she defaulted at the arbitration hearing or sought to otherwise undermine or circumvent the arbitration process. The court may require parties to make good faith use of arbitration before seriously considering a request for a new trial. The following are two cases in which courts considered requests for new trials. Compare the differing outcomes of each case based on the party seeking a trial de novo. The first case involves a plaintiff's lack of participation in a court-mandated arbitration hearing.

HONEYWELL PROTECTION SERVICES V. TANDEM TELECOMMUNICATIONS, INC.
130 Misc. 2d 130, 495 N.Y.S. 2d 130 (Civ. Ct. 1985)

FACT SUMMARY

A dispute between plaintiff Honeywell Protection Services and defendant Tandem Telecommunications, Inc., was referred to a court-annexed arbitration process. At the arbitration hearing, no representative of the plaintiff appeared. The plaintiff's attorney appeared but offered no witnesses or evidence either to support plaintiff's cause of action or to oppose the defendant's counterclaim. As a direct result of the plaintiff's failure to present evidence, the arbitral award was made dismissing the plaintiff's complaint and finding in the defendant's favor on the counterclaim. The plaintiff made a demand for a trial de novo, and the defendant then moved to vacate the call for a new trial.

OPINION: *JUDGE SILBERMANN*

. . . The res governing compulsory arbitration provide that a trial *de novo* may be demanded by any party not in default. (22 NYCRR 28.12[a]). The appearance by an attorney at the hearing does not excuse a default by a party in presenting evidence and proceeding with the hearing. An attorney cannot sit by, listen to his adversaries' proof and demand a trial *de novo* as a result of the failure to affirmatively participate.

The plaintiff herein, in effect, defaulted in proceeding to trial even though it appeared at the hearing by an attorney. The arbitrator noted an appearance by plaintiff's counsel but no appearance by the client.

Plaintiff's counsel contends that "there is no requirement that he must produce a witness at arbitration and a party may prove a claim or a defense by utilizing documents in its possessions [sic] and using the other party's witnesses." Indeed this would be true if the court were to believe that plaintiff had no witnesses or evidence to produce and had in fact presented its entire case before the arbitration panel. In such a case a plaintiff would not be in default and could demand a trial *de novo* (22 NYCRR 28.12[a]).

However, this court having been presented with two motions in separate cases on the same day wherein this same law firm proceeded in almost an identical manner before the arbitration panel has come to the conclusion that this is a ploy to circumvent mandatory arbitration. (citation omitted)

Mandatory arbitration for cases in which the *ad damnum* clause is under $6,000 has been successful in alleviating calendar congestion of the Civil Court. If permitted to succeed such a ruse would create a loophole which would completely undermine compulsory arbitration and incidentally waste the time of the arbitrators and the adverse parties. To permit an attorney to appear at a hearing, not present any evidence and then be free to demand a trial *de novo*, would circumvent the statute providing for compulsory arbitration and render such law a nullity thereby defeating the intent of the arbitration procedure.

. . . . This loophole allows a party to use compulsory arbitration as a forum for free discovery and not for the purpose it was established to resolve disputes and relieve court congestion.

Accordingly, defendant's motion is denied on condition that plaintiff serve and file an affidavit with the court within five days after service of a copy of this order with notice of entry stating that it will present no evidence or witnesses at trial not already produced at the [arbitration] hearing. In the event plaintiff fails to file such an affidavit the motion is granted.

Plaintiff may, if it so elects, move to vacate its default and have this case restored to the arbitration calendar.

Discussion Questions

1. Why did the court determine that the plaintiff was in default and, therefore, unable to request a new trial?
2. What were the intended benefits of the compulsory arbitration program?
3. How might a defaulting party abuse the arbitration hearing process to advance its own claim in a subsequent trial?

This second case considers a defendant's request for a trial de novo, when only the defendant's counsel appeared and did not introduce any evidence at the arbitration hearing.

SAN-DAR ASSOCIATES V. ADAMS
167 Misc. 2d 727, 643 N.Y. S. 2d 880 (1996)

FACT SUMMARY

The plaintiff brought a contract action for monetary damages amounting to $2,650. The action was referred to the court's compulsory arbitration program. At the arbitration hearing, only the defendant's counsel appeared and cross-examined the plaintiff's witness. An award of $1,629 was made to the plaintiff. The defendant made a demand for a trial de novo, and the plaintiff moved to strike the demand. The trial court granted the plaintiff's motion to strike, finding that the defendant's failure to appear at the arbitration was a default precluding him from a new trial. The defendant appealed.

OPINION: *JUDGE P. PARNESS,*
Judges McCooe and Freedman, concur.

. . . .

   While the failure of a plaintiff to appear or present evidence through his attorney constitutes a default for purposes of compulsory arbitration. . . . the same cannot be said when a defendant, by his attorney, appears and disputes the plaintiff's evidence at the hearing. As a general rule, the plaintiff bears the burden of proof in a civil case. . . . and the defendant is under no obligation to present evidence or witnesses.

   Here, the arbitrator's own case report indicates that the matter was contested, since the amount awarded ($1629) was substantially less than the amount demanded ($2650), and the box denominated "failed to appear" was not checked. We therefore conclude that the defendant's appearance by attorney was not a default which would forfeit the remedy of a trial de novo (*Valot v. Allcity Ins. Co.*, 131 Misc. 2d 814, 501 N.Y. S. 2d 597). "The arbitration rules, in particular the procedure governing trial de novo, should not be interpreted too narrowly since the compulsory arbitration program initially deprives the parties of their right to a jury trial." [*Valot*, at 815].

Discussion Questions

1. How does the burden of proof standard influence the court's view as to whether a party may seek a new trial?
2. Will the benefits of mandatory arbitration be lost if defendants need not appear or introduce evidence at the arbitration hearing?
3. Are you concerned that the defendant in this case may be using the arbitration hearing as a chance for free discovery as forewarned in *Honeywell*?

CHAPTER CONCLUSION

After decades of judicial disfavor, arbitration has developed into an important and accepted method for adjudicating business disputes. Statute and case law now look favorably upon both voluntary and court-annexed arbitration. Voluntary arbitration maximizes the opportunity for businesspeople to fashion and participate in an arbitration process that best meets their needs. Court-annexed arbitration helps to expedite and reduce the time and costs of disputes processed through the judicial system. Regardless of the method used, arbitrators bring their special legal and business expertise to the review of business claims and the determination of appropriate awards.

In determining how to best use arbitration, businesspeople should work with their attorneys to evaluate its overall advantages and disadvantages. If arbitration is the selected ADR method, the collaboration between businesspeople and lawyers should continue throughout the process to reap fully the benefits of arbitration.

BEST BUSINESS PRACTICES

Here are some practical tips on how businesspeople can effectively use arbitration to resolve business disputes.

- Work with your attorney or legal staff to create binding arbitration clauses in company contracts with suppliers, vendors, and employees that clearly identify the disputes covered and the processes to be used if conflicts arise.

- Consult your state attorney general's office, local courthouse, Better Business Bureau, or other reputable administering organizations to learn about their arbitration training programs and professional services and to request copies of their standard arbitration clauses and forms.

- Discuss the use of arbitration with other people in your industry to learn about their experiences with the process and to become aware of qualified and respected arbitrators in your field.

- Be prepared to actively participate in the arbitration process, including selecting the arbitrator, collecting relevant company documents, scheduling arbitration proceedings, preparing oral testimony, and coordinating on-site visits, if needed.

- Educate your employees, vendors, and suppliers about the mutual benefits of arbitration to resolve business disputes.

- Evaluate the time and cost savings of your arbitration program and consider updating or revising your procedures to improve its speed and cost-effectiveness.

http://

For example, you can find the University of Massachusetts Dispute Resolution Program at: http://www.umb.edu/disres

KEY TERMS

ad hoc proceeding, p. 161

ADR adjudicatory mechanisms, p. 155

arbitral award, p. 173

arbitration hearing, p. 177

arbitration remedies, p. 173

arbitrator or arbitral panel, p. 172

canons, p. 173

court-annexed arbitration, p. 188

disclosure, p. 174

Federal Arbitration Act (FAA), p. 158

high-low arbitration, p. 173

med-arb, p. 161

modify an arbitration award, p. 179

outcome-determinative, p. 188

pre-dispute arbitration agreement (PDAA), p. 162

pre-hearing preparation, p. 177

preliminary hearing, p. 177

presumption of arbitrability, p. 169

procedural arbitrability, p. 164

pro se, p. 177

rules by reference, p. 162

submission agreement, p. 162

substantive arbitrability, p. 164

trial de novo, p. 188

Uniform Arbitration Act, p. 158

vacating the arbitration award, p. 179

voluntary arbitration, p. 161

ETHICAL AND LEGAL REVIEW

1. Stuart is an arbitrator in an intellectual property dispute between two companies involving ownership of a revolutionary product. During the hearing process, the parties decide to settle the dispute, advising the panel that they intend to merge their companies to pursue this new market together. Later that day, Stuart contacts his broker and buys stock in the merging companies. He does not discuss the arbitration proceeding with his broker. Has Stuart violated any of his ethical obligations? [See Code of Ethics for Arbitrators in Commercial Disputes]

2. During a hearing, an arbitrator named Nancy suggests to the parties that she thinks they should consider settlement. Nancy tells the parties that they could settle the matter easily within a couple of hours and save themselves time and money. Nancy volunteers to help mediate the discussions between the disputing parties. She then directs the parties to dismiss their witnesses, so she can begin the mediation in a confidential setting. Should Nancy have recommended settlement to the parties? Should she have acted to mediate the settlement discussions? [See Code of Ethics for Arbitrators in Commercial Disputes]

3. Two parties, Tracer and NESCO, had entered into a licensing agreement for the use of Tracer's tank and pipeline leak detection process. The licensing agreement contained an arbitration clause covering claims "arising out of this Agreement." After termination of the licensing agreement, Tracer contended that NESCO continued to use its confidential information and trade secrets to market an alternative product. An arbitral panel dismissed Tracer's tort claims for misappropriation of trade secrets as not arbitrable. In turn, Tracer sought to

compel arbitration of these claims. Was a tort claim for the misappropriation of trade secrets arbitrable under the arbitration provision? [*Tracer Research Corp. v. Nat'l Environmental Services Co.* (NESCO), 42 F. 3d 1292 (9th Cir. 1994), *cert. denied,* 116 S. Ct. 37 (1995)]

4. Melinda Broemmer was a pregnant, unmarried, twenty-one-year old high school graduate earning only about $100 a week with no medical benefits. She was under a great deal of physical and emotional stress, since the father-to-be was pressuring her to obtain an abortion and her parents were advising against the procedure. Ultimately, she sought the abortion and, in doing so, was first required to complete three forms, one of which was a separate PDAA. Neither the PDAA nor the arbitration clause was explained to her, and the clinic never provided her with any copies of the documents. Broemmer alleged that she did not recall signing the arbitration agreement and still remains unsure about what arbitration means. Broemmer suffered a punctured uterus during the abortion, which required follow-up medical treatment. She filed a medical malpractice suit against the clinic doctor, and the clinic sought to compel arbitration. Will the court require her to comply with the terms of the PDAA? [*Broemmer v. Abortion Services of Phoenix, Ltd.,* 173 Ariz. 148, 840 P. 2d 1013 (1992)]

5. Antonio and Diana Mastrobuono were an assistant professor of medieval literature and an artist, respectively, who had entered into an investment contract that contained an arbitration clause. The arbitrator in the investment dispute found in favor of the Mastrobuonos and awarded them $400,000 in punitive damages. The dealer's standard investor agreement indicated that the arbitration would be in accordance with the National Association of Securities Dealers (NASD) rules, which allow arbitrators to award punitive damages. However, the agreement also included a choice-of-law provision, which selected the laws of the state of New York to govern any dispute. Under New York case law, arbitrators do not have the authority to award punitive damages. Will the arbitrator's award of punitive damages be upheld? [*Mastrobuono v. Shearson Lehman Hutton,* 115 S. Ct. 1212 (1995)]

SUGGESTED ADDITIONAL READINGS

Blackford, Jason C. "Arbitration Provisions for Business Contracts." *Arbitration Journal.* September 1993, pp. 47–52.

Coulson, Robert. "An Introduction to Commercial Arbitration." *Business Arbitration—What You Need to Know.* American Arbitration Association, 1991, pp. 7–33.

Hoellering, Michael F. "Arbitrability." *Commercial Arbitration for the 1990s.* American Bar Association, 1991, pp. 1–13.

10

BUSINESS DISPUTE RESOLUTION SYSTEMS

CHAPTER HIGHLIGHTS

In this chapter, you will read and learn about the following:

1. Establishing procedures to resolve internal disputes involving employees, managers, and shareholders, including employee training, employee contracts and handbook language, and company ombudsmen.
2. Establishing procedures to resolve external disputes involving customers, business partners, and competitors, including use and supervision of outside counsel, relations with insurance carriers, and customer contracts and agreements.

The preceding chapters have described in detail the various alternative dispute resolution processes used to resolve business disputes. ADR processes range from informal, settlement-oriented negotiation to formal, adjudicative arbitration. Each process has advantages and disadvantages as well as proper and improper applications. This chapter will provide guidance on incorporating ADR processes into an effective business dispute resolution program. We will address the creation of structures for resolving both internal and external business disputes. The chapter concludes with exercises designed to assist you in evaluating the needs of various types of businesses with respect to dispute resolution system design.

AN OVERVIEW OF BUSINESS DISPUTE RESOLUTION SYSTEMS

Ten years ago, Chief Justice Warren Burger wrote in an article entitled "Our Vicious Legal Circle," "The notion that ordinary people want black-robed judges, well-dressed lawyers and fine courtrooms as settings to resolve their disputes is incorrect. People with problems, like people with pains, want relief, and they want it as quickly and inexpensively as possible." The same can be said of businesses. Both businesses and individuals want a system that provides them some measure of humanity, a system that allows them to participate in resolving their own dispute. They seek to be heard directly, not eliminated from the process through expensive and arcane legal procedures. They desire, in short, access to the processes that are used to solve their problems. The premise of the preceding chapters has been that ADR processes provide such access. Consequently, wise businesspeople develop companywide, programmatic approaches to implementing dispute resolution.

http://

For information on the Foundation for Prevention and Early Conflict Resolution, see http://wwwz. conflictresolution .org/perg/index. html

Successful companies manage both internal and external conflict. Internal dispute resolution mechanisms resolve conflict between members of the organization, such as employees, while external dispute resolution mechanisms target disputes involving those with whom the company does business, such as vendors and suppliers. The best company dispute resolution policy is a comprehensive and pre-emptive one that addresses both types of disputes as early as possible.

In deciding to implement policies favoring ADR, companies must answer three initial questions relating to internal and external disputes. How should the company balance facilitative, evaluative, and adjudicative processes? Should the company favor binding or nonbinding processes? And, what benefits is the company most interested in achieving with an ADR program? These benefits, at minimum, often include economic savings, relationship preservation, and quick dispute resolution.

The most effective method of balancing facilitative, evaluative, and adjudicative processes, both binding and nonbinding, is to employ them in that sequence. Negotiation and mediation are the least expensive and most expeditious facilitative processes, and they pose no threat to future adjudication. When they prove unsuccessful, the minitrial or summary jury trial, evaluative processes that allow party-driven settlement but introduce an advisory third party charged with considering the merits of the case in an advisory capacity may be used. If the evaluative process fails, an adjudicative process, whether private arbitration or public trial, remains available. This progression of relatively simple processes saves time, money, and important commercial relationships by resolving many cases early. It also saves costly adjudication for cases in which early settlement proves impossible. This progression allows businesses to rely on nonbinding, negotiated processes that initially preserve party control over outcomes and to relinquish control in adjudicative processes only when necessary. Finally, this progression recognizes the fact that business dispute resolution is primarily concerned with economics. As such, length of time to resolution, reduction of resolution costs, and preservation of important commercial relationships contribute to both narrow process and broad policy decisions.

ADR IN ACTION

United Parcel Service Delivers an Employment ADR Program

Two years of research and planning by a core group drawn from the legal, human resources, employee relations, communications, training, and labor departments ended recently for UPS with the creation of its pilot Employment Dispute Resolution Program. This program covers approximately 5,000 nonunion management, administrative, technical, and specialist employees in two company regions. Ultimately, the program will cover all 70,000 workers in these categories around the world. The planning group visited six companies with similar programs, studied twenty-five additional corporate ADR initiatives, and consulted extensively with the American Arbitration Association before finalizing plans for the program.

The program, which complements other ADR efforts by the company, including incorporation of ADR into many company contracts and documents, covers claims such as discipline, discrimination, harassment, termination, and interference with other legal rights. The program moves a dispute through three internal and two external processes. A dispute may be sent through three in-house processes including "open door," facilitation, and peer review. Outside processes used to resolve disputes are private mediation and arbitration. The first four steps of the program, open door through media-

tion, are processes that allow voluntary negotiation of disputes and only end with mutually agreed-upon conclusions. It is only at the fifth and final stage that a third party may impose an outcome on the company or employee. "We want to do everything we can to maintain a positive relationship while the dispute is in process, so that ideally, when the dispute is satisfactorily resolved, we all go back to work and move forward," said Joseph Shaginaw, UPS corporate employee relations manager.

Extensive in-house training and promotion will accompany the rollout of the full program. UPS hopes the economic benefits of the program will be considerable. Indeed, they hope to shave as much as eighty percent from the $10 million spent annually on legal expenses. Still, Jeff Paquin, who handles ADR and litigation for the company, says, "A lot of companies start the process because they want to save money. But if you do it for that reason only, you're not going to get too far. We began with the principle that we wanted to do this to resolve disputes in a way that is fair to employees and the company. And if you save money, reduce the amount of time to resolve a dispute, maintain confidentiality, and do all these things, that's great. But always remember the real objective: preserving working relationships."

INTERNAL DISPUTE RESOLUTION POLICIES

http://

For information on training and simulations, see the Harvard Negotiation Project site: http://www.law.harvard.edu/Programs/PON/

In-house employee training is a significant effort companies can make to reduce **internal disputes** or conflict in the workplace. Training is preemptive inasmuch as it endeavors to empower employees to solve problems informally and early. Indeed, interactive training in interest-based and nonadversarial conflict resolution can improve the workplace by avoiding formal conflict resolution processes altogether.

Employee contracts and handbooks calling for ADR processes present two noteworthy opportunities to promote the ADR philosophy in the company. For many years, courts have enforced contract provisions and grievance processes that use ADR principles. In 1991, the U.S. Supreme Court decided in *Gilmer v. Interstate/Johnson Lane Corp.* that an arbitration clause requiring an employee to submit an age discrimination claim to arbitration and waiving a right to trial was enforceable. The Court held that an employee who signs such an agreement is simply choosing an alternative forum in which to resolve a claim. Courts have reached largely consistent results since then, although courts will decline to enforce agreements that they believe to be unconscionable or otherwise insufficient in contract terms. Indeed, some recent decisions have scaled back support for mandatory arbitration agreements. These provisions enable businesses to use rapid and cost-effective means offered by alternative dispute resolution to resolve claims and avoid litigation with and between employees altogether.

http://

The complete text of Gilmer v. Interstate/Johnson may be found at: http://caselaw.findlaw.com/cgi-bin/getcase.pl?court=US&vol=500&invol=20

Employers wishing to use handbook provisions and contracts for the purposes of ADR should be mindful of several potential pitfalls. They should not, for example, treat contracts and handbooks as equivalent. In *Heurtebise v. Reliable Business Computers,* 550 NW 2d 243 (1996), where a handbook allowed the employer to modify the contents at its sole discretion, a court declined to enforce an arbitration provision, finding that no intent to be bound was present. Although courts normally affirm such provisions, judges are willing to void them when they pose an injustice to the employee. To be effective and enforceable, ADR provisions in either a contract or handbook must be:

1. *Fair.* Provisions should, at a minimum, include an impartial third-party advisor, an opportunity for parties to state their case following a reasonable period of preparation, and a range of remedies generally equivalent to those available in a public forum. In *Stirlen v. Supercuts,* 60 Cal. Rptr. 2d 138 (1997), the court struck down a provision that provided that only actual damages could be recovered, and that those damages were subject to further limitations for mitigation.

2. *Inexpensive.* Courts have voided arbitration clauses that shifted a disproportionate amount of proceeding expenses to the employee. Companies are well advised to divide ADR expenses to avoid the appearance of placing an undue economic burden on the employee.

3. *Consistent.* The commitment to ADR should apply to all populations. If the provision appears to deprive a single class of employees from using the courts,

while ensuring the right of the business to do so, courts will be cautious about enforcing it. In *Stirlen v. Supercuts,* the court declined to enforce a provision that also allowed the company to avoid arbitration while requiring it of the employee.

4. *Voluntary.* Courts have expressed reservations about **adhesion contracts** that condition employment, new or continued, upon employee acceptance of an ADR provision that waives the right to court access.

5. *Clear.* The principles of contract are followed closely in analyzing pre-dispute clauses and handbook provisions, and these principles disfavor clauses that are not explicit and prominently displayed. They should, at a minimum, identify the employees covered by the provision, the case types covered, the nature of the procedure used to address each particular case, the allocation of process-related expenses, and the right to counsel.

The following case illustrates many of these principles as it considers the enforceability of an employment handbook and contract package requiring employees to use arbitration to resolve claims against the company.

GIBSON V. NEIGHBORHOOD HEALTH CLINICS
(7th U.S. Circuit, 1997)

FACT SUMMARY

Gibson, who had previously been employed by Neighborhood Health Clinics under circumstances not relevant to this case, was rehired by NHC on December 22, 1994. On December 30, 1994, at which time Gibson, although rehired, had not yet returned to work, NHC held a meeting at which all employees were presented with a new Associates Policy Manual and required to sign a new Associates Understanding. Gibson was not required to attend the meeting, and in fact, she did not. The Understanding included the following language:

> I agree to the grievance and arbitration provisions set forth in the Associates Policy Manual. I understand that I am waiving my right to a trial, including a jury trial, in state or federal court of the class of disputes specifically set forth in the grievance

and arbitration provisions on pages 8–10 of the Manual.

The Manual states that when an employee alleges a violation of his or her rights under the ADA or Title VII:

> Then it is clearly intended and agreed that the sole and exclusive means for the resolution of all disputes, issues, controversies, claims, causes of action, or grievances by an employee against neighborhood health clinics shall be through the process of arbitration.

The opening two paragraphs of the Manual include the following language:

> Neighborhood Health Clinics reserves the right at any time to modify, revoke, suspend, terminate, or change any or all terms of this Manual, plans, policies, or procedures, in whole or in part, without having to consult or

reach agreement with anyone, at any time, with or without notice. . . .

[W]hile Neighborhood Health Clinics intends to abide by the policies and procedures described in this Manual, it does not constitute a contract nor promise of any kind. Therefore, employees can be terminated at any time, with or without notice, and with or without cause.

The arbitration provisions were not part of the terms of employment during Gibson's previous tenure with NHC.

When Gibson was rehired in December 1994, she was told to report to work on January 9, 1995. On that date, she met with NHC's personnel director, Chris Baxter, who handed her a stack of papers to sign, including insurance and tax forms. Among the papers was the Associates Understanding. Gibson testified at her deposition that when she asked Baxter about the Associates Understanding, Baxter told her that it was a form that everybody signed so that complaints about time off could be settled through a grievance procedure. The Manual referenced in the Associates Understanding was not given to Gibson at that time; Baxter was only able to locate a copy of the Manual later that day, at which time she provided it to Gibson. Although she signed the Associates Understanding, Gibson never signed the Manual.

NHC fired Gibson on April 6, 1995. On May 15, 1995, Gibson filed a discrimination claim with the Equal Employment Opportunity Commission, alleging sex and disability discrimination. NHC was informed of this charge shortly thereafter. Gibson then filed her complaint in the district court. NHC moved to dismiss Gibson's complaint on the ground that she had waived her right to a judicial determination of her claims against NHC by agreeing to submit such disputes to arbi-

tration. The district court agreed, concluding that the Manual in connection with the Associates Understanding created an enforceable arbitration agreement, and granted the motion for dismissal. In addition, because Gibson failed to abide by the deadline for submitting her claim to arbitration, the dismissal effectively foreclosed her ability to obtain redress. The district court therefore entered final judgment, from which Gibson now appeals.

OPINION: *FLAUM, Circuit Judge*

On appeal, the parties debate an important issue: whether the prerogative of litigating one's ADA and **Title VII claims** in federal court is the type of important right the relinquishment of which requires a **knowing and voluntary waiver.** The Supreme Court indicated in *Alexander v. Gardner-Denver Co.*, 415 U.S. 36 (1974), that an employee could not forfeit substantive rights under Title VII absent a voluntary and knowing waiver. In *Pierce v. Atchison, Topeka & Santa Fe Ry. Co.*, 65 F.3d 562 (7th Cir. 1995), we applied the knowing and voluntary standard set out in *Alexander* to an employee's release of age and race discrimination claims against his employer. Thus, before an employee cedes a substantive right grounded in federal statutory law, she must understand and freely make the decision to do so.

Less clear is whether the right to have one's federal claims determined judicially rather than in an arbitration proceeding qualifies for this added protection. The Supreme Court has not reached this issue, but in dicta has stated that in agreeing to arbitrate a federal claim, a party "does not forgo the substantive rights afforded by the statute; it only submits to their resolution in an arbitral, rather than a judicial, forum." *Gilmer v. Interstate/Johnson Lane Corp.*, 500 U.S. 20 (1991). Conversely, we have noted that by being forced into binding

The complete text of Alexander v. Gardner-Denver may be found at:
http://caselaw.findlaw.com/scripts/getcase.pl?navby=case&court=US&vol=415&page=36

For the complete text of Pierce v. Atchison, Topeka, see this site:
http://caselaw.findlaw.com/cgi-bin/getcase.pl?court=7th&navby=case&no=943057

arbitration [employees] would be surrendering their right to trial by jury—a right that civil rights plaintiffs fought hard for and finally obtained in the 1991 amendments to Title VII. This issue is further complicated by the strong federal policy in favor of arbitration as embodied in the substantive provisions involved in this case. Thus, an employee's contractual agreement to submit her federal claims to arbitration implicates competing policy concerns.

Obviously, the strongest case for a court's finding that an employer and employee agreed to submit claims to arbitration will arise when the record indicates the employee has knowingly agreed to do so. If parties operate under these conditions, we believe that the twin goals of protecting federal rights and resolving claims where possible through arbitration will be effected. Moreover, the formation of arbitration agreements upon terms that both parties understand need not be unduly burdensome. The course that NHC undertook to alert those already employed to the change in policy (the convening of a meeting and the presentation of the appropriate documentation) demonstrates the feasibility of achieving this objective. While we therefore stress the advantage of arbitration agreements that are the product of an employee's knowing and voluntary consent, we decline today to decide whether such consent is a prerequisite to the validity of an agreement to arbitrate federal civil rights claims. To resolve this appeal, we need look no further than the state law of contract that generally governs arbitration agreements.

The parties agree that an employee and employer may contractually agree to submit federal claims, including Title VII and ADA claims, to arbitration. An agreement to arbitrate is treated like any other contract. If there is no contract, there is to be

no forced arbitration. In determining whether a valid arbitration agreement arose between the parties, a federal court should look to the state law that ordinarily governs the formation of contracts.

It is a basic tenet of contract law that in order for a promise to be enforceable against the promisor, the promisee must have given some consideration for the promise. Consideration is defined as bargained for exchange whereby the promisor (here Gibson) receives some benefit or the promisee (here NHC) suffers a detriment. Thus, in order for Gibson's agreement to be enforceable, there must be detriment to NHC or benefit to Gibson that was bargained for in exchange for Gibson's promise to arbitrate all disputes.

Often, consideration for one party's promise to arbitrate is the other party's promise to do the same. In the present case, however, NHC cannot point to its own promise to arbitrate in order to make enforceable Gibson's promise to do likewise. The Understanding contains no promise on NHC's part to submit claims to arbitration. It is worded entirely in terms of Gibson's obligation to submit her claims to arbitration (using phrases such as "I agree" "I understand" "I am waiving"); it contains no promise on NHC's part. In order for a contract to be enforceable, both parties must be bound by its terms. Although Indiana courts will not find that there was a lack of obligation on the part of one party when "a reasonable and logical interpretation will render the contract valid and enforceable," *Id.* at 645, there is no gloss we can apply to the language of the Understanding that would suggest that NHC was also required to forgo a judicial forum in favor of arbitration. To find that NHC was required to arbitrate any claim brought by Gibson would not give recognition to an obligation that was clearly present yet imperfectly expressed, but rather would lend arcane meaning to the clear language chosen by NHC; to find an obligation here would be to weave a contract out of loose threads. Therefore, we conclude that the Understanding itself did not contain consideration for Gibson's promise in the form of a promise by NHC to submit disputes to arbitration.

In contrast to the one-sided obligation contained in the wording of the Understanding, the Manual contains language that arguably could be read to bind NHC. We conclude, however, that any promise NHC made in the Manual cannot serve as consideration for Gibson's promise to arbitrate. The absence of a meaningful link between Gibson's promise, contained in the Understanding, and NHC's obligation, set forth in the Manual, precludes reading these provisions as complementary components of a bargained for exchange. To be sure, contract terms may be incorporated by reference to a separate document, including an employee handbook, and consideration for the promise in one instrument may be contained in another. Nevertheless, whatever the physical form by which a contract is memorialized (if any), proper consideration must consist of benefit or detriment given in exchange for the promise in question. The principal purposes of this consideration requirement are the "cautionary function of bringing home to the promisor the fact that his promise is legally enforceable and an evidentiary function . . . of making it more likely that an enforceable promise was intended." *Scholes v. Lehmann*, 56 F.3d 750 (1995). Neither of these functions is served when a promisor does not know of the promise that purportedly serves as consideration. Here, Gibson was unaware

of the terms of the Manual (even if the Understanding's reference to the Manual alerted her to its existence) at the time she signed the Understanding. The promise that she made in the Understanding, therefore, was not given in exchange for any promise that NHC made in the Manual. In addition, although the Manual contains language that could be read to bind Gibson as well as NHC, Gibson did not (even in the objective or constructive sense) assent to the terms of the Manual, either when she signed the Understanding (at which point the Manual was not made available), or when she received the Manual. Consequently, there is no promise on the part of NHC that can serve as consideration for Gibson's promise to arbitrate.

Nor was Gibson's promise to submit claims to arbitration supported by consideration in the form of NHC's promise to hire her or to continue to employ her, or by its reasonable reliance on her promise. An initial offer of employment may constitute consideration for an employee's promise, such as a covenant not to compete. However, NHC's offer of employment to Gibson was not made in exchange for her promise to arbitrate, for she had already been hired at the time she made the promise. Once again, the element of bargained for exchange is lacking. An employer's specific promise to continue to employ an at-will employee may provide valid consideration for an employee's promise to forgo certain rights. In the present case, however, NHC never made a promise to continue Gibson's employment in exchange for her promise to submit claims to arbitration. That is, it never communicated to her that if she signed the Understanding she could continue to work there, and that if she did not her status would be uncertain. It is true that NHC continued to employ her. Yet when an employer has made no specific promise, the mere fact of continued employment does not constitute consideration for the employee's promise.

Finally, while in the employment context it has been held that one party's partial performance in reliance upon the other party's promise may be sufficient consideration to make the promise enforceable, there is no indication in the present case that NHC was induced to rely on Gibson's promise. It had made its decision to hire her prior to her agreeing to the terms of the Understanding, and there is no evidence that its decision to continue to employ her following her signing of the Understanding (on the day she returned to work) was based upon her agreeing to the terms contained therein. We therefore conclude that Gibson's promise to submit her claims against NHC to arbitration did not give rise to an enforceable contract.

Reversed and Remanded.

Discussion Questions

1. Do cases involving civil rights present particularly compelling claims deserving of formal court adjudication, regardless of any ADR clause contained in an employment contract or handbook?

2. Does the interest in judicial economy and in support of ADR outweigh the employee's interest in public adjudication of statutory and constitutional claims?

3. Is employment, whether continued or new, an acceptable incentive to enter into an ADR agreement with an employer? How would consideration of public policy affect your answer?

4. Why should employees be compelled to arbitrate and thus forfeit their right of access to a court trial by a jury of their peers?

ADR IN ACTION

National Franchise Mediation Program

The CPR Institute for Dispute Resolution operates a National Franchise Mediation Program. A diverse group of fifty companies, including Burger King, UNOCAL, McDonald's, Dollar-Rent-A-Car, Holiday Inn, Jiffy Lube International, and Meineke Discount Muffler Shops, participate. The participating companies commit to resolving franchisor/franchisee disputes through direct negotiation and, in the event of failure, through a formal ADR process. Franchisee participation is voluntary, but franchisors must participate if a franchisee initiates a dispute resolution procedure. The program has addressed successfully a wide variety of disputes, including encroachment, lease claims, customer service matters, and contract violation allegations.

For a complete description of the CPR National Franchise Mediation program, including statistics and members, see this site: http://www. cpradr.org/fran _397.htm

Use of company ombuds is a long-standing method of internal dispute management and resolution. The **ombudsman** is a company-employed internal problem solver. Ombudsmen offer employees a confidential, relatively powerful office through which to resolve claims that they would otherwise have to address through formal grievance procedures or litigation. Likewise, they offer the employer an opportunity to diffuse potentially serious workplace disputes prior to the initiation of either in-house grievance procedures or external lawsuits. The ombudsman position is a difficult one to maintain in terms of loyalty and privilege, because it is normally one through which promises of neutrality and confidentiality are made to the employee and employer alike. The following two cases give opposing answers to the question of whether the files maintained by an ombudsman can later be discovered in litigation. Ironically, both cases involve the same company and ombudsman, but were decided by different courts.

KIENTZY V. MCDONNELL DOUGLAS CORPORATION
33 F.R.D. 570 (U.S.D.C. Eastern Dist. Miss, 1991)

FACT SUMMARY

Plaintiff Mary Kientzy alleges that McDonnell Douglas Aircraft Corporation (MDC) terminated her from her position as a security officer in violation of Title VII. The plaintiff has noticed Therese Clement for deposition and would depose other company personnel about their statements to ombudsman Clemente. Clemente is employed as a senior staff assistant in the ombudsman program of the defendant's subsidiary McDonnell Douglas Aircraft Company (McAir). Clemente has been employed in the McAir Ombudsman Office since the ombudsman program began in 1985. The purpose of the ombudsman program and office is to mediate, in a strictly confidential environment, disputes among MDC employees and between employees and management.

Plaintiff Kientzy was terminated from employment in August 1988, following the decision of a company disciplinary committee. After the committee made its decision, the plaintiff went to Ms. Clemente in her position as ombudsman; MDC nevertheless terminated her. The plaintiff argues that Ms. Clemente received information about her situation from company employees, including a member of the disciplinary committee who has since died.

This action is before the court upon the motion of Therese Clemente for an order under Federal Rule of Civil Procedure 26(c)(1), protecting from pretrial discovery by both plaintiff and defendant the communications she received in her position as a company ombudsman of defendant MDC. MDC argues in support of Clemente's position. The plaintiff argues that any such ombudsman **privilege** should not include the information sought.

OPINION: *DAVID D. NOCE, U.S. Magistrate Judge*

Plaintiff argues that the information received by Clemente is relevant to the trial of the action and is discoverable on two grounds. First, she argues that the statements made to Clemente by defendant's personnel may evidence discriminatory animus in the decision to terminate her. Second, she argues that the ombudsman program is a company procedure for appealing her dismissal and that the ombudsman thus participated in the final decision to terminate her. For the reasons set forth below, the court agrees with movant that the confidential communications made to her are protected from disclosure by Federal Rule of Evidence 501.

Rule 501 requires that this Court assay the ombudsman's claim of privilege by interpreting the principles of the common law "in light of reason and experience." Four cardinal factors have been discerned for this purpose.

> (1) The communication must be one made in the belief that it will not be disclosed; (2) confidentiality must be essential to the maintenance of the relationship between the parties; (3) the relationship should be one that society considers worthy of being fostered; and (4) the injury to the relationship incurred by disclosure must be greater than the benefit gained in the correct disposal of litigation.

First, ombudsman Clemente received the subject communications in the belief that they would be kept confidential. The McAir ombudsman office is constituted as an independent and neutral entity. It has no authority to make company policy. Its head has the position of company vice-president, independent of the company's human resources and personnel offices. The office has direct access to the company president. Ombudsman Clemente is bound by the Code of Ethics of the Corporate Ombudsman Association, which provides for the confidentiality of communications. The office has adopted procedures to assure such confidentiality. The McAir Ombudsman Office has given its strict pledge of confidentiality to all employees and to the company. All new employees are so advised and defendant has repeatedly restated to its employees that they may rely on the confidentiality of the ombudsman's office. Since it opened in 1985, the McAir ombudsman's office has received approximately 4800 communications. Defendant has sought, but has been refused, access to the ombudsman's files and records regarding plaintiff. The company has indicated it will not request them in the future.

Second, confidentiality of communications is essential to relationships between the ombudsman's office and defendant's employees and defendant's management. The function of the McAir ombudsman's office is communications and to remedy workplace problems, in a strictly confidential atmosphere. Without this confidentiality, the office would be just one more nonconfidential opportunity for employees to air disputes. The ombudsman's office provides an opportunity for complete disclosure, without the specter of retaliation, that does not exist in the other available nonconfidential grievance and complaint procedures.

Third, the relationship between the ombudsman office and defendant's employees and management is worthy of societal support. The Court takes judicial notice of the fact that MDC and McAir are very large federal government contractors in the aircraft, space, and other industries. It is important that their employees have an opportunity to make

http://

For a complete version of the Federal Rules of Evidence, including Rule 501, see the Cornell Law School site: http://www.law.cornell.edu/rules/fre/overview.html

confidential statements and to receive confidential guidance, information, and aid to remedy workplace problems, to benefit themselves and possibly the nation. This is true in spite of the possibility that such actions may be perceived by an employee to be against company or fellow employees' interests.

Fourth, the harm caused by a disruption of the confidential relationship between the ombudsman's office and others in plaintiff's case would be greater than the benefit to plaintiff by disclosure. A successful ombudsman program resolves many problems informally and more quickly than other formal procedures, including court actions. A court order that Clemente disclose the information communicated to her in confidence, or that her informants disclose what they told her in confidence about plaintiff, would destroy the reputation and principle of confidentiality that the McAir ombudsman program and office now enjoys and needs to perform its function. The utility of that program and office, in resolving disputes in this workplace and thus diminishing the need for more formal resolution procedures, is founded on the confiden-

tiality of its communications to and from company officials and employees. Federal Rule of Evidence 408 has recognized the utility of confidential settlement discussions. The societal benefit from this confidentiality is paramount to plaintiff's need for disclosure.

The Court is persuaded in the case at bar that the plaintiff's need for relevant information can be satisfied, in spite of the privilege, by deposing all relevant fact witnesses, including the remaining members of the disciplinary committee, about the events leading to plaintiff's termination. Indeed, the depositions of these persons is expected to occur soon. Plaintiff may not ask these witnesses to disclose their statement to the company ombudsman. Plaintiff may ask these witnesses about facts known by them, even though those facts were contained in their statements to the ombudsman. Because there has been no showing that ombudsman Clemente has nonconfidential, relevant information, plaintiff may not depose her at all.

For the reasons set forth above, IT IS HEREBY ORDERED that the motion of Therese Clemente for a protective order is sustained.

CARMAN V. MCDONNELL DOUGLAS CORPORATION
114 F.3d 790 (8th Cir. 1997)

FACT SUMMARY

In October 1992, McDonnell Douglas Aircraft Corporation laid off Frank Carman as part of a reduction in its management staff. Carman then sued McDonnell Douglas, claiming that his termination violated the Age Discrimination in Employment Act, the Missouri Human Rights Act, and the Employee Retirement Income Security Act of 1974. In the course of discovery, the District Court denied Carman's request for the production of certain documents, holding that they were protected by the "Ombudsman Privilege." The District Court later granted summary judgment to McDonnell Douglas, a decision which Carman now appeals. We hold that the District Court lacked sufficient justification for creating an ombudsman privilege and denying Carman's discovery request.

In June 1994, Carman requested 54 sets of documents from McDonnell Douglas. Item No. 53 was a request for "[a]ll notes and documents reflecting data known to . . . Clemente [a company ombudsman] . . . concerning "the plaintiff, a number of other individuals, and various topics, including "[m]eeting notes regarding lay-offs in Plaintiff's Division" and "[m]eeting notes regarding Plaintiff Frank Carman." McDonnell Douglas objected to this and many other requests as vague, overbroad, and irrelevant. McDonnell Douglas further objected with regard to documents known to Therese Clemente, because her activities as an ombudsman were considered confidential, and any information and documents relating to her activities are immune from discovery. In response, the plaintiff filed a motion to compel production of certain documents. The Court granted the motion in part and ordered the defendants to produce a number of documents, including those requested in Item No. 53. Two months later, however, in clarifying its order with respect to Item No. 53, the Court ruled that the "defendant is not required to produce documents protected by the Ombudsman Privilege."

OPINION: *ARNOLD, Chief Judge*

In the context of this case, the term "ombudsman" refers to an employee outside of the corporate chain of command whose job is to investigate and mediate workplace disputes. The corporate ombudsman is paid by the corporation and lacks the structural independence that characterizes government ombudsmen in some countries and states, where the office of ombudsman is a separate branch of government that handles disputes between citizens and government agencies. Nonetheless, the corporate ombudsman purports to be an independent and neutral party who promises strict confidentiality to all employees and is bound by the Code of Ethics of the Corporate Ombudsman Association, which requires the ombudsman to keep communications confidential. McDonnell Douglas argues for recognition of an evidentiary privilege that would protect corporate ombudsmen from having to disclose relevant employee communications to civil litigants.

Federal Rule of Evidence 501 states that federal courts should recognize evidentiary privileges according to "the principles of the common law" interpreted "in the light of reason and experience." The beginning of any analysis under Rule 501 is the principle that "the public has a right to every man's evidence." Hardwicke, L.C.J., quoted in 12 Cobbett's Parliamentary History 675, 693 (1742). Accordingly, evidentiary privileges "are not lightly created." *United States v. Nixon*, 418 U.S. 683, 710 (1974). A party that seeks the creation of a new evidentiary privilege must overcome the significant burden of establishing that permitting a refusal to testify or excluding relevant evidence has a public good transcending the normally predominant principle of utilizing all rational means for ascertaining truth.

The first important factor for assessing a proposed new evidentiary privilege is the importance of the relationship that the privilege will foster. The defendant argues that ombudsmen help resolve workplace disputes prior to the commencement of

http://

For a sample Code of Ethics, see this site: http://www-leland.stanford.edu/dept/ocr/ombudsperson/standards.html

expensive and time-consuming litigation. We agree that fair and efficient alternative dispute resolution techniques benefit society and are worthy of encouragement. To the extent that corporate ombudsmen successfully resolve disputes in a fair and efficient manner, they are a welcome and helpful addition to a society that is weary of lawsuits.

Nonetheless, far more is required to justify the creation of a new evidentiary privilege. First, McDonnell Douglas has failed to present any evidence, and indeed has not even argued, that the ombudsman method is more successful at resolving workplace disputes than other forms of alternative dispute resolution, nor has it even pointed to any evidence establishing that its own ombudsman is especially successful at resolving workplace disputes prior to the commencement of litigation. In recognizing a privilege for the McDonnell Douglas ombudsman's office in 1991, the court in *Kientzy v. McDonnell Douglas Corp.*, 133 F.R.D. 570, 572 (E.D. Mo. 1991), found that the office had received approximately 4,800 communications since 1985, but neither the court nor McDonnell Douglas in the present case provides us with any context to evaluate the significance of this statistic.

Second, McDonnell Douglas has failed to make a compelling argument that most of the advantages afforded by the ombudsman method would be lost without the privilege. Even without a privilege, corporate ombudsmen still have much to offer employees in the way of confidentiality, for they are still able to promise to keep employee communications confidential from management. Indeed, when an aggrieved employee or an employee-witness is deciding whether or not to confide in a company ombudsman, his greatest concern is not likely to be that the statement will someday be revealed in civil discovery. More likely, the employee will fear that the ombudsman is biased in favor of the company, and that the ombudsman will tell management everything that the employee says. The denial of an ombudsman privilege will not affect the ombudsman's ability to convince an employee that the ombudsman is neutral, and creation of an ombudsman privilege will not help alleviate the fear that she is not.

We are especially unconvinced that "no present or future [McDonnell Douglas] employee could feel comfortable in airing his or her disputes with the Ombudsman because of the specter of discovery." See Appellee's Br. 45. An employee either will or will not have a meritorious complaint. If he does not and is aware that he does not, he is no more likely to share the frivolousness of his complaint with a company ombudsman than he is with a court. If he has a meritorious complaint that he would prefer not to litigate, then he will generally feel that he has nothing to hide and will be undeterred by the prospect of civil discovery from sharing the nature of his complaint with the ombudsman. The dim prospect that the employee's complaint might someday surface in an unrelated case strikes us as an unlikely deterrent. Again, it is the perception that the ombudsman is the company's investigator, a fear that does not depend upon the prospect of civil discovery, that is most likely to keep such an employee from speaking openly.

McDonnell Douglas also argues that failure to recognize an ombudsman privilege will disrupt the relationship between management and the ombudsman's office. In cases where management has nothing to hide, this is unlikely. It is probably true that management will be less likely to share damaging information with an ombudsman if there is no privilege.

Nonetheless, McDonnell Douglas has provided no reason to believe that management is especially eager to confess wrongdoing to ombudsmen when a privilege exists, or that ombudsmen are helpful at resolving disputes that involve violations of the law by management or supervisors. If the chilling of management-ombudsman communications occurs only in cases that would not have been resolved at the ombudsman stage anyway, then there is no reason to recognize an ombudsman privilege.

McDonnell Douglas relies on the analysis of the court in *Kientzy*, supra, apparently one of only two federal courts to have recognized a corporate-ombudsman privilege. We do not find the reasoning of that opinion convincing. For example, the *Kientzy* opinion argues that confidentiality is essential to ombudsman-employee relationships because the function of that relationship is to receive communications and to remedy workplace problems in a strictly confidential atmosphere. Without this confidentiality, the office would just be one more nonconfidential opportunity for employees to air disputes. The ombudsman's office provides an opportunity for complete disclosure, without the specter of retaliation, that does not exist in the other available, nonconfidential grievance and complaint procedures. As we have said, the corporate ombudsman will still be able to promise confidentiality in most circumstances even with no privilege. To justify the creation of a privilege, McDonnell Douglas must first establish that society benefits in some significant way from the particular brand of confidentiality that the privilege affords. Only then can a court decide whether the advantages of the proposed privilege overcome the strong presumption in favor of disclosure of all relevant information. The creation of a wholly new evidentiary privilege is a big step. This record does not convince us that we should take it.

We disagree with the District Court's holding that employee communications to Therese Clemente were protected from discovery by an ombudsman privilege. The judgment is reversed, and the cause remanded for further proceedings consistent with this opinion. On remand, the District Court should order the production of the evidence it had believed the privilege protected, unless there are other reasons why discovery of this evidence would not be appropriate.

It is so ordered.

Discussion Questions

1. If ombudsman confidentiality is not preserved, is there any reason to believe that the use of ombuds has any long-term future? Under what circumstances do you expect that an employee would use an ombudsman if absolute confidentiality is not guaranteed?

2. Are the circumstances in these cases sufficiently dissimilar to justify the differing rulings? Is the absence of judicial certainty on this matter troubling?

3. Is private, outside dispute resolution an acceptable substitute for in-house, ombud dispute resolution in jurisdictions in which there is no clear judicial finding in favor of ombud proceeding confidentiality?

4. Would a statutory privilege be preferable to a judicial privilege? Why or why not?

ADR IN ACTION

Peers Judging Peers: A Corporate Cost-Cutting Strategy

Peer review programs, ones in which employees judge other employees in-house and without lawyers, have become a popular form of alternative dispute resolution for companies. Darden Restaurants, Inc., the owner of Red Lobster, the nation's largest seafood chain, and Olive Garden, the top casual Italian restaurant chain, is one of several companies, including TRW, Inc., Marriott International, Inc., and Rockwell International Corp., who have recently created peer review programs. Darden permits employees who have been disciplined or fired to appeal such decisions to a panel of several coworkers who may hear testimony from the appealing party and other employees. The panel receives evidence and, on the basis of that testimony and evidence, has the authority to affirm or overturn the management decision. The panel can even award money damages to any employee who brings a claim deemed to have merit by the panel. Each panel comprises volunteers from other restaurants as well as company management employees.

Darden, the largest casual restaurant dining group in the world, characterizes its program as highly successful. The company believes the program helps protect valuable employees from unfair dismissal and asserts that it has reduced racial tensions between employees and with customers. In addition, company General Counsel Clifford Whitehall claims the program cuts $1 million from annual legal expenses, which now total $3.5 million. The program saves on legal expenses by providing Darden's 114,500 employees with an alternative to employee litigation against the company. Indeed, although roughly 100 cases go through peer review each year, only about 10 or so ultimately result in litigation.

EXTERNAL DISPUTE RESOLUTION POLICIES

The Role of Outside Counsel

External disputes present a different set of options. Companies wishing to make broad use of ADR will likely need to closely supervise outside legal counsel. As this text has demonstrated, counsel—particularly outside firms—are sometimes reluctant to use ADR processes. Many are reluctant for substantive reasons, such as the absence of regulatory authority over most private ADR providers. Others, principally practitioners not schooled in law during the past decade, are unfamiliar with the processes and prefer to litigate in the familiar courtroom setting rather than learn new advocacy skills and process rules. Still others anticipate the potential loss of revenue through the use of ADR processes designed to eliminate the time and acrimony of the trial and its associated costs.

Companies have several options with respect to the use and supervision of outside counsel. First, they may require that in all cases a **choice of process memorandum** be created by counsel and reviewed in-house before any decision is made. In such a document, counsel must explain the reasons for choosing a particular dispute resolution process, whether trial or ADR. Second, companies may require that some percentage of all business referred to outside counsel be sent to an ADR process. Counsel could select from among the cases referred, but they would be required to show a good-faith effort to resolve a stated percentage of all cases through an ADR process. Third, companies could create a more significant role for in-house counsel, one that expressly includes managing cases through ADR processes. Cases on which a decision to litigate has been made in-house could be sent to outside counsel; many of the remaining cases could be managed to conclusion by in-house counsel. Finally, ADR agreements between companies that deal regularly with one another can eliminate the question of process choice altogether. When companies with ongoing commercial relationships agree to refer some or all cases to a form of ADR, perhaps using the following American Arbitration Association predispute contract clauses, counsel is only left with process execution, not with the process decision.

Enforcement of ADR provisions in commercial contracts is governed by essentially the same rules that were previously described for use in employee agreements. When such provisions are between business partners, courts virtually always enforce them because they are rarely adhesion contracts that raise the concerns of unilateral bargaining power found in some employment contracts. The appendix to this chapter includes a number of **predispute contract clauses** provided by the American Arbitration Association for use in commercial agreements. Most of the clauses are consistent with one another, so that they can be layered for different processes in a contract as described at the beginning of this chapter.

The Role of the Insurer

A solid working relationship with one's insurer is also helpful. Most carriers are intensely interested in reducing the cost of defending suits. Thus, where a business communicates its willingness to engage in ADR processes, the insurer is in a position to bring additional pressure to bear on the attorneys representing the company. Most business insurance policies cover both fees and settlements or judgments. Consequently, the insurer has, to a very significant extent, veto power over counsel's choice of a dispute resolution process.

The Role of Customers

Contracts with customers may specify the use of ADR processes. Many customers find it attractive to participate in less formal processes to resolve claims against a company. However, customers may wish to resolve a dispute in court. The following case examines the enforceability of a clause contained in a mail-order computer purchase contract requiring arbitration, rather than litigation, of all claims against the company. The case is presented for two reasons: (1) to further elucidate the nature of knowing and voluntary assent to an arbitration clause and (2) to provide a context in which to consider the impact on customer relations resulting from enforcement of such a clause.

HILL V. GATEWAY 2000, INC.
105 F.3d 1147 (7th Cir. 1997)

FACT SUMMARY

A customer picks up the phone, orders a computer, and gives a credit card number. Presently a box arrives, which contains the computer and a list of terms that apply unless the customer returns the computer within 30 days. Are these terms effective as the parties' contract, or is the contract term-free because the order-taker did not read any terms over the phone or elicit the customer's assent?

One of the terms in the box containing a Gateway 2000 system was an arbitration clause. Rich and Enza Hill, the customers, kept the computer more than 30 days before complaining about its components and performance. They filed suit in federal court arguing, among other things, that the product's shortcomings make Gateway a racketeer (mail and wire fraud are said to be the predicate offenses), leading to treble damages under RICO for the Hills and all other purchasers. Gateway asked the district court to enforce the arbitration clause; the judge refused, writing that "[t]he present record is insufficient to support a finding of a valid arbitration agreement between the parties or that the plaintiffs were given adequate notice of the arbitration clause." Gateway took an immediate appeal.

OPINION: *EASTERBROOK, Circuit Judge*

The Hills say that the arbitration clause did not stand out: they concede noticing the statement of terms but deny reading it closely enough to discover the agreement to arbitrate, and they ask us to conclude that they therefore may go to court. Yet an agreement to arbitrate must be enforced "save upon such grounds as exist at law or in equity for the revocation of any contract." 9 U.S.C. sec. 2. *Doctor's Associates, Inc. v. Casarotto,* 116 S. Ct. 1652 (1996), holds that this provision of the Federal Arbitration Act is inconsistent with any requirement that an arbitration clause be prominent. A contract need not be read to be effective; people who accept take the risk that the unread terms may in retrospect prove unwelcome. Terms inside Gateway's box stand or fall together. If they constitute the parties' contract because the Hills had an opportunity to return the computer after reading them, then all must be enforced.

ProCD, Inc. v. Zeidenberg, 86 F.3d 1447 (7th Cir. 1996), holds that terms inside a box of software bind consumers who use the software after an opportunity to read the terms and to reject them by returning the product. Likewise, *Carnival Cruise Lines, Inc. v. Shute,* 499 U.S. 585

(1991), enforces a forum-selection clause that was included among three pages of terms attached to a cruise ship ticket. *ProCD* and *Carnival Cruise Lines* exemplify the many commercial transactions in which people pay for products with terms to follow; *ProCD* discusses others. The district court concluded in *ProCD* that the contract is formed when the consumer pays for the software; as a result, the court held, only terms known to the consumer at that moment are part of the contract, and provisos inside the box do not count. Although this is one way a contract could be formed, it is not the only way: A vendor, as master of the offer, may invite acceptance by conduct, and may propose limitations on the kind of conduct that constitutes acceptance. A buyer may accept by performing the acts the vendor proposes to treat as acceptance. Gateway shipped computers with the same sort of accept-or-return offer ProCD made to users of its software. ProCD relied on the Uniform Commercial Code rather than any peculiarities of Wisconsin law; both Illinois and South Dakota, the two states whose law might govern relations between Gateway and the Hills, have adopted the UCC; neither side has pointed us to any atypical doctrines in those states that might be pertinent; *ProCD* therefore applies to this dispute.

Plaintiffs ask us to limit *ProCD* to software, but where's the sense in that? *ProCD* is about the law of contract, not the law of software. Payment preceding the revelation of full terms is common for air transportation, insurance, and many other endeavors. Practical considerations support allowing vendors to enclose the full legal terms with their products. Cashiers cannot be expected to read legal documents to customers before ringing up sales. If the staff at the other end of the phone for direct-sales operations such as Gateway's had to read the four-page statement of terms before taking the buyer's credit card number, the droning voice would anesthetize rather than enlighten many potential buyers. Others would hang up in a rage over the waste of their time. And oral recitation would not avoid customers' assertions (whether true or feigned) that the clerk did not read term X to them, or that they did not remember or understand it. Writing provides benefits for both sides of commercial transactions. Customers as a group are better off when vendors skip costly and ineffectual steps such as telephonic recitation, and use instead a simple approve-or-return device. Competent adults are bound by such documents, read or unread. For what little it is worth, we add that the box from Gateway was crammed with software. The computer came with an operating system, without which it was useful only as a boat anchor. Gateway also included many application programs. So the Hills' effort to limit *ProCD* to software would not avail them factually, even if it were sound legally which it is not.

For their second sally, the Hills contend that *ProCD* should be limited to executory contracts (to licenses in particular), and therefore does not apply because both parties' performance of this contract was complete when the box arrived at their home. This is legally and factually wrong: legally because the question at hand concerns the formation of the contract rather than its performance, and factually because both contracts were incompletely performed. *ProCD* did not depend on the fact that the seller characterized the transaction as a license rather than as a contract; we treated it as a contract for the sale of goods and reserved the question whether for other purposes a

http://
The complete text of ProCD v. Zeidenberg may be found at this site: http://caselaw. findlaw.com/cgi-bin/getcase.pl? court=7th& navby=case&no =961139

http://
The complete text of Carnival Cruise Lines v. Shute may be found at this site: http://caselaw. findlaw.com/ scripts/getcase. pl?navby=case& court=US&vol= 499&page=585

"license" characterization might be preferable. All debates about characterization to one side, the transaction in *ProCD* was no more executory than the one here: Zeidenberg paid for the software and walked out of the store with a box under his arm, so if arrival of the box with the product ends the time for revelation of contractual terms, then the time ended in *ProCD* before Zeidenberg opened the box. But of course ProCD had not completed performance with delivery of the box, and neither had Gateway. One element of the transaction was the warranty, which obliges sellers to fix defects in their products. The Hills have invoked Gateway's warranty and are not satisfied with its response, so they are not well positioned to say that Gateway's obligations were fulfilled when the motor carrier unloaded the box. What is more, both ProCD and Gateway promised to help customers to use their products. Long-term service and information obligations are common in the computer business, on both hardware and software sides. Gateway offers "lifetime service" and has a round-the-clock telephone hotline to fulfill this promise. Some vendors spend more money helping customers use their products than on developing and manufacturing them. The document in Gateway's box includes promises of future performance that some consumers value highly; these promises bind Gateway just as the arbitration clause binds the Hills.

Next the Hills insist that *ProCD* is irrelevant, because Zeidenberg was a "merchant" and they are not. Section 2-207(2) of the UCC, the infamous battle-of-the-forms section, states that "additional terms [following acceptance of an offer] are to be construed as proposals for addition to a contract." Between merchants such terms become part of the contract. Plaintiffs tell us that *ProCD* came out as it did only because Zeidenberg was a "merchant" and the terms inside ProCD's box were not excluded by the "unless" clause. This argument pays scant attention to the opinion in *ProCD*, which concluded that, when there is only one form, "sec. 2-207 is irrelevant." The question in *ProCD* was not whether terms were added to a contract after its formation, but how and when the contract was formed—in particular, whether a vendor may propose that a contract of sale be formed, not in the store (or over the phone) with the payment of money or a general "send me the product," but after the customer has had a chance to inspect both the item and the terms. *ProCD* answers "yes," for merchants and consumers alike. Yet again, for what little it is worth we observe that the Hills misunderstand the setting of *ProCD*. A "merchant" under the UCC "means a person who deals in goods of the kind or otherwise by his occupation holds himself out as having knowledge or skill peculiar to the practices or goods involved in the transaction," sec. 2-104(1). Zeidenberg bought the product at a retail store, an uncommon place for merchants to acquire inventory. His corporation put ProCD's database on the Internet for anyone to browse, which led to the litigation but did not make Zeidenberg a software merchant.

At oral argument the Hills propounded still another distinction: the box containing ProCD's software displayed a notice that additional terms were within, while the box containing Gateway's computer did not. The difference is functional, not legal. Consumers browsing the aisles of a store can look at the box, and if they are unwilling to deal with the prospect of additional terms can leave the box alone, avoiding the transactions costs of returning the package after reviewing its contents. Gateway's box, by contrast, is just a shipping carton; it is not on display anywhere. Its function is to protect the product during transit, and the information on its sides is for the use of handlers ("Fragile!" "This Side Up!") rather than would-be purchasers.

Perhaps the Hills would have had a better argument if they were first alerted to the bundling of hardware and legalware after opening the box and wanted to return the computer in order to avoid disagreeable terms, but were dissuaded by the expense of shipping. What the remedy would be in such a case—could it exceed the shipping charges?—is an interesting question, but one that need not detain us because the Hills knew before they ordered the computer that the carton would include some important terms, and they did not seek to discover these in advance. Gateway's ads state that their products come with limited warranties and lifetime support. How limited was the warranty—30 days, with service contingent on shipping the computer back, or five years, with free onsite service? What sort of support was offered? Shoppers have three principal ways to discover these things. First, they can ask the vendor to send a copy before deciding whether to buy. The Magnuson-Moss Warranty Act requires firms to distribute their warranty

terms on request; the Hills do not contend that Gateway would have refused to enclose the remaining terms too. Concealment would be bad for business, scaring some customers away and leading to excess returns from others. Second, shoppers can consult public sources (computer magazines, the Web sites of vendors) that may contain this information. Third, they may inspect the documents after the product's delivery. Like Zeidenberg, the Hills took the third option. By keeping the computer beyond 30 days, the Hills accepted Gateway's offer, including the arbitration clause.

The Hills' remaining arguments, including a contention that the arbitration clause is unenforceable as part of a scheme to defraud, do not require more than a citation to *Prima Paint Corp. v. Flood & Conklin Mfg. Co.*, 388 U.S. 395 (1967). Whatever may be said pro and con about the cost and efficacy of arbitration (which the Hills disparage) is for Congress and the contracting parties to consider. Claims based on RICO are no less arbitrable than those founded on the contract or the law of torts. *Shearson/American Express, Inc. v. McMahon*, 482 U.S. 220, 238-42 (1987). The decision of the district court is vacated, and this case is remanded with instructions to compel the Hills to submit their dispute to arbitration.

Discussion Questions

1. Is a company's interest in ADR sufficient grounds to enforce it over the objection of a customer under circumstances similar to the ones described in the case?

2. How prominently should ADR provisions that substantially affect the rights of a consumer be displayed? Do the facts in this case suggest a good-faith effort on the part of Gateway to communicate these essential terms? Does this case represent an example of an adhesion contract?

3. What is the long-term effect on ADR if provisions like the ones in this case are enforced? Is it possible that such an enforcement will work to the disadvantage of ADR? Why or why not?

CHAPTER CONCLUSION

Businesses that choose to use the full range of dispute resolution processes in a systematic fashion can expect to reap considerable gains. ADR offers the possibility of quick and inexpensive resolution of both internal and external disputes. Companies wishing to preserve important relationships in either setting may do so most effectively by designing dispute resolution systems that address problems preemptively and by choosing processes and legal counsel carefully.

BEST BUSINESS PRACTICES

Here are some practical tips for managers on the design of systems for the resolution of business disputes.

- In designing company dispute resolution processes, differentiate between internal and external disputes and understand the benefits of particular processes in each context.
- Do not be tempted to neglect internal and informal conflicts that may sap productivity and employee morale. The cost in confidentiality of an ombudsman's office is likely offset by the gains realized through employee productivity.
- Centralize decision making related to dispute resolution to ensure consistent application of procedural rules and maximum internal and external cost savings. In doing so, note the likelihood that corporate outside counsel will often neglect to use mediation, preferring arbitration and litigation instead.
- Mediation should precede adversarial processes in both internal and external systems, as it provides an opportunity for a negotiated settlement that may preserve important, ongoing business relationships.
- Understand that advocacy is important in the context of any dispute resolution process and that it must be tailored to the specific process being used to address a particular case.
- Anticipate the expectations and needs of international clients as you consider processes and methods for dispute resolution.

KEY TERMS

Adhesion contracts, p. 299

Arbitration within monetary limits,
 p. 321

Choice of process memorandum,
 p. 311

Discovery, p. 319

Dispute Review Board, p. 321

Employee contracts and handbooks,
 p. 298

External disputes, p. 310

Internal disputes, p. 298

Knowing and voluntary waiver, p. 300

Ombudsman, p. 304

Predispute contract clauses, p. 311

Privilege, p. 304

Title VII claims, p. 300

ETHICAL AND LEGAL REVIEW

Consider the needs of the following companies with respect to alternative dispute resolution policy. Design a system for each that describes responses to internal and external disputes. Create systems consistent with the needs and resources of each company.

1. Nichecom, LLP is a small, closely held family business that sells retail office machines. The company has a base of both corporate and individual clients who purchase machines, service contracts, and supplies. The company occasionally struggles to collect from clients, both corporate and individual, and is unsure how to address such occurrences short of collection lawsuits. In addition, Nichecom builds into its service agreements factory warranties for the machines it sells to clients, and it does repair work only when the warranty does not provide independent coverage. Nichecom's clients often struggle with manufacturers to obtain service, and Nichecom feels caught in the middle. With whom should Nichecom have ADR agreements? What sorts of agreements should the parties create and why should they create them?

2. Agile, Ltd. is a mid-sized, publicly traded manufacturing concern with a unionized production workforce of 100 and a managerial contingent of 20. The relationship between the company and the union is acrimonious, although there has never been a work stoppage. Although a grievance procedure is in place, it is rarely used and is subject to revision during the imminent collective bargaining round. In addition, Agile, a maker of rollerblades and other Generation X sports gear, is faced with mounting legal expenses related to use of its gear. What provisions should the Agile ADR program include?

3. Megalith Incorporated is an international conglomerate. It holds contracts around the world, has a large staff of in-house lawyers, and uses outside counsel extensively. Megalith designs and produces a variety of products and services and is an industry leader in research and development. Megalith operates in many highly competitive areas in which trade secrets are vital, and litigation

is to be avoided. What sorts of ADR clauses might Megalith include in contracts with its employees and vendors? What other uses of ADR might benefit Megalith? Why would ADR utilization benefit Megalith?

4. Expert Services, Chartered is a mid-sized consulting and service firm built on relationships with long-standing clients who rely upon experienced firm employees to service their accounts. Loss of a client has a significant impact on Expert, and maintaining high employee morale is therefore essential. What ADR approaches could Expert undertake to preserve both employee and customer loyalty?

SUGGESTED ADDITIONAL READINGS

Blake, Robert R., and Jane S. Mouton. *Solving Costly Organizational Conflicts: Achieving Intergroup Trust, Cooperation, and Teamwork.* Jossey-Bass, 1984.

Cooley, John W. *Mediation Advocacy.* National Institute for Trial Advocacy, 1996.

Cooley, John W., and Steven Lubet. *Arbitration Advocacy.* National Institute for Trial Advocacy, 1997.

Costantino, C., and C. Merchant. *Designing Conflict Management Systems: A Guide to Creating Productive and Healthy Organizations.* Jossey-Bass, 1996.

Gleason, S., ed. *Workplace Dispute Resolution: Directions for the Twenty-First Century.* Michigan State University Press, 1997.

Weise, R. H. "The ADR Program at Motorola." *5 Negotiation Journ. 381.* 1989.

CHAPTER APPENDIX 10A:

PREDISPUTE CONTRACT CLAUSES FROM THE AMERICAN ARBITRATION ASSOCIATION

Predispute Contract Clause Calling for Negotiation

In the event of any dispute, claim, question, or disagreement arising from or relating to this agreement or the breach thereof, the parties hereto shall use their best efforts to settle the dispute, claim, question, or disagreement. To this effect, they shall consult and negotiate with each other in good faith and, recognizing their mutual interests, attempt to reach a just and equitable solution satisfactory to both parties. If they do not reach such solution within a period of 60 days, then, upon notice by either party to the other, all disputes, claims, questions, or differences shall be finally settled by arbitration administered by the American Arbitration Association in accordance with the provisions of its Commercial Arbitration Rules.

Predispute Contract Clause Calling for Mediation

If a dispute arises out of or relates to this contract, or the breach thereof, and if the dispute cannot be settled through negotiation, the parties agree first to try in good faith to settle the dispute by mediation administered by the American Arbitration Association under its Commercial Mediation Rules before resorting to arbitration, litigation, or some other dispute resolution procedure.

Predispute Contract Clause Calling for Arbitration

Any controversy or claim arising out of or relating to this contract, or the breach thereof, shall be settled by arbitration administered by the American Arbitration Association in accordance with its Commercial [or other] Arbitration Rules [including the Emergency Interim Relief Procedures], and judgment on the award rendered by the arbitrator(s) may be entered in any court having jurisdiction thereof.

Clauses Providing Details Related to Arbitration

Arbitrator Selection.   Within 15 days after the commencement of arbitration, each party shall select one person to act as arbitrator and the two selected shall select a third arbitrator within 10 days of their appointment. If the arbitrators selected by the parties are unable or fail to agree upon the third arbitrator, the third arbitrator shall be selected by the American Arbitration Association.

or

In the event that arbitration is necessary, [name of specific arbitrator] shall act as the arbitrator.

Arbitrator Qualifications.   The arbitrator shall be a certified public accountant.

or

The arbitrator shall be a practicing attorney [or a retired judge of the [specify] Court].

or

The arbitration proceedings shall be conducted before a panel of three neutral arbitrators, all of whom shall be members of the bar of the state of [specify], actively engaged in the practice of law for at least 10 years.

Discovery.   Consistent with the expedited nature of arbitration, each party will, upon the written request of the other party, promptly provide the other with copies of documents [relevant to the issues raised by any claim or counterclaim on which the producing party may rely in support of or in opposition to any claim or defense]. Any dispute regarding discovery, or the relevance or scope thereof, shall be determined by the [arbitrator(s) or chair of the arbitration panel], which determination shall be conclusive. All discovery shall be completed within [45 or 60] days following the appointment of the arbitrator(s).

or

At the request of a party, the arbitrator(s) shall have the discretion to order examination by deposition of witnesses to the extent the arbitrator deems such additional discovery relevant and appropriate. Depositions shall be limited to a maximum of [three] [insert number] per party and shall be held within 30 days of the making of a request. Additional depositions may be scheduled only with the permission of the [arbitrator(s) or chair of the arbitration panel], and for good cause shown. Each deposition shall be limited to a maximum of [three hours, six hours, or one day's] duration. All objections are reserved for the arbitration hearing except for objections based on privilege and proprietary or confidential information.

The Award.   The award shall be made within nine months of the filing of the notice of intention to arbitrate (demand), and the arbitrator(s) shall agree to comply with this schedule before accepting appointment. However, this time limit may be extended by agreement of the parties or by the arbitrators, if necessary.

or

The arbitrators will have no authority to award punitive or other damages not measured by the prevailing party's actual damages, except as may be required by statute.

or

In no event shall an award in an arbitration initiated under this clause exceed [insert amount].

or

Any award in an arbitration initiated under this clause shall be limited to monetary damages and shall include no injunction or direction to any party other than the direction to pay a monetary amount.

or

If the arbitrator(s) find liability in any arbitration initiated under this clause, they shall award liquidated damages in the amount of [insert amount].

or

Any monetary award in an arbitration initiated under this clause shall include pre-award interest at the rate of [insert percentage] from the time of the act(s) giving rise to the award.

Confidentiality.   Except as may be required by law, neither a party nor an arbitrator may disclose the existence, content, or results of any arbitration hereunder without the prior written consent of both parties.

Predispute Contract Clause Calling for Final Offer Arbitration

Each party shall submit to the arbitrator and exchange with each other in advance of the hearing their last, best offers. The arbitrator shall be limited to awarding only one or the other of the two figures submitted.

Predispute Contract Clause Calling for Arbitration Within Monetary Limits

Any award of the arbitrator in favor of [specify a party] and against [specify a party] shall be at least [specify a dollar amount] but shall not exceed [specify a dollar amount]. [Specify a party] expressly waives any claim in excess of [specify a dollar amount] and agrees that its recovery shall not exceed that amount. Any such award shall be in satisfaction of all claims by [specify a party] against [specify a party].

or

In the event that the arbitrator denies the claim or awards an amount less than the minimum amount of [specify], then this minimum amount shall be paid to the claimant. Should the arbitrator's award exceed the maximum amount of [specify], then only this maximum amount shall be paid to the claimant. It is further understood between the parties that, if the arbitrator awards an amount between the minimum and maximum stipulated range, then the exact awarded amount will be paid to the claimant. The parties agree that this agreement is private between them and will not be disclosed to the arbitrator.

Predispute Contract Clause Calling for a Dispute Review Board

The parties shall impanel a **Dispute Review Board** of three members in accordance with the Dispute Review Board Procedures of the American Arbitration Association. The DRB, in close consultation with all interested parties, will assist and recommend the resolution of any disputes, claims, and other controversies that might arise among the parties.

Predispute Contract Clause Calling for a Minitrial

Any controversy or claim arising from or relating to this contract shall be submitted to the American Arbitration Association under its Minitrial Procedures.

Predispute Contract Clause Calling for Mediation-Arbitration

If a dispute arises from or relates to this contract or the breach thereof, and if the dispute cannot be settled through direct discussions, the parties agree to endeavor first to settle the dispute by mediation administered by the American Arbitration

Association under its Commercial Mediation Rules before resorting to arbitration. Any unresolved controversy or claim arising from or relating to this contract or breach thereof shall be settled by arbitration administered by the American Arbitration Association in accordance with its Commercial Arbitration Rules, and judgment on the award rendered by the arbitrator may be entered in any court having jurisdiction thereof. If the parties agree, a mediator involved in the parties' mediation may be asked to serve as the arbitrator.

Clauses for Use in International Disputes

Any controversy or claim arising out of or relating to this contract shall be determined by arbitration administered by the American Arbitration Association under its International Arbitration Rules.

Any dispute, controversy, or claim arising out of or relating to this contract, or the breach thereof, shall be finally settled by arbitration administered by the Commercial Arbitration and Mediation Center for the Americas in accordance with its rules, and judgment on the award rendered by the arbitrator(s) may be entered in any court having jurisdiction thereof.

Any dispute, controversy, or claim arising from or relating to this contract, or the breach, termination, or invalidity thereof, shall be settled by arbitration in accordance with the Rules of Procedure of the Inter-American Commercial Arbitration Commission in effect on the date of this agreement.

Any dispute, controversy, or claim arising out of or relating to this contract, or the breach, termination, or invalidity thereof, shall be settled by arbitration under the UNCITRAL Arbitration Rules in effect on the date of this contract. The appointing authority shall be the American Arbitration Association. The case shall be administered by the American Arbitration Association under its Procedures for Cases under the UNCITRAL Arbitration Rules.

Source: Reprinted with permission of the American Arbitration Association.

Appendix H

CPR CORPORATE POLICY STATEMENT
on
ALTERNATIVES TO LITIGATION©

COMPANY

We recognize that for many disputes there is a less expensive, more effective method of resolution than the traditional lawsuit. Alternative dispute resolution (ADR) procedures involve collaborative techniques which can often spare businesses the high costs of litigation.

In recognition of the foregoing, we subscribe to the following statements of principle on behalf of our company and its domestic subsidiaries.

In the event of a business dispute between our company and another company which has made or will then make a similar statement, we are prepared to explore with that other party resolution of the dispute through negotiation or ADR techniques before pursuing full scale litigation. If either party believes that the dispute is not suitable for ADR techniques, or if such techniques do not produce results satisfactory to the disputants, either party may proceed with litigation.

_____
CHIEF EXECUTIVE OFFICER
_____
CHIEF LEGAL OFFICER
_____
DATE

Our major operating subsidiaries are

_____

_____

Source: © 1998, CPR Institute for Dispute Resolution, New York, NY. Reprinted with permission. The CPR Institute for Dispute Resolution is a nonprofit initiative of 500 general counsel of major corporations, leading law firms, and prominent legal academics in support of alternatives to litigation. CPR develops new methods to resolve business and public disputes by alternative dispute resolution (ADR).

More than 4,000 operating companies have committed to the Corporate Policy Statement on Alternatives to Litigation©. The CPR Corporate Pledge obliges subscribing companies to seriously explore negotiation, mediation or other ADR processes in conflicts arising with other signatories before pursuing full-scale litigation. The list of companies subscribing on behalf of themselves and their major operating subsidiaries is available on the CPR Web site (www.cpradr.org).

CPR Institute for Dispute Resolution
366 Madison Avenue, New York, NY 10017 Tel (212) 949-6490
Fax (212) 949-8859 Internet: www.cpradr.org